IMAGE & LIKENESS

Religious Visions in American Film Classics

edited by
John R. May

Paulist Press
New York/Mahwah, New Jersey

Cover: Enthroned as a Mafia don, Michael Corleone (Al Pacino) is the American cinema's clearest reflector of the hypocritical human heart. Only if we see our own likeness in his icy gaze can we claim to have fathomed the depths of Francis Ford Coppola's cinematic variation on the American Protestant Puritan image of the demon within ourselves.

Cover design by Tim McKeen.

ACKNOWLEDGMENTS
The film stills are reproduced courtesy of the Museum of Modern Art, Film Stills Archive, with the exception of *City Lights* and *Sunset Boulevard* (courtesy of the Academy of Motion Picture Arts and Sciences).

Credits for the art reproductions are the following: Cole, *The Course of Empire: Consummation of Empire* (courtesy of the New-York Historical Society, New York); Rembrandt, *The Adoration of the Shepherds* and *Christ Crucified between the Two Thieves,* and Raphael, *The Alba Madonna* (courtesy of the National Gallery of Art, Washington); Grünewald, *Crucifixion* (courtesy of Marburg/Art Resource, New York).

Library of Congress Cataloging-in-Publication Data

Image and likeness: religious visions in American film classics/
  edited by John R. May.
      p. cm.—(Isaac Hecker studies in religion and American culture)
  Includes index.
  ISBN 0-8091-3286-9
  1. Motion pictures—United States—Religious aspects. I. May,
John R. II. Series.
PN1995.5.I46   1991
791.43'682—dc20   91-31249
                                                                CIP

Published by Paulist Press
997 Macarthur Boulevard
Mahwah, NJ 07430

Printed and bound in the
United States of America

IMAGE & LIKENESS

ISAAC HECKER STUDIES
IN RELIGION AND AMERICAN CULTURE

Contents

Dedication

for
John David

"De te fabula." Horace, *Satires*

"And God said,

Let us make man in our own image,

after our likeness."

King James Bible (Gen. 1:26)

Introduction

A line from *Beneath the Planet of the Apes* has an inordinate claim on my memory—a curiosity that continues to surprise and amuse any lecture audience I recall it for. Whatever one thinks of the *Planet of the Apes* series, one cannot deny that the scripts were on the whole quite literate, and I feel sure that the reason the line has lingered in my memory long after even the broadest details of the plot have vanished is quite simply because it was a good line. "When may we hope to go free?" asks the imprisoned Cornelius (Roddy McDowall), and his simian captor responds, "You may hope anytime you wish."

Being able to "hope anytime [we] wish" is what this collection is all about. It is a hope, moreover, that liberates the spirit, the irony of the remembered dialogue notwithstanding. Such a hope, the contributors to this volume feel, explains the durability of certain American films; indeed, it would be justifiable to claim that hope undergirds all canons of greatness. I am not speaking here of the hope that, in everyday usage, has an evident object, as in the expression, "I hope to finish this editorial project before the end of the millennium." It is rather the kind of hope that Gabriel Marcel has called fundamental hope, hope without a discernible object, the hope that supports survival and even, at times, sustains perseverance.[1]

This collection of essays is grounded on a traditional theory of art as communication, hence on the assumption that films have meaning—for us. Great films like high art both reflect and affect our lives in ways that we can discern, discuss and share. To the credit of the contributors I hasten to add that this assumption is by no means the facile belief, now properly discredited, that the meaning of a work of art can be reduced to a proposition or a theme or, for that matter, to any one of its complex elements. Yet, that moviegoers, even those apparently unfamiliar with the language of film, feel confident to comment on what a film was about or how it affected them—and to share their impressions with others—can be confirmed simply by attending to the comments one hears on

1

leaving a theater, or on a higher plane by the dialogue that develops among reviewers in the standard journals and often leads to a certain consensus. Moreover, because Hollywood's classic films are overdetermined as art, namely, the product of a wide variety of causes, we grasp their meaning, if at all, in a far less conscious manner apparently than we perceive the meaning even of a literary text.

If this is so, and we certainly feel that it is, we should reconsider T.S. Eliot's measured warning about the effects of reading on the life of the spirit. In an essay of his, published in 1936, that has become a classic statement about the relationship between literature and religion, Eliot all but denied the possibility of our reading books "merely for entertainment" (which we so often claim to be our sole reason for seeing films). "The common ground between religion and fiction," he wrote, "is behaviour."[2] Although he seems now to have been overly ethical in his understanding of that common ground, he was nonetheless precise in his estimate of the manner of literature's inevitable effect upon us: "If we, as readers, keep our religious and moral convictions in one compartment, and take our reading merely for entertainment, or on a higher plane, for aesthetic pleasure, I would point out that the author, whatever his conscious intentions in writing, in practice recognizes no such distinctions. The author of a work of imagination is trying to affect us wholly, as human beings, whether he knows it or not; we are affected by it, as human beings, whether we intend to be or not" (228).

Eliot supports his assertion by asking us to examine "the history of our individual literary education," particularly the time in our youth when we were "completely carried away by the work of one poet" (229). Indeed, he describes the "seductions of poetry" in a manner that is *a fortiori* appropriate to the seductions of cinema. "What happens," he wrote, "is a kind of inundation, of invasion of the undeveloped personality, the empty (swept and garnished) room, by the stronger personality of the poet" (229). Roger Angell has described cinema's variation on this experience of seduction, in which the metaphoric empty room of the undeveloped youth becomes the literal dark interior of the movie theater. "Movies are felt by the audience long before they are 'understood'," Angell points out. "Going to the movies, in fact, is not an intellectual process most of the time but an emotional one. Any serious, well-made movie we see seems to wash over us there in the dark, bathing us in feelings and suggestions, and imparting a deep or light tinge of meaning that stays with us, sometimes for life."[3] Cinema's capacity, therefore, to affect our view of the world, our attitudes toward self and neighbor, our hopes and fears is all the more potent.

In the spirit of Eliot, I would be inclined to add to Angell's statement, "Movies are felt by the audience long before they are 'understood' *if indeed they are ever fully understood.*" The emotional impact has nonetheless been experienced in the darkness of the theater; whether we are consciously aware of it or not, *we have been affected*—personally, wholly. The inexperienced moviegoer must therefore develop the analytical skills for conscious reflection upon the seductiveness of film, or at least be guided by knowledgeable critics to the best films available, those that are faithful to the values of our religious tradition. We are not concerned here, of course, with censorship of any sort, but with the discrimination that leads with reason to the establishment of a canon of greatness—because, in their classical canon, films may finally have become the most potent vehicle of teachers and parents for imparting the values of our heritage.

The video-cassette revolution makes it possible at the beginning of the 1990s for us to rent film classics from our local video outlet just as our ancestors for generations, indeed centuries, have taken books home from the bookstore or library. At the risk of being overly apocalyptic, I wonder if video tapes will not shortly become the principal texts that our children and grandchildren take home. Premiere movie channels may already have become our cable home libraries, and when one considers the appalling banality of most of the films that cable systems and satellites make available, we have reason enough to worry about the level of popular culture. Even as I write these lines during the summer of 1989, my inclination toward dire predictions about the general decline of American cinema is confirmed by the evident proliferation of cynically-numbered sequels. Whereas genre was traditional Hollywood's answer to the popularity of certain types of story, the movie industry seems determined now to standardize its product by repeating *ad nauseam* specific narrative formulas that have spelled financial success, and for every artistically-conceived sequel like *Indiana Jones and the Last Crusade,* there would seem to be ten of the likes of *Ghostbusters II, The Karate Kid Part III,* and *Eddie and the Cruisers II,* not to mention the atrocities *Friday the Thirteenth VIII* and *A Nightmare on Elm Street V.* If our assumptions in this collection are correct, however, we shall not have lost touch with our heritage if we continue to be discriminating in what we watch, and in what we encourage our children to see, show our students and present to study groups at synagogue or church.

Given the inevitable diversity in the arena of film criticism today— and the tensions resulting from the rivalry of opposing schools—it is important for us to explain our critical intentions initially by making clear precisely what we are not attempting in this collection. This is neither a history of American film classics nor a formal analysis of what makes them classics. Nor is it an attempt to demonstrate precisely what is American about our acknowledged classics; that has already been done in provocative fashion by a variety of critics, the most notable recent essay in this vein being Robert B. Ray's *A Certain Tendency of the Hollywood Cinema, 1930–1980.*[4]

Ray builds his analysis of Hollywood's classic cinema by demonstrating its "systematic subordination of every cinematic element to the interests of a movie's narrative" (32). The "certain tendency" he identifies (the phrase was Truffaut's about French cinema) is Hollywood's inclination to reflect and perpetuate an ideology—in this instance, an American cultural mythology, that Ray feels is best understood in Marxist, structuralist, and psychoanalytic terms—namely, our American disposition to avoid choices, reflected formally in realistic filmmaking's concealment of cinematic choices. Final choices, Ray suggests, following Frederick Jackson Turner and Erik Erikson, are unnecessary violations of our national spirit (67).

We too are concerned with "ideology," although admittedly current usage of the term, especially in Ray and related Marxist studies of American cinema, carries with it unmistakable suggestions of a worldview that is by design materialistic, thus denying the very possibility of our principal concern for the religious ideologies inherent in American cinema. Now as the subtitle of this collections announces, "visions" seemed to us a more appropriate term for that "system of . . . representations (images, myths, ideas or concepts, depending on the case) endowed with a historical existence and role within a given society" that is referred to simply as "ideology" by Ray (quoting Althusser's definition, 14). "Visions" seems especially suitable for an analysis of film inasmuch as it is principally a visual medium in which we see images of images—the visual representation, in our instance, of the religious images, myths, and concepts of the films' creators.

It is for this reason that I found the verse from Genesis (1:26) to be a fitting epigraph to this volume. It is one of the earliest reflections in the religious text cherished above all others in America that analogy plays a significant part in our elaboration of religious beliefs. According to the Priestly account of creation that became the first chapter of Genesis, we are images of God because he has made us in his likeness. This is, of course, a proposition taken by Jew and Christian alike to be a matter of God's revelation. Now as centuries of rabbinic and scholastic theological commentary on this passage prove, the direction of analogical reflection has also been reversed, not of course in the sense that we have made God in our image, but rather in the sense that since we know ourselves more directly than we know God, theologians have freely—and it would seem appropriately—attributed to God the very best that they found in his rational, loving creatures. Hence our thesis: each of these films is an image of the religious sensibility of an American filmmaker, and thus a likeness of the transcendent in his vision.

We are concerned with the *religious* visions in American film classics precisely because the religious questions that we ask are the most fundamental. Dedicated as we are to the critical assumption that films like literature convey their profoundest meaning indirectly, we have not focused narrowly on the morality of actions portrayed (as did Eliot), or on films that deal explicitly with religious faith or use theological language (in the tradition of Bergman or Fellini) because this has never been the way of the best American films. What we have dealt with usually is story itself—the way that the stories of the Jewish and Christian scriptures (the textual basis of American religious belief) relate to the stories that films tell—because classic Hollywood, as Ray demonstrates convincingly, subordinates "every cinematic element to the interests of a movie's narrative" (32).

We have aimed therefore, as Nathan Scott urges us, at Mark Van Doren's simplicity in *The Noble Voice* when he asks about poetry:

> What is a given poem about? What happens in it? What exists in it? If too little of the world is in it, why is that? If all of the world is there, by what miracle has this been done? Is tragedy or comedy at work, and what is the difference between the two, and what the resemblance? Are the facts of life accounted for in the unique way that poetry accounts for them, and is this poem something therefore that any man should read? Does its author know more, not less, than most men know? Such seem to me the great questions, though they are not regularly asked by criticism.[5]

Although I have resisted here as earlier the temptation to substitute "film" for "poem" and "director" for "poet," the passage bears rereading in that manner. If we as critics claim then to be knowledgeable about "the facts of life" or about what "most [Americans] know," it is because religion as well as film is our academic discipline. If anyone contests our implied judgment of the facts of American religious life or our estimate of what should be known, we have achieved at least one of our goals—namely, the initiation of a dialogue about lasting values in American films.

In our analyses, we have allowed our reflections to be suitably overdetermined. However much we have been enlightened by the auteur school of film criticism, it is not simply to the director as author that we have looked in exploring the origin of the images, ideas, and concepts that contribute to the film's final effect. We have, as evidence dictated, looked to the whole company of those who participate in the cinematic venture—the scriptwriters and their sources where known (novelists and playwrights), the cinematographers, the designers, the editors, and so forth.

Like Hollywood's classics themselves, the norms that went into the selection of the films in this collection were overdetermined. The project was conceived during the summer of 1986 and developed through the following summer in a dialogue among the earliest contributors. The truth about our final list of films is that it represents our own personal choices within certain discernible, though loosely conceived limits. Initially, we consulted lists, especially those prepared by the American Film Institute,[6] then compared our own individual lists of the top ten, keeping in mind our principal interest in the values central to our Jewish-Christian religious heritage. One clear preference of ours, which made a mere tally of individual lists impossible, was to produce a list of films that would represent a reasonable pantheon of great American directors, old and new. We also agreed we would limit ourselves to American feature films, indeed to those that are predominantly realistic in technique, but in the aftermath of Robert Ray's analysis of Hollywood cinema that qualification may be tautological.

Certain dominant characteristics that emerged from my dialogue with the contributors are evident in the films included in this collection: generally speaking, the films are noble in vision and artistically significant; they portray characters or settings that are recognizably American; they are all of lasting appeal (as classics should be), if not perennially popular; and they are representative of a variety of film genres. There are of course some exceptions, but each is, we feel, of the sort that "proves the rule" of dominant characteristics I have just noted. *Ben-Hur*, for instance, though scarcely American in setting, is indispensably American, that is, Jewish-Christian, in both theme and tone.

A certain artificiality accompanies any attempt at classification, and the arrangement of the essays in this collection is no exception. Unlike Ray, we have not, for obvious reasons, sought a single overriding religious ideology in American film classics. There are many reflections of our shared religious story in American cinema, as one might expect, just as there are many uniquely creative minds reflecting the boundless goodness of creation and our apparently limitless human capacity for marring it. Yet, to emphasize our determination to relate formal and thematic elements, I have arranged the essays, I hope without unnecessary distortion, under four headings that reflect the dominance of certain formal elements to related thematic concerns. The ordering of the parts, from one through four, has a more systematic basis inasmuch as I was guided by the progression of the religious visions of the films from the generic to the specific, from fundamental religious attitudes through to the heart of the redemptive experience in Judaism and Christianity. Within each part, I resorted to the simple expedient of arranging the essays in the chronological sequence dictated by the release of the film.

Mise-en-scène or composition of frame emerges as the principal cinematic element that in Part I draws our attention to thematic centers. In *City Lights*, Jack Coogan demonstrates, the final close-up of the tramp's enigmatic smile elevates hope over despair as the film's overriding mood. Proxemic patterns of closeness are at the heart of *The Grapes of Wrath*, in Philip Rule's analysis; John Ford uses the two and three shots of the Joad family members to highlight the triumph of mythic idealism over the film's prevailing documentary realism. For Ann-Janine Morey, an unidentified quivering hand rivets our attention in *High Noon* and becomes the visual signature of uncertainty as an evident propensity of our religious disposition. And in *2001: A Space Odyssey*, James Wall suggests, the way the black monolith is framed from time to time by its fascinated observers is the type of our persistent human search for the ultimate.

Film is preeminently capable, in the director's choice of physical reality to be photographed, of making allusions to other texts. In Part II, the dominant visual allusions are to Jewish and Christian biblical sources as well as to western classics, medieval and modern. *Citizen Kane* appeals to Dante's *Inferno* and Conrad's *Heart of Darkness* in its exploration of the demonic heart, George Garrelts explains, while Michael Morris discloses the centrality of the image of the veil—an obvious appeal to the evangelical narrative of Salome and the Baptist—as *Sunset Boulevard*'s way of destroying our illusions of divinity. In *The Godfather* films, I attempt to show, the sacramental framework makes Genesis 2-4 the most reasonable source for illuminating Coppola's indictment of hypocrisy as the rotten core of our human history of sin.

Cinema is of course the visual art that moves, although not every film employs movement—either within the frame or of camera itself— with precisely the same centrality. Some, like the films in Part III, raise movement to mythic heights, to the level of spiritual quest, and in each instance the quest yields a rebirth of sorts. Scott Cochrane traces the parallels between Dorothy's experiences along the Yellow Brick Road in *The Wizard of Oz* and the stages of universal religious rites of passage, and discovers the death of an outmoded image of God that is a rebirth of the religious imagination. In *The Treasure of the Sierra Madre*, a quest for gold, Peter Valenti indicates, ultimately reveals the essential superiority of selflessness over greed; a new spirituality for "man" is the genuine treasure of Mother Mountain. The journey of *On the Waterfront*, writes Neil Hurley, is a spiritual quest for personal wholeness, that in the pattern of the messiah comes only through suffering. *Ben-Hur*, as Diane Apostolos-Cappadona presents it, is more of a passage through art history than a narrative spanning two lands—Palestine and Rome—and the sea between; we perceive the film's theme of the unexpected touch of new life through its allusions to religious art history.

Editing or montage, as Europeans use the term, is an indispensable element of every feature film. However, in Part IV, editing is viewed as the dominant formal element in the four films treated in this volume that come closest to the heart of the Jewish-Christian religious experience— the power of love to transform self and others. For Mara Donaldson, nostalgic lighting, music, and the flashback are the pivotal elements in *Casablanca*'s presentation of self-sacrificing love. Carefully-edited narrative sequences in *Notorious*, with drinking as the visual link, suggest to Harold Hatt that Hitchcock was appealing, at least unconsciously, to the sacrament of penance—contrition, confession, and satisfaction—as a paradigm for transforming love. Robert Lauder reveals the way that parallel editing and flashbacks support Capra's celebration of neighborly love in *It's a Wonderful Life*, while Charles Ketcham demonstrates how the juxtaposed images of death and resurrection in *One Flew Over the Cuckoo's Nest* are unmistakable references to our biblical narratives of sacrificial love and redemption.

Although I had discussed with the original contributors the desirability of our doing an essay and a brief note apiece on a couple of films, this proved to be unmanageable as a project. I must, therefore, claim full responsibility for the final list of twenty films included in Part V—"Other Forms, Other Visions"—as well as for the short analyses of the films. In their selection, I was constrained by a near absolute—the desire to include, with one exception (*Star Wars*), all the films in the 1977 AFI List that were not covered by the principal essays. Beyond that, I confess that I consulted my own list of favorite films, among which, you'll notice immediately, are some that reflect my predilection for distinctly American settings and for works adapted from other media, and others that expand the traditional pantheon of great American directors. Films like *Bonnie and Clyde*, *Midnight Cowboy*, and *Slaughterhouse-Five* have in recent years achieved something of a cult status.

I am deeply indebted to my contributors for their patience and encouragement throughout the editorial process, and to Gloria Henderson of the English department staff at LSU for her untiring help in the preparation of the final manuscript. Once again, I acknowledge loving gratitude to my wife, Janet, my most enthusiastic reader and gentle critic. Finally, a special note of thanks to three close friends and trusted advisors—Jim Hietter for suggesting the title, and Alexis Gonzales and Del Jacobs for helping to supplement the stills gathered by the contributors.

John R. May
Louisiana State University
March 2, 1991

PART I

Composition and Fundamental Attitudes

City Lights
(1931, Charles Chaplin)

Her sight restored through his efforts, the blind girl sees the tramp (Charlie Chaplin) for the first time, and through her eyes we see—for the first time too—the irony in his smile and the ambiguity of their future. Chaplain audaciously projects the rhythms of traditional comedy into a world where tomorrow is increasingly shrouded in meaninglessness and despair.

Comic Rhythm, Ambiguity, and Hope in *City Lights*

Jack Coogan

Those who subscribe to the cyclical theory of history will be grati-
fied by the patterns which appear to govern the development of film
criticism. The striking achievements of early filmmakers like Griffith,
Chaplin, Flaherty, and Eisenstein focused critical attention on film as the
extension of a single personality. But the growing importance of the
studios throughout the 1920s, reinforced by the economic upheavals
attendant upon the coming of sound, gave rise to genre criticism, genre
being a convenient way that corporations conceive and standardize their
products. Postwar critical work, particularly that of François Truffaut
and Andrew Sarris, returned to an emphasis on the work of individual
filmmakers through the application of the critical principle that satisfac-
tory imaginative forms generally exhibit unity of purpose and design, and
the simplest way of achieving this unity is to have each work shaped and
controlled by a single mind—a commonplace, it must be admitted, in
relationship to older art forms, but stimulating in relationship to this new
collaborative art. Contemporary criticism, on the other hand, has shown
renewed interest in the social, economic, and ideological environments
which influence the creation of individual films or groupings of films.

But the work of Charles Chaplin has resisted this critical ebb and
flow, perhaps because it is rooted so solidly in Chaplin's own intuitive
understanding of his environment and his experience, an understanding
significant and coherent enough and certainly expressed forcefully
enough to merit consideration as a religious worldview. Indeed, in his
mature work Chaplin seems almost obsessed with religious problems:
the possibility of meaningful relationships (*The Kid, The Gold Rush, The
Circus*), the problem of a just social order (*Modern Times, The Great
Dictator, Monsieur Verdoux*) and, finally, the meaning of failing powers
and of death (*Limelight*). These issues are addressed from the perspective
of his own experience: the recollection of childhood poverty, the world

and style of the English music hall, the shock of sudden fame and wealth, all filtered through a mind actively interested in the meaning of experience, and transformed by a unique talent into an equally unique vision.

City Lights offers an ideal vantage point from which to survey the Chaplin worldview, for in it he not only displays all his traditional virtues—Agee has called its last few seconds "the greatest piece of acting and the highest moment in movies"[1]—but also solves the structural problems which in his other feature films diminish both statement and impact. This structural achievement proved to be exceptional, for Chaplin never really duplicated it; but the fact that *City Lights* succeeds in functioning on so large a scale gives weight to its articulation of values, and enables it to touch our lives in the significant, transforming way we expect of a major religious statement.

So we have in *City Lights* a work which expresses a distinctive vision of the world in a remarkably uncompromised way, and on a scale which commands serious attention. This alone is enough to merit careful, repeated viewing, and such viewing is in itself the only completely adequate access to the religious insight which the work offers. It may be possible, though, with care to identify some elements in this film which contribute to its religious significance; care is needed because, like all successful art works, *City Lights* functions on its own terms, and efforts at describing it risk reducing it to what is expressible in ordinary language, a particular irony in the case of a silent film. In place of description we might prefer "suggestions for perception," to paraphrase Gene Blocker's excellent phrase,[2] by which we would draw attention to key aspects of the world which Chaplin has created, without presuming to define them exhaustively.

The obvious importance of Chaplin's work has seen to it that this task is already well under way. The figure of the clown has traditionally been viewed as a religious metaphor, and the clown-like aspects of Chaplin's tramp have been noted in this respect. More strikingly, Neil Hurley has given us a catalogue of Jewish-Christian images which Chaplin appears to have incorporated in his work;[3] and many of these find a prominent place in *City Lights:* "concern for the underdog," "the theology of reversal," and even the healing of a blind person.

The larger structure of the film also seems to reflect a biblical conceptuality. S.K. Langer's work in theory of drama offers a helpful way of getting at this structure; and although it may seen curious to approach a film from the standpoint of drama, it can be shown that Chaplin uses film primarily as a way of extending a fundamentally theatrical art, rather than exploiting its peculiar characteristics as Keaton likes to do.

Langer locates the significance of art in the forms which it presents to us, and identifies these forms as symbolic projections of human feeling. As such, they offer the best tools we have for presenting to others the affective dimension of our inner lives. To the degree that a religious conception of the world functions in affective as well as rational categories, it normally relies upon these symbolic forms to explore, organize, and communicate affective elements; this is one reason why religion and the arts are so ubiquitously linked. And since the symbolic forms of art are more easily manipulated than is actual feeling, these offer the possibility of proposing novel patterns of feeling, which may finally be as significant to the development of the life of the imagination as comparable theoretical work in the natural sciences is to that realm. In fact, one of the most important aspects of *City Lights* is precisely the manner in which it projects an original way of feeling in relationship to a key religious problem of our time, as our analysis will reveal.

In Langer's analysis, drama shapes a representation of human behavior in such a way as to embody forms of feeling; an important work can thus offer a fresh conception of feeling which adds to the richness of human experience. Beyond this, dramatic representation permits the symbolization and presentation of rational as well as affective elements, and the fusion of both of these into a more comprehensive envisioning of experience quite similar to that which religion has traditionally sought. And because this process can articulate the affective elements which characterize value, it can also contribute to the shaping of value structures which finally motivate or even transform behavior. Here is another reason for the historic relationship between religion and the arts, and the special affinity of religion and drama.

Langer draws our attention primarily to the structure of the dramatic action, modeled on patterns of human awareness: "human beings, because of their semantically enlarged horizon, are aware of individual history as a passage from birth to death."[4] Tragedy stresses one aspect of this passage, "the deathward advance of . . . individual lives . . . a series of stations that are not repeated; growth, maturity, decline."[5] Thus a typical tragedy introduces us to its protagonist in full career, and traces that career toward death. Langer calls this rhythm "Fate," and its linear, purposive character seems to control situation as well as character.

But the comic rhythm, equally drawn from "life as it feels to the living," represents a quite different abstraction. It is seen in the smaller upsets and victories of life, in meeting and overcoming obstacles, in the struggle toward survival. Langer sees two aspects of the most basic life processes mirrored in the structure of comedy: the movement from equilibrium to disturbance and then back to equilibrium, and the characteristic ability "of organisms to seize on opportunities" and use them to advantage.⁶ Thus the comic protagonist repeatedly encounters, but one way or another survives, a series of disruptions, often by a show of ingenuity and resourcefulness. It should come as no surprise to find these comic rhythms present in so much myth and ritual action, for the imaginative representation and interpretation of life forces, of survival, growth, and development have always been a central religious theme. That such rhythms can be traced both in "secular" forms like popular films and in traditional modes of religious expression is one of the key links between religion and film.

The environments surrounding these rhythms are equally distinctive. The tragic world is highly ordered, controlled, dependable; the action often begins with some breach of social order, and ends with this order emphatically reestablished, as for instance with a coronation as in *Hamlet* or *Macbeth*. Hamlet himself takes note of this aspect of his environment when he laments, "The time is out of joint. O cursed spite/That ever I was born to set it right!" In contrast, the comic world is disorderly, almost chaotic, characterized by coincidence, chance, and "Fortune."⁷ Whatever fitful order there may be results from the hero's resourcefulness, not from any intrinsic structure of meaning. In a happy phrase which might have been coined to describe *City Lights*, Langer sums up that aspect of the human adventure which gives rise to comedy: "a brainy opportunism in the face of an essentially dreadful universe."⁸

Reflecting on "an essentially dreadful universe," *City Lights* offers among other things a bosom buddy who suddenly, repeatedly, and inexplicably has one thrown out of the house, a parade of elephants to vex a neophyte street cleaner, a lucky charm which brings disaster, a prison term as reward for charitable action—its setting bears an uncomfortable resemblance to that legendary place where no good deed goes unpunished. "The perpetual misery of the world he believes to be unredeemed and unredeemable"⁹ is Robert Payne's description of the atmosphere of Chaplin's *City Lights;* its potential for despair "reaches depths which are visible in no other film composed by Chaplin."¹⁰

But "a brainy opportunism" is also fully in evidence. A statue to "peace and prosperity" may not be much help to the homeless, but viewed with imagination, as it is by the tramp, it can be used as a tent, a bed, and an opportunity for thumbing one's nose at bureaucracy. A prize-fight can with advantage be transformed into a ballet; the transformation is simultaneously hilarious and strangely beautiful. Although this may be the harshest environment in which we ever see the tramp, his resourcefulness and comic invention never flag; he responds to each new crisis with the courage and grace which seem to be his birthright.

F. Thomas Trotter has noted some interesting parallels between these comic elements and the way we have conventionally understood our own experience. Since the renaissance, European culture has given pride of place to tragic forms, and long before that had attempted to achieve in its social and political life the order and stability of the tragic world. But the worldview of the Christian scriptures, Trotter points out, seems really much closer to that of comedy—"random," "disorderly," characterized by "natural chaos."[11] The comic figure embodies not only the Langerian rhythms of survival, but also something "similar to the gospel . . . that into a disorderly world God entered in the person of Jesus and introduced a principle that is other than order—freedom, grace, trust, faith, courage."[12] In this context, Chaplin in *City Lights* offers us insight into patterns of endurance and survival as well as, and more importantly, into those rhythms of transformation and renewal which are at the heart of the Jewish-Christian tradition.

The film moves beyond even this, however, to engage a contemporary fragmented world. As Kerr points out, "it is the most ingeniously formed, immaculately interlocked of Chaplin's experiments in combining comedy with pathos. The comedy and the love story depend utterly on each other; neither can move until the other requires it to do so."[13] Chaplin has here succeeded in integrating two quite different patterns of human feeling into a larger, more inclusive whole, an achievement which points toward a new way of conceiving the human situation. This is at the heart of the most famous sequence of the film, the meeting between the tramp and the now-seeing flower girl. Traditional comic forms ended happily, often with a wedding and a dance,[14] and most of the practitioners of silent comedy were content to follow the tradition. But Chaplin's experiments in integrating the darker aspects of human experience into his comedy apparently began to involve the rethinking of this convention.

One sees a possible prefiguring of this in the ironic implications of the closing reel of *The Gold Rush;* significantly, when Chaplin rereleased the film in a sound version in 1942, he shortened the ending and made it even more ambiguous. Kevin Brownlow in his film *Unknown Chaplin* suggests that this may have been motivated by Chaplin's changing feelings toward Georgia Hale, and David Shepard reminds us that the 1942 version was constructed "almost entirely from outtakes,"[15] which may somewhat have limited Chaplin's options. Even so, the effect of the new ending is to weaken further any sense of a conventional happy ending, and in some ways even to blunt the irony because of its ambiguity. The last sequence of *The Circus* is even bolder: As the circus moves on, taking with it the girl he loves, the tramp is left behind in the dusty ring; as he sets out on new adventures, his jaunty walk does not entirely efface the sense of loss.

But the ending of *City Lights* goes still further. Released from prison, the tramp by chance encounters the girl whose sight he has helped to restore. At first she does not recognize him, but in offering him some money she touches his hand and realizes who he is. Now for the first time she sees him, and in turn he scans her face intently for signs of her reaction. With this exchange of glances, in enormous close-up rare in Chaplin, the film ends.

What are we to make of this? Kerr offers a provocative interpretation: the film has been full of role reversals, and this is the ultimate. The impoverished flower girl now has a nice shop of her own, while the "millionaire" has become a shabby tramp, and a continuing relationship between them is now impossible. "Without the least loss of laughter," Kerr writes, "Chaplin has remade the world in his own despairing, but unyielding, image."[16]

This is, however, a rare lapse in his superb book, for Kerr seems here to discuss not what Chaplin has done, but what he would perhaps have done had he continued his narrative.[17] The film ends with the famous close-up of the tramp's anxious smile. If we accept Chaplin's actual ending, as indeed we must, then he has given us his boldest experiment in comic rhythm and form. Looking back, we recall that, throughout *City Lights*, moments of comic reversal or transformation have been presented unemphatically or ambiguously. Compare the tramp's capture with his effortless rout of authority in dozens of earlier films, for one of many examples; the unprecedented defeat in the comic prizefight is another. Over and over again, in place of triumph or resolution, we are offered ambiguity: reasons for hope and reasons for despair. It is as though Chaplin wanted to push comic rhythm toward ambiguity as far as it would go without collapse, and thus do the fullest possible justice to what seems more than ever a hostile, meaningless world.

But, at the same time, he is unyielding in maintaining the underlying comic structure, both in individual sequences and in the total shape of the film. Win, lose, or draw, the tramp is back at the beginning of virtually every new sequence, armed with imagination and grace. Even the last sequence, an apparent exception, is actually shaped by this comic rhythm; the tramp's unusually bedraggled appearance and sour mood at its beginning become an important ingredient in the quite magical transformation of its last few shots. And its very contrast with the rest of the film reminds us again how strong the comic structure is throughout, the promise of survival and hope juxtaposed decisively against the ambiguity and despair.

A final question remains: Can this way of conceiving and, more importantly, of feeling about human experience be taken seriously? Chaplin has often been proclaimed a genius, and nearly as often dismissed as a sentimentalist, a paradox visited in reverse proportions upon Capra and Disney. What does it mean to be a "sentimental genius"? Usually, the implication is that the artist is asking us to entertain feelings which are thought to be exaggerated or otherwise inappropriate to the subject under consideration; an instance might be the tramp's attitude toward his foundling in *The Kid*. But such criticism is flawed when it takes an aspect of a work out of context, and then compares it with a conception of appropriate feeling external to the work. Thus, those who find *The Kid* sentimental appear to assume general agreement about the way one ought to feel about small children, and then to find Chaplin's treatment excessive.

The integrity of a work is better served, however, when its details are seen in relationship to its larger structures. If Langer is right, this is the only way for us to grasp the distinctive mode of feeling which the artist is proposing and, in turn, to be grasped by it; otherwise, we risk finding only what we were looking for. At the climax of *The Kid*, the tramp rescues the boy from the orphanage truck, and they embrace with tears running down their cheeks. No doubt a sentimental image considered abstractly, but in the context of the splendid conception of the whole sequence and of its pantomime, this shot is felt as both inevitable and absolutely right, a feeling confirmed by the wonderful last shot of the sequence in which the tramp disposes of the driver.

Where the larger structure of a work really does fail, as in the case of the bathetic self-pity which appears to swamp whole tracts of *Limelight*, then the film fails because no grander conception of feeling is articulated. But when that structure succeeds, as it does brilliantly in *City Lights*, then such a work in turn can be brought into dialogue with our everyday experience in a way that is powerful and transformative. Like other important religious conceptions, it has the ability to affect the very fabric of our lives.

City Lights is Chaplin's grand success, for in it he provides us with a vision of the world rooted in the ancient celebration of comedy, but without the easy reversals and triumphs which seem trivial or unbelievable in the context of the contemporary world. Equilibrium is maintained with far greater difficulty; chaos is barely survived rather than banished. But the underlying courage and imagination and grace are still present and, because of them, so is that hope of which John May speaks in the introduction to this volume. The famous last shot can be read as Kerr does, but it can also be read in the context of the tremendous energy toward the future which the film's larger structure has generated. It is this affirmation of a possible and even hopeful future which is at the center of *City Lights,* and which offers the fullest justification of Agee's claim that Chaplin has given us in "the tramp, the most humane and the most nearly complete among the religious figures our time has evolved."[18]

The Grapes of Wrath:
The Poor You Always Have with You
Philip C. Rule, S.J.

When *The Grapes of Wrath* opened in January 1940, New York *Herald Tribune* critic Howard Barnes wrote that "for once in a long, long time the screen has made electric contact with the abiding verities of existence."[1] In an age when few films violated the happy-ending formula, Edwin Locke, another contemporary critic, wrote that although film-makers assumed audiences "want nothing for their money but entertainment," people were "crowding the box office and breaking into spontaneous applause after each screening of the picture."[2] The film did indeed touch something deep in the hearts of its audiences. Why else would people who were just beginning to emerge from the suffering and depri-vation of the Great Depression flock to see a film which, in Locke's words, "dramatized and memorialized one wretched section of our na-tion," the Okies driven from their dust-bowl farms to California where they found not the anticipated land of milk and honey but one of back-breaking labor at starvation wages? What are those abiding verities Barnes mentioned and what artistry could so dramatize and memorialize the plight of those oppressed men and women that their fellow Ameri-cans flocked to see them on film? What pleasure can we derive from watching the pain and suffering of fellow human beings if it is not the realization of our solidarity in the human predicament, that when one of us suffers we all, in a very real sense, suffer with that person?

Nothing is more fundamental to a religious vision of human exis-tence than the recognition of this human solidarity. "No man is an is-land," poet and preacher John Donne reminded us centuries ago. Our lives are related and intermingled. No individual develops a religious vision or myth. It grows, rather, out of the shared experience of a commu-nity whose hopes and aspirations find common voice in a system of common symbols. Every human community must answer for itself a

21

The Grapes of Wrath
(1940, John Ford)

Medium two- and three-shots are Ford's recurring visual emblem for his myth of the solidarity of the human family. Here Tom Joad (Henry Fonda), Ma (Jane Darwell) and Rosasharn (Dorris Bowdon) reveal their relative thematic significance—Tom representing drive and forward vision, Ma with stubborn determination at the heart of the family (and the frame), and Rosasharn fearfully learning the mother's role she must assume.

number of "ultimate" questions: What shall we do with our dead, i.e. where do they go after life as we know it? What shall be the common norm of right and wrong, good and evil? Is there a common transcendent sanction for our behavior? Do we stand alone and naked in an impersonal universe or do we stand together in the presence of an absolute mystery which is personal? There are, of course, other questions and other answers. But to the extent that they, too, are "ultimate," they are religious.

One of the most vexing questions that has confronted human society, both secular and sacred, from the dawn of recorded history, is the discouragingly persistent disparity between the haves and have nots, the rich and the poor. Whether one looks to the ancient past or the contemporary present, whether one looks far away to the third world or here at home in our own country, the terrible problem persists. We have found no socio-economic system that eliminates poverty, that guarantees a fair distribution of wealth. Even in our land of great prosperity, the farm problem "dramatized and memorialized" in *The Grapes of Wrath* still dogs us fifty years later as we have seen recently recorded in films like *Country* and *The River*. Taken out of context, Jesus' remark to his disciples, "the poor you always have with you," might seem banal if not cynical in its obviousness. Certainly Tom Joad sees through its glib use by religionists who point out pie in the sky to the poor and hungry of this world. "An' I got to thinkin'," he says, "most of the preachin' is about the poor we shall have always with us, an' if you got nothin', why just' fol' your hands an' to hell with it, you gonna git ice cream on gol' plates when you're dead."[3] These words and some others like them are left out of the film, as we shall see, as part of a process of toning down the anti-religious elements in the novel.

In their recent study of American society, sociologist Robert Bellah and his colleagues point out that "the litmus test that both the biblical and republican traditions give us for assaying the health of a society is how it deals with the problem of wealth and poverty."[4] In concluding his penetrating study of Marxism, philosopher Arthur McGovern similarly observes that "all religious faiths and political ideologies share in common some vision of a truly just and human society."[5] This imbalance of wealth and poverty existing in the same society is recorded at the dawn of civilization as we know it. In the ancient Code of Hammurabi, that "perfect king" tells his subjects he has promulgated his law "to cause justice to prevail in the land, to destroy the wicked and evil, that the strong might not oppress the weak." Among other things, masters must treat their servants justly; widows and orphans must be protected.[6] The Jewish and Christian scriptures echo the same exhortations. God strictly forbids the oppression of the weak: the poor, the widowed, and the orphaned. To the extent that this perennial problem is seen solely in the light of socio-economic causes, the solutions offered will be specific and in fact secular, if they are indeed forthcoming. To the extent that it is viewed as arising from pervasive evil that has afflicted the human heart, the solutions will always sound somewhat vague and general; for what the religious solution ultimately urges is that the wealthy and the powerful have a profound change of heart, a change which as Jesus pointed out might not even be effected by the return of someone from the dead (Lk 16:19–31).

I think it is this very association of the religious dimension with what is somewhat vague and general which has led John May to write that Ford's film "is just slightly more sophisticated theologically than John Steinbeck's novel and only because it is less specific" in its laying blame for the evil depicted at the feet of "society or its institutions." I disagree slightly, however, with May's statement that the film "scrupulously avoids the novel's clear accusations,"[7] for a series of vividly clashing images (the fedora-wearing, cigar-smoking land repossessors, hiring agents, and lawmen driving around in big roadsters contrasted with the simply clad migrants piled in their jalopies and trucks) silently points an accusing finger at big business just as in *Stagecoach* the presence of the self-righteous banker who has embezzled from his own bank suggests the hypocrisy of wealth and power. Nevertheless, Ford does raise more questions than he answers; and, like Steinbeck, he does not even mention the issue of poor farming methods which contributed as much as drought to the soil erosion in the dust bowl. In a written prologue flashed on the screen, the plight of the Okies is simply attributed to "drought, poverty, and economic change beyond anyone's control." Where Steinbeck's novel is a grimly detailed description of the status quo and a harsh indictment of big business, Ford's film is a realistic portrayal of the farmers shot from a more humane and nostalgic point of view which focuses less sharply on the causes of their condition and rather looks ahead to a better society in which such injustices may be eliminated.

It is, in fact, the transformation of Steinbeck's harsh social realism into Ford's affectionate vision of good people driven together in common suffering that gives the film a certain mythic and thereby religious dimension expressed as a vision of hope. Significantly, Ford dropped the final two chapters of the novel in which Steinbeck with oppressive detail narrates the further savaging of the life of the migrants by torrential rains and Rose of Sharon's giving birth to a stillborn child. In sharp contrast, Ford chose to end the film with Tom running off in search of a solution to society's problems and the family driving off to find work. Tom will, in fact, articulate a vision in which men will, in the words of William Faulkner's Nobel acceptance speech, not only survive but prevail. Ford's powerful images of goons and lawmen clubbing those early farm unionizers would prophetically anticipate the fate of Gandhi and his followers in India, and Martin Luther King and American Blacks who were galvanized into solidarity by King's dream that "We Shall Overcome." As a matter of fact, socio-economic solutions to human problems usually follow rather than precede deeply moving visions and sustaining myths that sink deep into the human imagination and heart.

While it is often neither fair nor profitable to compare a film with its literary source, there are striking and significant differences between the style and theme of the film and the novel. Andrew Sarris, for example, summarizes neatly the contrasting treatment of characters in pointing out that "where Steinbeck depicted oppression by dehumanizing his characters into creatures of necessity, Ford evoked nostalgia by humanizing Steinbeck's economic insects into heroic champions of an agrarian family and community."[8] Ford, in fact, did more than this. As I have already pointed out, he raised a story told in a style of harsh social realism, if not naturalism, to the level of life-sustaining myth without in any way ignoring the grim reality of his characters' lives.

In producing a script for the movie, Ford and scriptwriter Nunnally Johnson left out some fourteen chapters of descriptive interludes that chronicled in harsh detail life in the 1930s and constituted a strongly worded authorial commentary on the family saga narrated in the novel. Certain religious elements, mostly negative, were either eliminated or toned down: Uncle John's periodic benders as he tries to drown his guilt-ridden conscience with alcohol, Casy's boasting about the sexual escapades associated with his revival meetings, and comments like the one Tom makes about the hypocritical uses of scripture. Key religious elements do remain, however. The title, derived immediately from "The Battle Hymn of the Republic" and ultimately from the Bible, suggests that God will wreak vengeance on those who oppress the poor and the downtrodden. For in Jeremiah we read that "the cup of the wine of God's wrath" will be given to alien nations who oppress God's people (25:15), and Revelation says that idolators "shall drink the wine of God's wrath" (14:10). The message is profound in its vagueness: someone is definitely going to pay dearly for this kind of evil behavior.

While Ford's and Johnson's script and Alfred Newman's wonderfully evocative musical score (which summons up images of an America

gone by) establish tone and mood, nothing is more central than the cinematography in establishing Ford's point of view. Fresh from his recent
experience in making government documentary films and inspired by his
Irish-Catholic immigrant love of America, Ford shifts the emphasis from
harsh realism and social criticism to the tension between hope and despair experienced by those facing overwhelming odds, precisely by
counterpointing documentary realism and mythic vision. What Parker
Tyler called "a sort of newsreel coarseness"[9] conveys a keen sense of the
reality of the suffering of the migrants and translates into visual images
much of the harsh tone of the long descriptive passages omitted by Ford
and Johnson. A contrasting set of images embodies the polar idea of
hope. As the ships which brought hopeful pilgrims to the Atlantic shores
were later replaced by "prairie schooners" that bore still more hopeful
pilgrims westward after the Civil War, now once again in the 1930s the
Joads and other farmers are borne still farther westward to a new promised land of milk and honey, bursting with grapes and oranges.

No image dominates the film as does that of the truck chugging
along Route 66 from Oklahoma to California, first to the tune of an
upbeat and optimistic musical background, then in stark silence. The
journey motif, familiar to most readers of western European literature,
finds a ready-made religious analogue here, one that symbolizes Ford's
vision of American civilization. The similarity of the Joads to the chosen
people leaving their home and journeying through the desert to a promised land is not strained. The handbills like some distant divine call
beckon the Joads with the promise of work in a land "flowing with milk
and honey." At the final meal before leaving the farm, Grandpa Joad
dreams of eating oranges and especially grapes, which are rumored to
grow in great abundance in the Golden State. "There's a thing I ain't
never had enough of," he says. "Gonna get me a whole big bunch of
grapes off a bush, or whatever, and I's a gonna squash 'em on my face an'
let 'em run offen my chin." When the family arrives at the Colorado
River and stands looking at California on the other side, Pa Joad exclaims, "Thar she is, folks, the land of milk and honey, California."

In the dilapidated truck rides not only a family but the future hopes
of our country.[10] The family is the microcosm of society, of the solidarity
and cooperation and trust that make society possible. If the family survives, so will society. Here again Ford tones down certain negative
aspects of the novel. Where Steinbeck details the disintegration of the
family, Ford shifts the emphasis visually to Ma as the sustaining source of
unity and survival. In the novel, for example, we learn that Noah Joad,

one of the older brothers, runs off when the family first reaches California. In the film he is introduced only to be silently omitted from the trip west. The departure of Rose of Sharon's husband is noted, but not anticipated as it is in the novel. And at the end Al is going to get married—leaving only Uncle John, the Joads, and three younger children, two generations of the four who started out (if one includes Rose of Sharon's then unborn child). But at the end of the film, there is a strong sense that the family is still together, struggling, surviving because the hopes of the dead and of those who have gone away live on in this brave remnant.

In a long passage Ford omitted, Tom explains to Ma that Casy the Preacher "went out into the wilderness to find his soul," and what he discovered was that each individual soul is part of a larger common soul. Casy formulated his insight in verses taken fairly literally from Ecclesiastes: "Two are better than one, because they have a good reward for their labor. For if they fall, the one will lif' up his fellow, but woe to him that is lone when he falleth, for he hath not another to help him up." And, again, "if two lie together, then they have heat: but how can one be warm alone? And if you prevail against him, two shall withstand him, and a threefold cord is not quickly broken."[11] Why Ford left this out is, of course, a matter of conjecture, but one might suspect that, in spite of the film's firm biblical basis, such veiled hints at unionizing of the farm workers were too hot an item for the filmmakers to handle. As John May has noted, "big business threatened to withdraw its financial support from the film venture."[12] The issue is not, however, entirely suppressed. Besides the strong visual images of oppression already mentioned, at several points in the film Tom shakes his head quizzically at the persistent charges of "reds" and "agitators" leveled against anyone who objects to or in any way questions the labor practices of the ranchers and hiring agents. Early in the film when Mulie describes for Tom and Casy the repossession of the land, the blame is laid first on "the company," then "the banks," and finally and somewhat cryptically "the East." But the oppressors are no less real for all their anonymity, and individual farmers and workers cannot withstand their economic power.

In taking leave of Ma, Tom amplifies Casy's insights mentioned above. When Ma asks, "What are you gonna do?" Tom says he has been doing some thinking "about our people living like pigs, and good land lying fallow, or maybe one fellow with a million acres, while a hundred thousand good farmers is starving. And I been wondering if all our folks got together and yelled. . . ." He has decided to run away and "scrounge around and find out what's wrong and maybe do something about it."

And then in a passage taken almost verbatim from the novel, he articulates a dream of human solidarity and compassion:

> I'll be around in the dark. I'll be everywhere—wherever you look. Wherever they's a fight so hungry people can eat. I'll be there. Wherever they's a cop beatin' up a guy. I'll be there. I'll be in the way guys yell when they're mad—and I'll be in the way kids laugh when they're hungry and they know supper's ready. And when people eat the stuff they raise an' live in the houses they build, I'll be there.

Although Ma says she doesn't understand all this, a few scenes later she enunciates a similar belief. In the closing scene, far more hopeful and upbeat than Steinbeck's grim closing picture of Rose of Sharon's nursing a starving man with her useless mother's milk, Ma says that the individualistic rich will die out, but "we're the people that live. We'll go on 'cause we're the people." Here is expressed the core of Ford's myth, which is a mixture of sacred and secular hope.

Tom's and Ma's language evokes both the biblical and the republican spirit of this country encapsulated in such slogans as "we the people," "united we stand divided we fall," "one people under God," and "*e pluribus unum.*" Our hope is not in the selfish individualism of the rich, but in the generosity and solidarity of the common people. Ford's faith was in the "common man," the decent, caring, trusting, law-abiding, God-fearing person. He believed in the validity and efficacy of a democratic system that guaranteed the policy of one person, one vote. He believed that if enough good people realized this, respected one another and worked together in mutual cooperation, things would work out—if not today, then tomorrow. A glimpse of what might be is, of course, presented during the almost Edenic stay in the government camp where a democratic process and respect for one's neighbors provide a peaceful and decent living, however temporary it might be.

In staging this myth of American society, Ford turned again and again to a cadre of favorite actors. Two in particular represent the hero of the Ford myth: John Wayne and Henry Fonda. Wayne appeared in Ford films as the silent but tough hero who spoke best with fists and guns. His articulation of the vision was limited to down-to-earth observations drawled out in his own laconic manner. Henry Fonda was a different kind of hero. Although he too played in many westerns, he seems, unlike Wayne, to have transcended the stereotype of the cowboy. Although he often appeared as a soft-spoken, shy, almost gentle figure, there was a deep, quiet inner strength about him and his ability to express, in however halting a manner, the hopes and dreams of the people he represented: as a national leader in *Young Mr. Lincoln,* as an angry and defiant farm worker in *The Grapes of Wrath,* or, as later in Sidney Lumet's *Twelve Angry Men,* the ordinary decent American seeking justice. Fonda, like Jimmy Stewart, always seems to speak for the common man, *homo Americanus.*

Ford, in fact, increasingly focuses the film on the actions and thoughts of Ma and Tom Joad. Where the other characters are either naturally diffident or increasingly silenced by adversity, Ma and Tom become more angry and articulate as the film reaches its climax. Close-up shots of them individually or together may in fact constitute a formal paradigm for the meaning of the film. Louis Giannetti, working with anthropologist Edward T. Hall's concept of "proxemic patterns," argues convincingly that close-ups visually define "intimate distances" which suggest "love, comfort, and tenderness between individuals,"[13] the very basis for the human solidarity which I have intimated lies at the heart of Ford's myth. Few images in the film remain more indelibly fixed in the viewer's mind than the closing shot of Jane Darwell staring resolutely through the windshield of the truck as the remnant of the family drives off to find work. The major movements of the film each conclude with close-ups of either Tom or Ma or the two of them together, visually underlining their thematic importance in the film. For this is a film about both a specific family and a common dream of the human family. It is, as the prologue tells the audience, about the plight of one family "and their great journey in search of peace, security, and yet another home," words that contain the seed of Ford's myth which grows up out of the soil of Steinbeck's realism.

If Ma Joad represents the solid, practical stubbornness that survives the present affliction, Tom represents the forward-looking aspect of Ford's vision. Ford's Irish Roman Catholic heritage, blended with the democratic ideal in the melting pot of American society, transformed the secular realism of Steinbeck into a transcendent myth. If this seems like replacing the concreteness of the actual with the vagueness of the possible, the charge is not without warrant. The Romantic poet Percy Shelley originally closed his great drama *Prometheus Unbound* with a third act that presented a revolutionary vision of social reform which specified the current sources of human oppression: monarchy, religion, superstition, and social status. But then he added a fourth act, less specific and timely, but far more emotionally and imaginatively powerful and in fact timeless in its passionate assertion of the final victory of hope over despair.

It is, however, precisely the tension between the film's texture of documentary realism and the organizing and visual patterns of Ford's myth that keeps these two elements humanly significant and, thereby, genuinely religious. I say genuinely religious because a move toward either extreme runs the risk of ignoring the reality of the social evil or trivializing the myth—or reducing it to sheer sentimental wishful thinking. An excessive focus on social realism can lead to pessimism and paralyzing despair. Excessive focus on the mythic element can lead to false hopes and a kind of revolutionary utopianism that vainly attempts to realize heaven on earth. Ford's documentary treatment, therefore, expresses our inhumanity to one another; his visionary treatment expresses our humanity at its deepest level—its real, albeit often suppressed instinct to transcend itself.

High Noon: On the Uncertainty of Certainty

Ann-Janine Morey

The formula for the story of *High Noon* contains all the elements of the classic western yarn. It owes much to *The Virginian* (1929), one of Gary Cooper's earliest movies, and it is obviously the inspiration for the several more recent Clint Eastwood films in which the true western made an effective comeback. Just as retiring marshal Will Kane (Gary Cooper) and Quaker Amy Fowler (Grace Kelly) are celebrating their marriage, outlaw Frank Miller is returning to town on the noon train to take vengeance upon Kane. The tension of the movie is tightened in several directions beyond the obvious drama of the anticipated show-down. His wife threatens to leave him if he stays for the confrontation, and his deputy Harvey (Lloyd Bridges) quits because Kane refuses to let him take over as marshal. At the same time Kane slowly realizes that public support for him is minimal as well. Faced with crises of both public and private spheres, and often unable to articulate his reasons for persisting, he finally faces the four killers alone, and triumphs.

In this plot we are presented with "good guys" and "bad guys," and the irony that violence is necessary to protect the civilization that professes to abhor such methods of resolution. Women and ministers usually speak for some sort of ethic of peace and non-violence, and as with many western tales, the ineffectiveness of Christianity to offer any meaningful mediation is underlined. There is the courageous, lone male who triumphs over evil against daunting odds, and his triumph resolves at least two confrontations—the gun battle with the outlaws and the verbal battle with his wife or sweetheart. The classic western is usually keyed about some clear antinomies: the blonde angel/passionate dark lady, the church/saloon, the rugged individual/community, order/anarchy, hero/villain, good/evil. It is a combination of the scenery and the formula that makes the western such a cherished statement of American identity. The scenery provides a visual affirmation of grandeur and possibility; the

31

formula is powerful for its certainty: that good will triumph; that men know what they are doing, and that the good men will be brave and skillful and loyal when they do it; that women will acknowledge the necessity and superiority of this kind of moral order, and if they don't, they along with the outlaws will be punished; and that violence is a regrettable good in establishing the security of this moral order.

Today most people think of *High Noon* as one of several quintessential westerns, but despite much of its structural predictability, *High Noon* is much more than the epitome of a beloved genre. The film was reviewed as an "anti-western" movie, and John Wayne called it "un-American." Many interpreted the film as a daring critique of McCarthyism and the failure of people to stand up to villainy, a kind of statement that would hardly have been expected from the genre at that time. How, then, is *High Noon* so different?

One way to answer the question is briefly to compare the movie to a near and popular contemporary, George Stevens' *Shane* (1953). *Shane* fulfills every romantic, mythic expectation one could have about the west and what it represents to Americans. It was filmed in the Grand Tetons and the scenery is breathtaking, the color vivid and tender. The gunman (Alan Ladd) is chivalrous, fatherly, sure, deadly; the farmer's wife (Jean Arthur), an ineffective voice for pacifism. Shane always knows what he must do, and he does so with consummate skill. Fight scenes are slow and even ballet-like, the brutality of the encounter subordinate to the joy and mastery exercised by the hero. The threatened, dispirited community of homesteaders is resurrected in response to the gunman, who makes a graveside speech about the importance of families, and so encourages them to renew their claim to life and land. He then rewards their efforts by doing what they cannot, and secures their kingdom by violence. Both the community and the gunman get high marks for principle, loyalty and courage. With great sensitivity, Shane rides into the sunrise once the killing is done, for he knows his salvific actions have also forfeited his place in the human community.

But *Shane* is a story for children, not because it is told from a child's point of view, but because it tells what a nostalgic adult would like for a child to see, what an adult would still like to believe. The only moment of truth in the film occurs during the scene between the hired gun Wilson (Jack Palance) and the impetuous Irish farmer Torry. The scene is shot so that Wilson, lounging outside the bar on a raised porch, is in the shadow of a receding storm, although the muddy street before him is partly in the sun. The farmer, skidding in the slop of the street, slowly approaches from the sun into the shadow with the killer. He is taunted, draws, hesitates, and is shot. Torry's body jerks violently into the mud, and as the camera draws away, the corpse becomes indistinguishable from the muddy, rolled furrows of the rain-gouged street. A horrified companion drags his body from its sodden grave. Next we see the friend riding home with the body of the farmer slung across a second horse. The corpse is perfectly clean, and we know we have been returned to the world of romance.

In contrast, *High Noon* is simply an ugly film. It was made in black and white, with an effort toward a documentary style of film narration. The landscape offers no romance or exaltation. The sun is pitiless and hot, the sky cloudless, the town dusty and barren despite the various businesses that form the main street. As the story progresses, there are other things about the formula that are dislocated as well. The church and the saloon show themselves to be the same kind of resource—neither gathering will act on Kane's behalf, and the public owner of the saloon is a prominent church member. The "dark woman," Helen Ramirez (Katy Jurado), despite the convention of her questionable past, has been Kane's lover. Even more surprisingly, she befriends the bewildered but determined blonde who has succeeded her, and with warmth and dignity coaches her in the role she must assume. The alliance between the two women is oddly touching, and although Kelly's character has been tenderized—in the script she announces herself to be a feminist, a speech which does not appear in the movie—she is given room to demonstrate her own intelligence and courage.[1]

But Kane himself is the biggest dislocation to the formula, for Fred Zinnemann, the director, uses the convention of the strong, silent male to create a portrait of bewilderment, awkward resolution, and even pathos. Zinnemann said that, amidst much protest, he used "flat lighting for Cooper to make him look as moth-eaten as we could, which was then a great departure for a western hero."[2] In addition, Kane is an older man leaving his profession of force to become a shopkeeper, an unlikely domestic outcome for any serious western hero.

Overall, it was Zinnemann's intention to let the audience make up its own mind about the story, and that makes *High Noon* a film for adults in a way that most westerns are not. It was Zinnemann's contention that "rooting interest" where the director tells the audience who is good and who is bad is "almost mechanical in the writing. . . . I don't really believe in heavies and heroes personally." Zinnemann was interested in the motivations and processes of the Cooper character, and the film was made with that unfolding in mind, an approach that is highly subversive of the conventional western movie. As Zinnemann said, "if a character in a situation does something, I want to know why. I'm not interested in a man shooting a gun, I'm interested in why he does it . . . and the conflict of the person becomes the landscape that I work from."[3]

Zinnemann's interest in Kane focuses on why he is staying and how he struggles with his sense of self-respect and duty, and he dramatizes the complexities of the situation by using the convention of the strong, silent hero to act as its own critical chorus. Kane is a man of so few words he is simply clumsy, although when he does speak, he says all the right western hero sorts of things. Yet the accumulation of his silences is not decisive or strong, but crippling. As Kane moves from individuals and groups to seek assistance, it becomes clear that he has managed to alienate various constituencies, and he is awkward and self-defeating in these encounters with his wife, the saloon crowd and the church congregation. He has annoyed the preacher by his infrequent appearances in church, and by his failure to let him know why he was not married in the church. He never explains to the congregation why there are only two deputies when there used to be six (and we don't know either; we see only one of them in the film). He goes to a saloon filled with Frank Miller's friends to appeal for help, and begins by punching out the bartender for an injudicious remark. Then he refuses to explain why his deputy has quit. He is unable to make his wife understand his motivations, nor does he seem to take seriously her objections, just as he never seems to hear the arguments of various friends and townspeople. The most we know about his motivations are summarized in the opening song, and fragments of the song reappear at crucial moments to speak on his behalf. When the song speaks up for him, it tells us he is torn between love and duty, and must face "that deadly killer or . . . lie a coward in [his] grave." For an audience of the western movie, this is a predictable motivation, but it is not particularly apparent to his new wife, or to the innumerable townspeople who urge him to leave as though they'd never heard of this manly code of the west. Only his ex-lover, Helen Ramirez, seems to understand, and she is unable to help him, having been replaced by the suitable blonde. What makes his inner struggle worth a story is not that he acts in loyalty to this principle, but that he is acting upon a principle that seems to be largely unnameable, and that even he doesn't seem to fully understand. In response to questions about why he is staying, his repeated response is, "If you don't know, I can't explain it to you."

He persists, and does so in the face of opposition, practical wisdom, and the pull of his own heart, but he is not sure what he is doing, and his own inability to articulate his motivations speaks of his growing confusion, doubt, and anger. Kane—and this was a key objection to the movie—doesn't always know what he is doing. He is not omniscient, and although the weight of the film is sympathetic to his struggle, it is not always clear that his position is right. The churched members of the community finally agree that his presence in town will inflame Frank Miller and so endanger the whole town, whereas if he leaves perhaps there will be no trouble. Kane has already said that Miller will hunt him down wherever he is, so this tactical suggestion from the good folk in the church may amount to the much maligned Pharisaical argument that it is better one man should die that a people may live. This mode of sacrifice does not occur to Kane, and there is enough truth to their concerns to make the situation ambiguous. Kane's refusal to consider their view of their own welfare looks as selfish as their position looks cowardly. Is he, finally, pigheaded and self-centered in his masculine individualism, or is the human community too self-interested and complacent to protect the life and dignity of the individual or to stand up for its own future? What is the principle at stake—his self-respect? his manhood? their survival? the efficacy of group action? the triumph of the individual over the community? the necessity of violence? the ineffectiveness of turning the other cheek? There is just enough ambiguity in the presentation to set this movie outside the genre of certainty that a western movie usually occupies.

The complexities of Kane's self-defeating silences are brilliantly augmented by the gestures and compositions that comprise the visual script. *High Noon* could almost run as a silent movie, so skillful is the non-verbal narrative, for the script does not do that much to advance the characters. Toward the end of *High Noon* there is a montage of portraits, driven by the magnified ticking of the clock. The shots flash with rhythmic urgency from face to face as each character measures the narrowing space between life and noon, an ironic sequence of profiles in ambiguity. An early scene in this tightening montage shows us the drunk who was one of the few people to volunteer his services to Kane. The scene is a close-up, although he is in the background, sitting at a table huddled over a whiskey glass. He seems to be the reason for the shot. But foreground left, virtually on top of the camera, is a man's shoulder, arm and hand, barely discernible in the shadows. Just before the shot is succeeded, the hand twitches. It is a minute gesture, the only movement in this brief shot, involuntary, too close and too ambiguous for us to gain any comfortable meaning from its presence. This silent, anonymous twitch of a hand (nervous? anticipatory?) could be seen as a signature for this film, for it is this sort of attention to gestural detail that also sets *High Noon* apart from the usual western. Later in this same sequence of portraits, the three outlaws crowd the camera, so close as to suggest distortion without there actually being any, except perhaps the psychic distortion of their malevo-

High Noon
(1952, Fred Zinnemann)

This frame is typical of Zinnemann's visual representation of the loneliness and uncertainty of Will Kane's situation—and of the life of faith. Though no longer marshal of Hadleyville, he interrupts his wedding day to defend the town and himself from returning outlaws; the tautly-edited film is intersected with images of Kane (Gary Cooper) walking the dusty streets alone in a fruitless quest for assistance.

lence. This is a visual effect that also manages to compress time into space, for a claustrophobia of the lens space makes us feel the time pressing upon us, too close. The reality of the menace Kane perceives is affirmed in this shot, just as the shakiness of the town's allegiance is registered in that twitching hand and the unreliable alcoholic, and the argument of the town begins to look like cowardly wishful-thinking.

Cooper himself provides some of the most effective of these mute, eloquent gestures—his clenched fists as he agonizes in the office, and then tries to hide his hands under the desk when he realizes the teenage boy is watching; the disbelief and flicker of his eyes when an unhappy wife lies for her husband; the wistful smile that appears only for a second as he talks with Harvey in the stable, wishing he could believe in somebody's good will. After the train whistle blows, the montage cycles back through the primary portraits—Helen Ramirez, Amy Kane, the killers, the tracks, and then very close upon Kane. The music ceases, and in the silence all we hear is the rattling of Kane's paper as he prepares his will, and the fragile scratching of the quill pen on the paper, the delicate sounds of life shattered yet again by the siren sound of the train at high noon. Kane, stiffly and with evident fatigue, goes out to meet his killers in the glaring, dusty street and in silent agony watches the two women drive by in the buckboard. Amy looks ahead with sorrow, Helen looks back in longing at the lonely man. As the two women board the train, the killers prepare for the hunt. Then, in one of the most famous shots in the movie, we are returned to Kane. He is standing alone in the bleak street, alone in the town altogether. He fidgets for a moment, his hands rising almost involuntarily, then returning to his side. He turns nervously, and the camera dollies high and away, leaving him utterly isolated and small in the empty street.

The genius of Zinnemann's film, and its enduring contribution to American cultural and religious values, is how he has used a formula which has always been a didactic expression of assurance and certainty to make the formula ask questions rather than provide an answer. *High Noon* is a film about the efficacy of individual and community action, the efficacy of violence and force to uphold peace and non-violence, and, perhaps secondarily, the positions of women and men in the working out of such questions. It asks questions about the risk and value of community, about what price is necessary for self-respect, and by what token we proclaim courage. It asks just what it is we think we will answer to and for.

In the sum of these things, *High Noon* is a film about the uncertainty of certainty. Zinnemann's approach is part of the best American Jewish-Christian tradition, but not necessarily the most popular. From the context of a landscape much like that of the western film, the children of Israel demand humanly conceived certainty from a God who has something else in mind. Periodically they flee toward the security of the predictable, the familiar, the tangible, only to be driven toward a different kind of faith by a deity who stakes the divine identity upon a shattering of formulas and conventional images. The challenge of this deity is articulated in law, although it is often the human presumption of legal certainty that violates the risk-taking imperative of the original legal event. God's law for the Jews is first a commandment of risk—one need only recall Abraham to verify this—and this invitation to the uncertainty of faith has been a poignant reality for twentieth century Jews.

Ironically enough, Christians sometimes stereotype Jews for adhering to the "letter" of the law, while flattering themselves that Christians represent the formula-breaking "spirit" of the law. Yet, all too often, Christians are no better than their Jewish brethren in preferring the rigidity of certainty. Jesus is always more reassuring when he is making pronouncements than asking questions; fundamentalists are happier with John than with Mark, and none of us is that comfortable with the necessity of doubt. We like our heroes omniscient; we want no ambiguity from the savior. In short, we want all of the comforts of faith, and none of the risk. A rather implausible source, this classic American western gives us more of a classic than we'd bargained for, affirming simply in its structure and existence, if not in the story line, the necessity and the right to ask questions and to doubt and to test courage while balancing this affirmation against that yearning to know, to be sure, to be safe. This is a perilous venture, whether we are talking about eternal life or our American future.

2001: A Space Odyssey and the Search for a Center

James M. Wall

In his lifelong quest for a unifying principle, Henry Adams turned to a variety of significant moments to see which one would bless him with a grace-filled solution. His autobiography, *The Education of Henry Adams*, was a book by a man in search of the ultimate. Filmmaker Stanley Kubrick, working in a different medium, pursues the same elusive goal.

Adams was a writer who related in a variety of ways to makers of public policy. He was also an artist who longed to find what would fill the spiritual void at the center of his existence. In this quest he stands in a long line of modern artists driven toward the ultimate even as they hold to a conviction that as earth-bound creatures they must suffer the agony of living without final answers.

Stanley Kubrick is—to suggest a metaphor from one of his own films—something of a reincarnation of Henry Adams, working not with the printed word, but with cinema. Although the focus of this essay is on Kubrick, we can gain a unique perspective on him by looking briefly at Adams.

Both men want to believe in something other than the sum of the rational reality surrounding them, and both share a sense of desperate uneasiness that they are not succeeding in their search. Henry Adams lived his adult life from the American Civil War to the early part of the twentieth century. Moving easily among the intellectual and political leaders of his time, Adams developed a reputation as a highly complex man in personal despair, always searching, but never finding. He was the quintessential modern man, believing in a rational approach to life, but harboring the suspicion that while rationality might produce his daily bread, it could not satisfy his longing for ultimate meaning.

Richard Palmer Blackmur (1904–1965), a Princeton University professor and literary critic, saw in Adams a man who wanted desperately to believe in that which was ultimate, but who was blocked from that belief because he was trapped in the mindset of modernity. Adams looked back to two central moments in history, the twelfth century fervor of belief in the Virgin Mary and the construction in the middle ages of Mont-Saint-Michel and Chartres. The energy involved in these events captivated Adams and left him longing for a similar energetic performance for his own life in the nineteenth and twentieth centuries.

From Blackmur's perspective, Adams had actually found the unity he sought in "the imaginative and artistic unity of the 12th century's Virgin [and in his] masterpiece, *Mont-Saint-Michel and Chartres*"[1] in which, according to Blackmur, Adams felt that

> truth was not a relation in the 12th century, as it tends to seem in the twentieth century, but the source of the relatedness of things: and the difference between two kinds of universe, that in which unity is grasped precariously by faith, and that in which centralization is imposed by incessant and always inadequate measurement of relations. Adams seemed to feel that it was not man who had changed the universe, but that it was the universe, by showing a different aspect as it moved, that changed man's mind.[2]

For Adams, then, something other than rational man had shifted the focus of reality. That "something" left man trapped in a search for which his modern mind has lost the tools to conduct a searching expedition. Modern man is driven to find unity not by faith, since the rational mind must rely on logical approaches to reality, but by "incessant and always inadequate measurement of relations."[3]

One could infer that neither Adams nor Stanley Kubrick finds any solace in traditional religion since both employ their artistic efforts to find unity in a universe which functions without a metaphysical anchor. As artists they demand intellectual integrity and hold no brief for unexamined pieties. Adams looks back to the glorious moments of intellectual energy in the past for his examples of those occasions when unity could be realized. Kubrick attacks the shame of his own time to demonstrate the emptiness of individual lives and social patterns that pretend a unity they do not possess. Adams looked in vain for a temporal authority worthy of respect in the political leadership of the late nineteenth and early twentieth century. What he sought was ultimate meaning in the structures of political leadership.

Working in his own medium a half century or more later, Stanley Kubrick has given up on finding anything meaningful in the societal structures of this century. His bitterest satirical shots are aimed at those persons who live as though their duties have inherent value because they possess temporal authority. Adams wished it were possible to find ultimacy in the well-ordered structures of his time; Kubrick knows this is impossible.

Adams thought he had failed in his quest; Kubrick's bitter, cool cinematic artistry would suggest a similar conviction that the ultimate unity he seeks is not to be found. R.P. Blackmur's reading of Adams applies as well to Kubrick. In their search they strip away the surface of inauthentic answers and in this process they create works of art that announce the presence of an ultimate unity through voices that insist there is no unity.

In the novel *Democracy*, one of Adams' characters longs for the "great American mystery" to restore virtue to the public order. Kubrick's films appear to fight the presence of mystery and in the process— through his artistic rendering—offer to the viewer a mysterious presence which enters the consciousness even as the filmmaker appears to deny its existence. Kubrick, for example, in his *2001: A Space Odyssey*, seems to be denying the presence of an ultimate mystery at the core of reality. But his style and the manner in which his film unfolds belie that denial. "Something" has pulled at man and beast from the beginning of time. What do we call that "something"? Kubrick leaves that to his viewers. A closer look at *2001* suggests a man who, like Henry Adams before him, is much closer to the unity he seeks than he is prepared to acknowledge.

When *2001* was released in 1968, it was received with less than enthusiastic reviews from the popular press. Clearly, a film that unfolds for over twenty minutes before a human character speaks a line was going to have to work to win a following. But gradually the film's special nature became apparent and in time it took its place as a major breakthrough in film history. James Monaco, in a book that focused on American films, summed up the positive regard with which Kubrick was held by critics when he wrote: "*2001: A Space Odyssey* transcends all science-fiction films."[4]

Not everyone agreed, of course, even after enough time had passed for the film's innovative style to become more apparent. Pauline Kael acknowledges the religious motif in the film, but she has little patience with Kubrick's work. The picture, she wrote, "has the dreamy somewhere-over-the-rainbow appeal of a new vision of heaven. . . . It says man is just a tiny nothing on the stairway to paradise, something better is coming, and it's all out of your hands anyway. There's an intelligence out there in space controlling your destiny from ape to angel, so just follow the slab."[5] An acerbic writer, Kael would appear here to be hostile to any film that seeks to explore metaphysics. Her comments suggest Kubrick is giving God a chance, something she resents.

To Kael, *2001* is a "monumentally unimaginative movie."[6] That assessment was in the minority, however, since most critics agreed with the general public which has made the film one of the all-time box office successes. Marsha Kinder and Beverle Houston described it as "a brilliant film. . . . Stanley Kubrick extends the boundaries of the technological resources of cinema; his own process of creating the film and solving its technical problems is the ultimate expression of the film's theme. He fully exploits the knowledge of the past and present in order to create a masterful illusion of the future, which has a striking authenticity."[7]

Kubrick is a superb technician. He is a director who assembles the parts of his film with the precision of a man moving knights and queens on a chess board—a game, by the way, to which he is devoted. He has developed his own visual style through which to convey his vision, a style that refuses to cater to popular taste. Because he knows that long journeys into space will be boring and tedious, he makes the early part of *2001* both boring and tedious. He relieves the boredom with small touches of humor (a fountain pen floats away from a passenger who falls asleep strapped in his seat; the same passenger studies a sign that explains how one is to use a "zero gravity toilet").

The initial views of ships moving gracefully through space—to the rhythm of the "Blue Danube Waltz"—are awesome, but even these grow tedious, as indeed they would on a long journey. Kubrick employs technology to establish an emptiness of the human spirit, and he does so with a resolute determination that defies an audience to stay with him long enough to discover his ultimate purpose: to reach for the ultimate.

Kubrick's view of the men and women who have developed technology is not nearly as positive as his portrayal of the ape creatures which begins the film or of HAL, the computer, whose dedication to the task at hand leads to his destruction.

"Ultimately the film seems to posit two contradictory views: that man has progressed very far and that he is still basically the same."[8] And that sameness to Kubrick is nothing less than a deadness at the center of the human condition, a self-deception created by the assumption that superiority belongs to the face one confronts in the mirror each morning. Kubrick conveys this point in the second segment of *2001* when he delivers the depressing message that travelers and stewardesses in the twenty-first century will still be conversing with one another with the same banality and false friendliness employed in the twentieth century.

The similarity between man and beast is noted in the transition scene between the opening "Dawn of Man" segment and the film's second section, in which Dr. Heyward Floyd is flying on his secret mission from the earth to the moon. The beasts grunt to communicate, and they discover the power of force when one of them picks up a bone and realizes that it will serve him as a weapon. The bone is cast into the sky, and from that slow-motion movement, Kubrick cuts to a spaceship floating lazily through the heavens. In this transition millennia are covered, but the nature of the human being does not improve. Banalities replace grunts, and technology is used to create force and conquer others. The bone as a weapon defines the human condition.

Kubrick's vision of human nature is bleak, consistent with other films he made before and since. But there is an irony in this assertion since Kubrick makes this point through a medium that is remarkable for its creative achievement, and he presents his personal vision in a manner that celebrates creativity itself. The bleakness comes, therefore, from Kubrick's belief that creativity is tainted at the center.

In scene after scene Kubrick celebrates the technology that man has developed to transcend his earth-bound condition, but he uses the same technology to underscore the vacuity of his characters that French critic and scholar Michel Ciment notes: "the exchange of banalities, outmoded forms of politeness, hollow speechifying, reciprocal suspicion, the Howard Johnson lounge, the souvenir snapshots taken by the moon explorers, the ridiculous 'Happy Birthday' intoned thousands of miles away by parents proud of their astronaut offspring, the father who no longer knows how to talk to his little girl."[9]

Kubrick, the artist, deplores the shallowness of the hollow men who made the journey, but nevertheless he takes them upward, in search of the mystery which he seems to feel ought to be available to the seeker, or at least he joins a long list of artists who insist on seeking "as if" an answer were available.

Like Henry Adams, who found meaning in the concrete achievements of the building of magnificent church structures, Kubrick celebrates the tangibility of twentieth century technological creations. But with that sense of exaltation comes also the fear of the human who has been involved in the creation alone in the universe, or living with the presence of others, perhaps a supreme other?

Arthur C. Clarke, the science fiction author whose work is the basis of *2001*, made a statement to which Kubrick says he also ascribes: "Sometimes I think we are alone in the universe and sometimes I think we aren't; in both cases, the idea makes me dizzy."[10] There is no conclusive answer to this dilemma provided in *2001*, for as Michel Ciment has indicated, "the strength of *2001* is that it confronts our civilization with another without ever dissipating the mystery of the encounter."[11]

2001: A Space Odyssey

(1968, Stanley Kubrick)

Sent from a moon base to discover the source of unidentified signals, astronauts are confronted by a "black monolith," Kubrick's recurring symbol for the experience of mystery that confounds human intelligence. The film clearly suggests that we are not alone in the universe, but just as persistently—like life—denies our curiosity any satisfying explanation.

Kubrick employs the "black monolith" at every crucial juncture in the film to evoke this sense of mystery without providing any conclusion as to its meaning. Again, he is with Henry Adams in asserting that he doesn't know, but also that he is not content with not knowing. Of one thing he is sure, however, and that is the inevitability of the imperfection of both humans and the technology they design. In religious language, Kubrick is presenting his conviction that "sin" is a part of the human condition and of all that is touched by human creativity.

In the marvelously photographed third segment of the film, where astronauts David Bowman and Frank Poole are introduced, along with their traveling companion, HAL 9000, the "perfect" computer that has never made a mistake, we see Kubrick's contrasting celebration of the perfection of technological creation with the recognition of the inevitable flaw in that creation and in human nature.

Both the inside of the spaceship and the module unit used to repair the "mother" ship are depicted as smooth, nicely rounded and comfortable. There is an eroticism in this presentation of technical beauty. Whiteness dominates these scenes, underscoring the sense of perfection which is implied by HAL's assertion that "mistake" is not a part of his makeup. This garden of Eden has its flaw, though, and that is the same as is found in the biblical version, the belief that perfection resides in human structures. Mission Control, speaking from earth, introduces doubt into this garden with the observation that HAL has made a mistake in determining that a part is going to malfunction. With the red eye of HAL ever present to the conversation, the two astronauts hear the disturbing news that, in Mission Control's opinion, HAL was "in error predicting default." With HAL in complete control of every aspect of the ship's operations, distrust creeps into this technological paradise. The two men hide away in a module, thinking they are free of HAL's surveillance. Speaking in the emotionless monotones that characterize all the film's conversations, they conclude that if it becomes apparent that HAL is not perfect, they will have to remove his higher brain parts; in short, they will have to recapture control of the ship.

Then, in one of the picture's most chilling moments, the camera gives us a glimpse of HAL's red eye staring at the two men. A close-up of them speaking, but not being heard, reveals that HAL has a programmed skill; he can read lips. Perfect he is not, but his creators gave him an ability to transcend his human traveling companions. They also gave him the ability to dominate his companions, which the film foreshadowed in its first segment. HAL is capable of murder, and in the name of what he feels is the higher mission of saving the ship, he ejects Frank Poole into space.

Only by tricking HAL is David Bowman able to carry out his planned destruction of the computer's brain function and regain control of the ship, thus setting up the film's fourth and final segment in which Bowman confronts that which is "beyond infinity."

The monolith, which awed apes four million years earlier and led six astronauts to act like tourists in front of a monument when they encounter it on the moon, appears twice to Bowman in the film's final segment—first in space and then again in a room where Bowman lies in bed, dying in preparation for what appears to be a return to life in the form of a fetus in space—the so-called Star Child.

This mysterious monolith defies easy explanations. Is it God? Is it some other cosmic force? Kubrick's film does not want to provide an answer. Rather, as he himself has said, our thought processes necessitate our thinking in human "standards," but we are compelled to thrust ourselves beyond those standards. Then, he notes, human thought becomes impotent in trying to form coherent expressions to address that which transcends our limited mode of thought. It is a cycle that feeds back on itself. So is there such a thing as a cosmic intelligence? "Once you begin discussing such possibilities you realize that the religious implications are inevitable because all the essential attributes of such extra-terrestrial intelligence are the attributes we give to God," says Kubrick. "What we're dealing with here is, in fact, a scientific definition of God."[12]

Without knowing the answer, Kubrick is nevertheless driven to postulate that humans are not alone in the universe. But the human condition is such that driven further by a conviction of possible perfection, humans create misery for themselves by claiming to possess a unity which, if it is to be found at all, rests only with the transcendent. Artists have always presented contentious humans in a quest for the eternal, driven by the belief that they will find perfect unity through their own efforts. But in this quest failure is inevitable, because perfection is not available to the earth-bound.

As Michel Ciment has noted, Herman Melville sent Captain Ahab on another odyssey, chasing his understanding of evil, Moby Dick.[13] Ahab is the quintessential ambiguous man, in quest of that which will inevitably evade him because he will not let go and accept his limited place in the universe. Stanley Kubrick's *2001: A Space Odyssey* involves the same artistic quest, a journey into space to seek the truth about the nature of the humans and beasts that inhabit this limited planet.

PART II

Mythic Allusions
and the Demonic Heart

Citizen Kane
(1941, Orson Welles)

    Although Charles Foster Kane's "pleasure dome" in Florida seems closer in the classic western religious imagination to Dante's Mount Purgatory, Xanadu evokes Welles' image for the hell of Kane's final isolation from humanity. The inevitable result of attempted self-deification is the exposure of his descent into the demonic.

Citizen Kane:
Descent into the Demonic

George Garrelts

Citizen Kane begins with a shot of a NO TRESPASSING sign on a grim iron fence set in the midst of an ominous fog. The music is equally ominous. The camera searches through that menacing fog, probing, picking out the details of an obviously neglected feudal estate, while the dirge-like music continues. An immense, many-turreted castle sits darkly in the background, and in the foreground we see monkeys abandoned in their cages. The camera moves rapidly on to the stagnant moat of the castle which is crowded with weeds and empty gondolas.

Thus the early camera work in *Citizen Kane* insistently records the decay, neglect, disrepair and despair that pervade this castle and its environs. No voice has spoken, but the camera and sound track are strident in their proclamation that something tragic has happened to this vast medieval anomaly and to its creator. A fall from a great height must have taken place here for so much darkness to abound. Indeed, there has been a fall from innocence into the demonic, and the story of that fall is the substance of *Citizen Kane*. This once great garden of Eden, which seems to have contained every delight, has fallen into the state of the diabolic which separates, isolates, and destroys. As Charles Higham expresses it, the message of *Citizen Kane* is clear: "the corrupt destroy themselves, and riches and power utterly corrupt."[1]

After its tour of the many signs of "the fall," the camera leaves the murk and gloom surrounding the castle and takes us into the bedroom of Charles Foster Kane, deep within the castle. There is a long shot of an enormous bed silhouetted against a spacious window. We pass through a snowy white-out from which the camera then draws back so that we can see that the snow was actually contained within a glass ball that has been shaken. The camera pulling even farther back, we can see, from above, the enormous lips of Charles Foster Kane, and we then hear the film's first word, Kane's last, spoken as he dies: "Rosebud!" In death Kane's hand falls over the side of the bed, releasing the novelty-shop ball with its contents of snow and a small house. The ball rolls down two carpeted steps onto a marble floor where it breaks and effects its last snowstorm. A nurse comes quietly and efficiently onto the scene and pulls the sheet over Kane's head, shrouding him in death. It is clear that Kane's fall is complete. Now the business of the film can begin—its quest, on our behalf, into why and how Kane descended into such an isolated, diabolic state.

In savage parody, Kane's life is presented in the form of a *NEWS ON THE MARCH* sequence complete with *March-of-Time*-type commentary and music. Its highly charged satire calls Kane an American Kubla Khan, and the private pleasure dome that he "decreed" is compared to the legendary Xanadu. Kane is considered an emperor and an empire builder. In its glory, we are told, his empire controlled thirty-seven newspapers, thirteen magazines, a radio network, grocery chains, apartment complexes, numberless objects of art, factories and ocean liners; he also allegedly manipulated public opinion as well as the people who worked on his newspapers and in his many enterprises. Kane is said to have been in touch with every important event in the western world; it is even suggested that he was responsible for some of them. He had an opinion about everything and apparently thought of himself as being close to infallible even though it was often clear that he was at times seriously—and foolishly—mistaken as when a reporter, prior to World War II, asked him if there would be a war in Europe, Kane responded: "Young man, there'll be no war. I have talked with all the responsible leaders of the Great Powers, and I can assure you that England, France, Germany and Italy are too intelligent to embark upon a project that must mean the end of civilization as we now know it. There will be no war!"[2]

NEWS ON THE MARCH takes us rapidly through the main events in the life of Charles Foster Kane (Welles himself). He had been married first to a president's niece named Emily Norton (Ruth Warrick), who divorced him in 1916 as a result of his affair with Susan Alexander (Dorothy Comingore). Kane's liaison with Susan not only cost him his marriage, but also caused him to lose a gubernatorial election, ending his political career. After marrying his would-be diva, Kane built a three million dollar opera house for her in Chicago and forced her to perform despite her evident lack of talent. His life at home and abroad as a newspaper tycoon, art collector, politician, and man of affairs is quickly sketched. But when the screening of *NEWS ON THE MARCH* ends, the editor is dissatisfied with it. It lacks cohesion, he feels; so he sends a reporter named Jerry Thompson (William Alland) to find out, if he can, what Kane's last word refers to, thinking that "Rosebud" may provide the clue to Kane's life.

Thompson's search constitutes the body of film. Through his encounters and interviews with people who were close to Kane, we begin to learn about Kane's fall from innocence into the demonic. Thompson finds Susan Alexander in Atlantic City in a cabaret called El Rancho that she purchased after leaving Kane, where she performs "twice nightly." She is drunk and unwilling to tell him anything. The head waiter, when bribed, admits that she has mentioned Rosebud and that it means nothing. After this abortive encounter with Kane's second wife, the fourfold pattern of the film's flashbacks into Kane's life begins. Thompson goes to the Walter P. Thatcher Memorial Library, then on to interviews with his business associates Mr. Bernstein (Everett Sloane) and Jed Leland (Joseph Cotten), and finally to a return visit with Susan Alexander.

In Thatcher's journal Thompson discovers an account of Kane's childhood and the story of how he came to be raised by Walter Parks Thatcher. The camera takes us into the snowbound front yard of Mrs. Kane's boarding house in Colorado where five year old Kane is playing on his sled, while his parents are shown inside the boarding house talking to Thatcher (George Coulouris). Mrs. Kane (Agnes Moorehead) has inherited a gold mine known as the Colorado Lode. A lodger left her the deed in payment for board and room. The mine was considered worthless at the time, but was later discovered to be the third-richest gold mine in the world. Thatcher has been hired to administer the estate because Mrs. Kane is afraid to allow her husband to be involved. The implication is that Mr. Kane is a violent man and that in his hands such wealth would be lost to the boy—and to his mother. So his mother entrusts the "raising of Kane" to Thatcher and his bank. The father is brushed aside, and all the trappings of innocence—home and hearth, mother's love, the sled, the snow—are left behind. The boy, however, does not go without a struggle. He strikes Thatcher in the chest with the sled and knocks him to the ground. But the die is cast. Kane is taken to Chicago where Thatcher and Co. control his life until he turns twenty-five.

Jed Leland, friend and business associate, calls his version of Kane's descent "Charlie's story." Thompson finds Leland in a psychiatric facility, living in the shadows of the past. Like Susan he was discarded by Kane when he ceased to be useful. Thompson asks Leland if Kane ever loved Susan Alexander. Kane sought love but never found it, Leland says, because he had no love to give, dooming him to alienation from everyone and everything. In answer to Thompson's question about Susan, Leland explains:

He married for love (a little laugh). That's why he did everything. That's why he went into politics. It seems we weren't enough. He wanted all the voters to love him, too. All he really wanted out of life was love—that's Charlie's story—how he lost it. You see, he just didn't have any to give. He loved Charlie Kane, of course, very dearly—and his mother, I guess he always loved her.[3]

It is this inability to love together with an obsessive desire to be loved that forms the context of the demonic and the instrument of its creation in the life of Kane. After reaching twenty-five, when he takes control of his fortune, Kane moves onto the self-centered, ruthless road to the demonic. He pledges himself as the new owner of the *Inquirer* and its editor to tell the truth and to defend human rights, but in practice he does exactly the opposite. He treats his wife and family as a stepping stone to power. He is interested in Jed Leland and Susan only insofar as he can force them to do his will. He buys expensive objects of art but is more interested in controlling them than in their beauty. Most of the things he buys end up in warehouses. He installs himself and his wife in a castle in Florida. By this time Kane has perfected the Mephistophelian touch. Everything and everyone he touches he turns into a thing possessed.

We get a clearer idea of how Welles came to his presentation of the life of Kane as a descent into darkness when we realize that the first picture he intended to make in Hollywood was to have been based on Joseph Conrad's *Heart of Darkness*. When at age twenty-five he was hired by RKO Studios and given carte blanche to make whatever picture he chose to, he went vigorously to work on an adaptation of *Heart of Darkness*. It is against this background that we can understand the international significance and the diabolic context of *Citizen Kane*. Kane's rapacity and ruthlessness were not limited to America. His fall into the demonic, like Mister Kurtz's, has affected the world.

Heart of Darkness is basically the story of European greed and lust for power extended to Africa and exercised upon helpless natives.[4] Kurtz himself is the most striking example of exploitation in the story, but he is also the representative of a vicious system that destroys and discards people when they are no longer useful. Kane's diabolism is not quite on the same scale or of the same intensity and horror but there are strong and recognizable similarities.

In *Heart of Darkness*, the French start wars by random firing into the jungle. In *Citizen Kane*, it is suggested that Kane starts our war with Spain to boost the circulation of his newspaper. In *Heart of Darkness*, the narrator Marlow, a river boat pilot, discovers a dark grove where blacks have been tossed aside to die after their European exploiters were finished with them. Kane hires people from other newspapers just to destroy those papers and then fires the people he has hired when he has achieved his destructive goals. Kurtz's genius at gathering ivory in *Heart of Darkness* reminds us of Kane's obsession with collections. What was said of William Randolph Hearst by the *Saturday Evening Post* could be said of Kane, that he bought whatever "touched his fancy—newspapers, mummies, monasteries, people."[5]

Welles' *Heart of Darkness* project was never finished because the studio feared it would not do well financially without a European audience, which the beginning of World War II had effectively cancelled out. The planned film was considered too dark for American audiences. Welles maintains a much lighter touch in *Citizen Kane,* yet the dark heart of Conrad's work is discernible there. Welles too is concerned with the dark groves and broken bodies created by greedy tyrants. Despite his often playful touch, there is behind the lives of the people and institutions which Kane manipulates an analogous feeling for "the horror, the horror" that Conrad conveys in *Heart of Darkness.*

The self-deification of tyrants is very much on the mind of Orson Welles, not only in *Citizen Kane* but in all of his films. James Naremore notes that a move toward self-deification is made by most of the egotists Welles depicts in his films.[6] *Citizen Kane* was completed in 1940, so Welles did not have the advantage of watching men like Mussolini and Hitler come to their bloody ends before he finished his film, but he clearly has the conviction that men who become so obsessed with power and who apotheosize themselves eventually fall into the destructive patterns of the demonic no matter how promising they seem at the beginning. Also Welles knows, as Conrad knew, that they take many with them into that darkness. Everything and everyone they touch is maimed in some way or simply destroyed. Although they seem amiable and full of promise early on, as they proceed their destructive tendencies become more obvious and more effective.

Early in the film Kane wears a benign mask. He espouses "the truth," human rights, and unpopular causes. Thatcher is so misled that he emphatically brands Kane as a communist. The early Kane reminds us of the early Kurtz, who is described by James Naremore as a "latter-day Renaissance man—a painter, writer, musician, and a public speaker with an hypnotic voice."[7] Kurtz gradually debases those talents by claiming magical powers, by extreme cruelty and, as Naremore points out, by giving himself over "to acts of lust and violence that Conrad cannot even name."[8] Kurtz loses all interest in human development. After his political defeat, Kane also becomes totally preoccupied with his own exercise of power, interested only in those things and those people whom he can control absolutely. Kane, like Kurtz, descends into the demonic via his own self-deification.

According to Robert Carringer, this movement of Kane into "the heart of darkness" is emphasized by the way that Gregg Toland, the photographer of *Citizen Kane,* has shot the film. Carringer rightly points out that most of the scenes in the latter part of Kane's story, after he has presumed to make his own rules about everything, are shot in a way that is "harshly expressionistic," so as to emphasize Kane's tyranny.[9] Xanadu is also managed by the camera as a symbol of Kane's failed attempt at divinization. Kane is shown there as alone and aloof, seeking to exercise absolute authority over everyone, but managing only minimal service and little respect from his staff and his fiendish valet. Toland's crowning touch comes in the way that he manages the flames into which Kane's possessions are tossed by insensitive workmen, including Kane's memorial of his brief experience with innocence—his sled. The way Toland composes the furnace and the flames makes it clear that Xanadu itself has turned into an active inferno. Only the audience learns what Kane has known from his childhood—the identity of Rosebud.

Some critics allege that Rosebud was a name that scriptwriter Herman Mankiewicz gave to his bicycle or to one of his female friends. Welles himself maintained, according to Higham, "that Rosebud was the name Marion Davies gave to her nose (or her private parts)."[10] Pauline Kael brands Rosebud as banal and calls it a "minor gimmick" or, in Welles' own phrase, "dollar-book Freud," inasmuch as it symbolizes the attempt to link Kane's lust for power to a frustrated childhood.[11] These observations aside, Rosebud stands as the film's major symbol of innocence. Thompson's editor is proven correct in his recognition of its importance. Kane's loss of innocence and fall into the demonic is effectively symbolized by his dissociation from Rosebud and the sled's ultimate destruction—which we alone see.

For Kane, like Sartre's characters, there is no exit. He is trapped in his own lovelessness and lust for power, a condition in which there is no room for improvement or helpful change. Xanadu is a perfect symbol for such a demonic condition. In the opening frame of the film, the NO TRESPASSING sign appeared on the outer fence of the estate. That sign should read ABANDON HOPE ALL YOU WHO ENTER HERE. Welles carefully ends the film with the same no-exit setting so as to leave no doubt in our minds that Kane has made his own descent into the demonic.

Welles' film is an exercise in negative ethics or negative theology. It communicates by telling us what is not operative in Kane's life and by making it blatantly obvious what Kane needs. If we see *Citizen Kane* as a contemporary version of the parable of Dives and Lazarus, we realize that Kane should have shared his talents, his power and his money with those who were in need. Kane is threatened with damnation if he cannot find a way to live a life of service rather than a life of unrelieved self-indulgence. When we compare Kane to William Randolph Hearst, whom Mankiewicz reputedly used as a model for the screenplay, the film seems excessive and exaggerated. But when we compare Kane to his *Heart of Darkness* avatars such as the robber barons of our own time who are raping and polluting our land, air, oceans, lakes, food, cities, and water, and who have built munitions capable of annihilating everyone and everything, Welles' presentation of his ruthless American mogul is appropriate. When we bring Kane up to date, it is clear that we desperately need symbol systems capable of persuading the tycoons of this world to give of their talents and wealth to the improvement rather than the diminishment of our human condition. The exaggerations of *Citizen Kane* blend easily into reality when we observe that the Kanes of our time are still collecting art and putting up museums rather than cleaning up the Love Canals, the Bhopals, the Cubatos, or stopping their destruction of the rain forests and the ozone layer.

Citizen Kane is an exercise in what Marc Alyn calls the absence of God.[12] There is no room for God in the film because Kane has presumed to take on the role of God. Kane, like each of us, desperately needs some model other than himself or Thatcher. Welles makes it painfully clear how empty Kane's life is of a sound orientation, even of minimally inspiring, humanistic models. The Colorado Lode takes him over as a boy of five and in the grip of its influence he falls from innocence. When he reaches out to grasp the only other sources of meaning he knows, the glass ball and Rosebud, they are powerless to effect his, or anyone's, salvation.

The film begins and ends with these symbols of innocence—snow and Rosebud. The glass ball filled with snow is broken and the snow scatters; the sled is burned in the fire that consumes Kane's possessions. Kane had been catapulted into the world by the fortune of the Colorado Lode. He left the innocence of his childhood to be corrupted by money and the lust for power. Innocence, gone from his life, is replaced by the destructive forces which bring him and his empire to ruin. The final note of his demise is sounded when the sled Rosebud crackles in the inferno fashioned by Welles to create a memorable image of the demonic state into which Kane has descended.

Sunset Boulevard:
Twilight of the Gods

Michael Thomas Morris, O.P.

In the history of motion pictures it was the silent era which first gave birth to the gods. From the beginning, movie stars have been created out of the combined efforts of beauty, talent, marketing, and money—the last being the nectar on which the entire industry has grown. Names like Pickford, Chaplin, Fairbanks, and Valentino became loved and adored by millions as the new film medium projected their images around the world. Silent films accompanied by music became the great communicator. The global village had been formed.

Nobody anticipated the power of movies in those early silent days. The journalist Adela Rogers St. Johns recalled that "everybody had an excitement about the whole thing that I've never seen since. None of us had any idea that this picture business had come to be the greatest form of art and entertainment the world has ever known."[1] The actors and actresses who performed in the early photoplays became bigger than life. There was something superhuman about them as their images were magnified on the screen. These were dreamlike and unattainable images without a voice. They were not tied to any particular accent or geographical group. They were universal, and that universality made them stars.

Then came the "talkies" and the stars fell down to earth. Sound brought with it a naturalism and immediacy which broke the magic spell created by pantomime. Overnight the gods and goddesses of the silent screen, renowned for their opulence and exoticism, were brushed into obscurity.

Billy Wilder, Charles Brackett, and D.M. Marshman Jr. wrote *Sunset Boulevard* as a type of Hollywood *Gotterdammerung*. They were acutely aware of the fact that the film capital of the world had been swept by a social change as profound as that which destroyed the Old South during the Civil War. The highly theatrical film culture of the silent era seemed far removed from the concerns of modern movie-making circa

1948. Charles Brackett, a patrician with an ivy league background, felt this gulf between the old and new Hollywood could be bridged with humor. His story was originally meant to be a comedy about a silent movie queen who attempts a comeback in talking films and who, despite many amusing obstacles, ultimately triumphs over her enemies. But Wilder, the most cynical member of the team and fresh from service in the psychological warfare department of the armed forces, changed the focus of the story in order to expose the wretched underbelly of Hollywood's dream factory. As a result, *Sunset Boulevard* turned into a bitter commentary on the film industry's manners and morals.

Sunset Boulevard is more than just the evocation of a mythic, bygone era. It is a cinematic morality tale that draws its inspiration from an historical—albeit biographical—perspective of the Hollywood experience which is both grotesque and relentlessly pessimistic. It is grotesque insofar as it exposes the excesses and hollowness of Hollywood artifice. It is pessimistic because in its demythologizing rigor it tears away at fantasy and illusion only to find a number of human weaknesses (pride, greed, and lust among them) acting as the motivating factors in the narrative.

The film begins with a view of a corpse floating face down in a Beverly Hills swimming pool. The dead man's voice narrates the events which led to his demise, and his story unfolds in the best *film noir* tradition. Joe Gillis is a down-on-his-luck scriptwriter who is delinquent in his automobile payments. One day when he fails to find work with an ulcer-ridden producer and likewise strikes out in getting a loan from his agent, he is spotted driving down Sunset Boulevard by the men sent by the finance company to repossess his car. A chase ensues with Joe's vehicle suffering a fateful blow-out. Quickly he turns the crippled auto into the nearest driveway in order to elude his pursuers. What he stumbles upon is the fantastic estate of the once-great silent film star, Norma Desmond. There she is attended by her factotum, Max von Mayerling, who was once her husband, her director, and her Svengali. Max ushers Joe into the gloomy mansion, mistaking him for the undertaker who had been recently summoned to bury Madam's pet chimpanzee. Joe meets the aging film star and immediately likens her to Miss Havisham in Dickens' *Great Expectations*. The actress is surrounded and enslaved by memories of her past. Over one hundred framed images of herself at the height of her fame litter the antique pleasure palace. She has been plotting her comeback role in pictures by writing a script about Salome, the adolescent princess of Judea, who danced for King Herod in order to obtain the head of John the Baptist. When Norma discovers that Joe is a scriptwriter, she persuades him to stay and help her with her project. He agrees, but falls victim to her rapacious needs and ultimately his own greed. Over a period of time he becomes not only her helper, but her reluctant lover. When at last he is so disgusted by his prostitution that he attempts to leave her, she blasts him into her swimming pool with three shots fired from her handgun. As the authorities arrive to take her away, they find her in the throes of a total cinematic fantasy. In her dementia she believes that she is a star again playing Salome. Max pretends to direct her one last time as he coaxes the pathetic vamp down the grand staircase of her mansion to the reporters and police below.

While *Sunset Boulevard* is considered a classic film, its dark and cynical mood marks a new direction in movie-making by mid-century. The argument can be made that classic American cinema between 1930 and 1945 was the product of a shared Jewish and Christian creative effort. This collaboration was based, for the most part, on a mutual optimism and respect reflective of the strong Jewish-Christian religious heritage of the nation. But by the post-war years, a number of factors weakened that Jewish-Christian domination of American culture: a disillusionment arising from the war's devastations abroad and the horrendous revelations of the holocaust, the popularizing of the theological notion that "God is dead," the rise of agnosticism and atheism, and an industrial prosperity that unleashed a commercial materialism unparalleled in the history of the western world.[2]

Going beyond the limits of good taste, of propriety, for the sake of a new brutal realism became the very reason for conflict in the creation of *Sunset Boulevard*. Charles Brackett produced the film, and Billy Wilder directed it. For fourteen years the two had shared a reputation for being a successful writing team, and they collaborated on such works as *Midnight, What a Life, Hold Back the Dawn, Ninotchka, The Lost Weekend, The Emperor Waltz*, and *A Foreign Affair*. While they worked amazingly well together, they were opposite in temperament. Brackett came from a WASP background and was the privileged product of Harvard Law School. He was an elegant gentleman with a reserved disposition. The galvanic Wilder, on the other hand, was the son of poor Austrian Jews. He worked briefly in the German film industry before fleeing the Nazis. When Wilder arrived penniless in Hollywood, his first "home" was the lavatory of an old hotel on Sunset Boulevard.[3] He worked his way up in the film capital by taking a series of odd jobs and working as a scriptwriter. The desperate condition of the character Joe Gillis would seem to have roots in Wilder's own Hollywood beginnings. Thus one can understand the reason for Wilder's insistence that *Sunset Boulevard* become a mordant drama of people willing to risk everything—even their own dignity—for the sake of success in an industry filled with rampant opportunism. Wilder's increasingly caustic viewpoint in the story caused a strain in his relationship with Brackett. At one point the two even came to blows as Brackett felt powerless in his efforts to curb Wilder's indelicate realism.[4] They never worked together again, and Brackett harbored a bitterness over the break that lasted until his death.[5]

The perils of casting the part of Norma Desmond further illustrated how true to life Wilder's creation had been drawn. He first approached Mae West. She declined. At fifty-five she felt that she was in her prime and not yet old enough to play an aging actress. Then he asked Mary Pickford, who also declined because she felt that the role was not big enough for a star of her stature. Then he asked Pola Negri, who reacted with a silent star's tantrum over the fact that Wilder was implying that her glory days were over. When finally Gloria Swanson was cast to play Norma Desmond and Erich von Stroheim was chosen to play Max von Mayerling, Wilder had fused the real life circumstances of his principals to the reel life story of *Sunset Boulevard:* Swanson had been one of the biggest stars in the 1920s, yet she hadn't made a film in over a decade; von Stroheim had been one of the silent era's greatest directors and he was now reduced to playing subsidiary roles as an actor. For cameo appearances Wilder threw in Cecil B. DeMille (who, like von Stroheim, had directed Swanson in the past), and three phantoms of the silent screen: Buster Keaton, H.B. Warner, and Anna Q. Nilsson, whom the film cruelly refers to as "the waxworks." For the part of Joe Gillis, Wilder hired William Holden, an actor whose own fledgling career in Hollywood had been saved by the help of an older actress.[6]

In the western world both Judaism and Christianity have placed a high value on the past, on tradition, and the respect owed to one's elders. But in the modern consumer society of the mid-twentieth century, the past was often seen as the history of outdated products. During that period the dictum "you're only as good as your last picture" was coined in Hollywood. *Sunset Boulevard* reflects that mid-century mind-set so at odds with the contemporary interest in film history, preservation, and nostalgia. When Joe Gillis first spots Norma Desmond's mansion—an architectural extension of her being—he dismisses it by saying, "It was a great white elephant of a place, the kind crazy people built in the crazy twenties." In Wilder's movie the past and the present are in a constant state of war. "You used to be big," Joe tells Norma. "I am big!" she spits back, explaining, "It was the pictures that got small." After lamenting the smashing of the old movie idols by the modern day movie moguls, the silent screen star then turns on Gillis' screenwriting profession with all the fury of Saturn devouring his children: "Words, words, more words! Well you've made a rope of words and strangled this business, ha ha, but

Sunset Boulevard
(1950, Billy Wilder)

Norma Desmond (Gloria Swanson), has-been movie goddess, thinking she has begun her screen comeback as Salome, dances before the cameras that record instead the extent of her madness and her apprehension by authorities for the murder of her lover. Wilder's film reveals the dark side of the star system: in allowing others to control her image, she lost control of her life.

there's a microphone right there to catch the last gurgles, and technicolor to photograph the red swollen tongue!" That conflict between Swanson and Holden is the conflict of dated illusions clashing with contemporary pragmatism. It also represents a conflict of generations. *Sunset Boulevard* ushers in the generation gap of the 1950s, a decade which produced such classic rebellion films as *The Wild One* and *Rebel Without a Cause.*[7]

This conflict between generations was further supported in the film by Franz Waxman's music. He invokes a former age in his main theme which is derived from tango music made popular in the 1920s. Early in the picture Norma Desmond makes reference to the fact that she used to dance the tango with Valentino in her ballroom. The musical theme reflects the state of mind of a woman who is desperately clinging to the past. For the final scene of her mental breakdown when she imagines that she is making her great comeback as Salome, the theme is transformed into a grotesque parody of a silent film score. It is a bitter note to end with, but one that is appropriate for the tragic undertow to the film.

The cinematography of John Seitz (with an assist from Gordon Jennings) enhances Wilder's demand for brutal realism. The restrained lighting throughout the film leads the viewer to focus on the performances which are subtle in themselves. Wide-angle shots which involve an extreme depth-of-field are forcefully used in the film, especially in one scene where the bandaged wrists of the neurotic and suicidal actress clearly dominate the foreground while her lover is kept in sharp focus in the background.

In the scene which shows Holden's bullet-ridden body floating downward in the swimming pool, it was Wilder's desire to have the face of the victim photographed with the same clarity as that of the police looking down at the corpse from the pool's edge. Photographing the scene from the bottom of the pool would not have worked since the water's surface would have acted as a reflector blocking any image outside the pool from being seen. Seitz solved the problem by placing a gigantic mirror at the bottom of the pool. He then photographed the scene from above with a poolside camera, and caught a clear image of the corpse and the police looking down at it from the reflection in the mirror. Thus through cinematic trickery was the illusion of graphic reality enhanced.

The art and set decorators of *Sunset Boulevard* draped the film in an eerie gothicism: rats on the swimming pool floor, a midnight burial by candlelight of the pet chimpanzee, the dark shadowed mansion with its early Balaban and Katz interior, the heavy velvet curtains and overstuffed furniture, the stained-glass windows in the front hall, the decrepit pipe organ moaning in the wind, the gilt frames scattered throughout the house acting as reliquaries for the actress' youthful image. Norma Desmond's mansion is made to look like an ancient temple precinct, a veritable shrine to her film legend, with Max filling the role of high priest.

Indeed, it is not inappropriate that the atmosphere which surrounds Norma Desmond's stardom be heavy-laden with religious overtones. It was her generation which established the gods and goddesses of the silver screen, making the very act of movie-going a quasi-religious experience. It was her generation which built the gigantic cinematic cathedrals with all their architectural splendor. They were baroque, Moorish, or Egyptian sanctuaries with row after row of seats arranged pew-like before the magnificent tabernacle curtains which veiled the holy of holies. Popcorn and cola became the ritualistic meal as the lights dimmed and the faithful watched those curtains part. The cinematic deities played out their mythic tales amidst all the numinous trappings of a cultic experience.

Joe Gillis, by contrast, represents the first wave of post-war iconoclasts, the demythologizers who care more about money than mystique. "She had her career," he protests, as if the actress' moment in the sun meant that she could now pack up and die. A man without illusion, Gillis knows exactly what he wants when he agrees to work on Norma Desmond's hopelessly bad script about Salome and moves into her all-consuming web: "I wanted the job. I wanted the dough, and to get out of there as quickly as I could." He seems unmoved when Max tells him in solemn tones that Madam was the greatest of them all, that in one week she received 17,000 fan letters, that men bribed her hairdresser to get a lock of her hair, that a maharajah came all the way from India to beg for one of her silk stockings only later to strangle himself with it. The litany falls on deaf ears. Gillis' pragmatic breed would later usher in the money grabbers who would desecrate those temples, tear down or hide their glorious detail, rip away the tabernacle curtains, and divide the sanctuary into a multiplex. In cultic terms, Gillis is a liturgical spoiler.

As a morality lesson *Sunset Boulevard* is also a tale of prostitution, and this makes Joe Gillis' character all the more contemptible. If Norma's tragedy is based on her insatiable desires, then Joe's is based on wanting too little and taking advantage of others in order to get it. "If I lose my car, it's like having my legs cut off," he complains as he eludes the repossessors. He's not above stealing his buddy's girlfriend, just as he's not above taking money from Norma Desmond. "As long as the lady's paying," a sales clerk whispers into Joe's ear as he convinces him to buy a more expensive overcoat. Joe's weak, jaded, and opportunistic character is finally filled with so much nausea and self-disgust that he confesses his worthlessness and walks out on Norma. But it's too late.

"I'm a star," Norma reminds herself as her brain snaps and she descends into madness. "No one ever leaves a star!" Joe's bullet-bled carcass gives visual testimony to the fact that "great stars have great pride."

It was a stroke of genius that Wilder included, as a continual reference in the film, the story of Salome on which Norma Desmond hangs her hopes for a cinematic comeback. For just as Salome was instrumental in the death of John the Baptist, so too would this aging screen actress become the means by which the young screenwriter would meet his sorry end. When Norma Desmond first meets Joe Gillis and presents him with her script, she marvels at the theme and identifies with the character: "Salome! What a woman and what a part! The princess in love with a holy man, she dances the Dance of the Seven Veils. He rejects her so she lands his head on a golden tray, kissing his cold dead lips."

But the love interest between Salome and John, the Dance of the Seven Veils, even the name of Salome herself are elements not found in the biblical record of the Baptist's beheading. Wilder ignored the strict scriptural account and made reference instead to the elaborations created by Oscar Wilde for his controversial play *Salome* written during the *fin-de-siècle* as a vehicle for another aging actress, Sarah Bernhardt. Just as Wilde's play is imbued with the perfumed decadence and exotica of a previous culture, Wilder's film invokes that elaborated story both as a point of reference for the passage of time in Hollywood history and as a foreshadowing of Joe Gillis' demise by a calculating *femme fatale*.

When Joe Gillis first hears Norma Desmond's voice calling to him in front of her house, her image is veiled behind a curtain made of bamboo. When finally he sees her, she is wearing dark glasses. Elsewhere in the film Norma wears hats with veils: when she dances the tango with Joe on the night her love is consummated, and when she returns to Paramount Studios to meet DeMille. The interior of her house is likewise veiled from the heavy draperies guarding her windows to the silk and chiffon streamers that decorate her bedroom. The prevalence of veils not only is appropriate for the Norma Desmond as Salome theme, but acts as a protective guard sheltering the aging screen goddess from the scrutinizing eyes of the film faithful.

Her house is a palace, but it is also a cage—a veritable trap from which Joe Gillis finds it increasingly difficult to escape. A baroque iron grill protects the front door from outside intruders and becomes a visual symbol of his incarceration. But the feeling of entrapment is best demonstrated visually by the way Swanson uses her hands in the love-making scenes with Holden. Although her hands appear to be petite, she arches those delicate fingers with their painted nails and transforms them into talons which grasp her prey by the head and draw him in close to her.

Like Oscar Wilde's biblical seductress of old, Norma Desmond trapped her man and snuffed the life out of him. But in turn this silent screen luminary had herself been trapped by the very machine that had made her a star. The motion picture camera captures an image and grants it a miracle reserved to the gods: bilocation. She could be seen in two places (or more) at the same time by different people. This was the process which created her legend. She assumed a god-like status through a cinematic apotheosis. Through film she was able to transcend the human confines of time and space. But the price mere mortals must pay for this deification, as primitive peoples will tell you, is that the camera also practices spirit theft. As a consequence Norma Desmond discovered that she was no longer in control of her life because she was not in control of her image. The new Hollywood had vanquished that image to the storage vaults where over the years it disintegrated with the film on which it was printed. The *coup de grace* for Norma Desmond was madness, for only then could she soften the blow she had suffered in falling from the cinematic Olympian heights and safely enter into her own private world of myth and magic.

The *Godfather* Films:
Birth of a Don, Death of a Family
John R. May

In an interview with William Murray after the release of *The God-father, Part II,* Francis Coppola admitted his disappointment with au-dience reaction to *The Godfather:* "I felt I was making a harsh statement about the Mafia and power at the end of *The Godfather I* when Michael murders all those people, then lies to his wife and closes the door. But obviously many people did not get the point I was making. And so if the statement I was trying to make was outbalanced by the charismatic aspects of the characters, I felt *The Godfather II* was an opportunity to rectify that."[1] The reason why audiences resisted *The Godfather*'s indict-ment of Michael is as obvious perhaps as a corollary of a fundamental principle of religious psychology: If it is easier to see the mote in an-other's eye than it is to acknowledge the beam in one's own, it is safer by far to ignore the other's mote altogether—if seeing it is going to require admitting one's own beam. To accept *The Godfather*'s condemnation of Michael, one must see him the way he is portrayed—as a reflector of the hypocritical human heart—and who finds it easy to admit his kinship with the demon?

In lecturing over the years on the religious implications of texts, both literary and cinematic, I've found myself time and again referring students by way of illustration to what I consider to be the most obvious meaning of the oldest and most accessible story in the Jewish scriptures —namely, the repudiation of hypocrisy that's implied in the narrative of the fall in Genesis 3. After the man and his wife have eaten the fruit of the tree of the knowledge of good and evil and discovered their nakedness, they cover themselves and hide from the Lord God as he walks through the garden in the cool of the evening. When God asks the man if he has eaten from the forbidden tree, the man blames his wife: "It was the woman you put with me; she gave me the fruit, and I ate it."[2] And when God asks the woman, "What is this you have done?" she points to the

The Godfather
(1972, Francis Coppola)

Standing beside his son, yet towering over him, Vito Corleone (Marlon Brando) instructs Michael (Al Pacino), who has succeeded him as Godfather. Although their eyes never meet, the sense of causality and collusion is unmistakable. The elder Don's eyes seem to pierce his son's skull; Michael's blank stare encompasses—and accepts—the dark reality of his fatal commitment.

serpent. "The serpent tempted me and I ate," she says. Our cultural indebtedness to this passage from Genesis ends apparently with a variation on the woman's reply—"the devil made me do it"—a saying that has become the comic refrain of the hypocritical finger-pointer. It is curiously indicative of the perennial difficulty we have in admitting our own fault that we have almost universally blocked out of our religious memories the conclusion to the story. Without further questioning, the Lord God passes sentence, working his way back along the collusive line, punishing serpent, woman, and man in succession—all without exception to blame. My point here is simply this: that the evidence in support of Coppola's claim about *The Godfather* is just as obvious as the implications of this biblical narrative.

Although at least one critic prefers to think that *The Godfather* succeeds only as "one of the finest gangster films ever made," most have readily accepted the Corleone "family" as a metaphor for American economic and political life.³ No one perhaps has put it as clearly as Pauline Kael: "In *The Godfather* we see organized crime as an obscene symbolic extension of free enterprise and government policy, an extension of the worst in America—its feudal ruthlessness."⁴ The evidence abounds. At crucial moments in the narrative, killing is linked to "business as usual." When Tessio realizes that his defection to Don Barzini's camp is known and that he will be eliminated, he calmly instructs Tom Hagen, "Tell Michael it was only business. I always liked him." And Tom replies, "He understands that." Then Tessio pleads, "Tom, can you get me off the hook, for old times' sake?" When Tom says simply, "Can't do it, Sali," Tessio turns and walks compliantly to his own death. Realignment is betrayal, and death is the accepted consequence of discovery.

A more pointed extension of the syndicate as metaphor occurs as Michael responds to Kay's worries about the legitimacy of the Corleone business. After his return from Sicily, he tells her, "I'm working for my father now, Kay. He's been sick, very sick." "But you're not like him, Michael," she answers, "I thought you weren't going to become a man like your father." Michael, already adept at wearing the don's inscrutable mask, explains, his visage chiseled in ice: "My father is no different than any other powerful man who's responsible for other people . . . like senators, or a president." "You know how naive you sound?" she asks foolishly, because Michael is anything but naive. "Senators and presidents don't have men killed," she adds, and Michael's response provides the film's ultimately ironic observation about America: "Oh? . . . Who's being naive, Kay?"

As I have implied, there are more universal extensions to the metaphor. To appreciate the full meaning of *The Godfather* films, an awareness of Jewish-Christian myth and Christian ritual is, in fact, necessary. Vito Corleone is a Sicilian immigrant; his children—Santino (Sonny), Fredo, Michael, and Connie—are first generation Sicilian-Americans. No immigrant population is more obviously centered on the family; none, more obviously Catholic. Ironically, the family is the heart of religious practice as well as the core of the Mafia operation. Baptisms, weddings, and funerals are the family rituals par excellence; shown together as they are in *The Godfather,* they suggest the family's ritual unity —its beginning, middle, and end. Less obvious perhaps than ritual is the manner in which the films become texts about the human family that can be read with mythic fullness only against the backdrop of the Yahwist narrative in Genesis 2–4. Both ritual and myth, I hope to demonstrate, are integral to the narrative structure and symbolic fabric of *The Godfather* films. Coppola's principal cinematic devices emphasizing ritual are intercutting and framing; the family is at the center of his narrative just as it is in Genesis 2–4.

To my mind, the most stunning instance of the use of Catholic ritual for ironic purpose in any Hollywood film that I am aware of is the riveting sequence toward the end of *The Godfather* that intercuts the baptism of Michael Corleone's godson with the new don's systematic pogrom against the rival Mafia families.[5] The Latin prayers intoned by the priest, reminding us of the antiquity of the ritual as well as suggesting the universality of the human problem, yield at the climactic moment to the English of the threefold profession of faith and its complement, the triple renunciation of Satan—questions ritually addressed to the infant being baptized, but appropriately, and with devastating irony here, answered by the one whose role it is to speak for the infant, his godfather, Michael Corleone.[6]

The threefold renunciation of Satan is the final act of the exorcism that precedes the actual baptism.[7] "Michael Francis Rizzi," the priest asks the infant—and from this point on, we see the godfather as we hear the priest—"do you renounce Satan?" (Cut to Victor Stracchi gunned down as he steps out of an elevator.) Michael Corleone says without emotion, "I do renounce him." (Moe Green, on a massage table, is shot through the lens over his right eye.) "And all his works?" the priest continues. (Carmine Cuneo is riddled through the glass of a revolving door.) Michael answers, "I do renounce them." (Philip Tattaglia and his mistress are strafed through the sheets on their hotel bed.) "And all his pomps?" the priest asks finally. "I do renounce them" is Michael's third expressionless protestation. (The cut, climactically, is to Emilio Barzini's assassination as he descends the courthouse steps to his waiting car.) The ritual expulsion of demons—that is to say, of enemies—completed, the priest asks, "Michael Rizzi, will you be baptized?" The godfather responds, "I will," and after a brief shot of the priest pouring water on the infant's head, there is a rapid triple cut to scenes of carnage (hotel bed, revolving door, and courthouse steps) corresponding to the priest's voice-over invocation of the Trinity ("in nomine Patris, et Filii, et Spiritus Sancti"). Michael Corleone's threefold renunciation is a solemnized lie signalizing the demonic bond of hypocrisy that holds together the human race; the matter and form of his sacrament of rebirth as the Godfather are not water and the Spirit of truth, but blood and deception.[8]

The pattern of threefold repetition continues through to the film's final, chilling shot of Kay, excluded from the darkness of the family business by the closing door—a shot that is reprised in *The Godfather, Part III* with stunning effect.[9] Just as the extermination of Michael's enemies outside of the family is accompanied by the triple renunciation of the church's public ritual, the internal purification of the family has its own ritual pattern of threes, first of deeds, then of words. Michael initiates the cleansing of his household with three acts of exclusion—Tessio for going over to Barzini, Carlo for betraying Sonny, and finally Connie for protesting Carlo's murder. Tessio is sent to his certain death, as Tom Hagen, who has delivered the muted sentence, watches from a window of the compound; we are spared the sight of his being killed. Carlo, for whose son Michael has just acted as sponsor, is garroted in the front seat of a car, his foot going through the windshield; Michael, standing apart, calmly witnesses the actual slaying. Finally, Connie, like Tessio, is sent away, though not to her physical death; for her hysterical refusal to understand business as usual, Michael commits her to the care of physicians.

More compelling even than these acts of excommunication is Michael's lie to Kay, itself solemnized by ritual repetition. Kay, awakening to the horror of Michael's intensification of the family vendetta, but too irresolute as yet to revolt against it, asks him, "Michael, is it true?" Has he had Carlo killed as Connie claimed? Twice, Michael responds vehemently, "Don't ask me about my business, Kay." Then he pauses and adds, "All right, this one time, this one time, I'll let you ask me about my affairs," and his condescending formula becomes an oath validating his response. A third time, scarcely vocalizing the words, Kay asks, "Is it true?" and Michael, perjuring himself, says simply, "No." Lying complements murder; Michael's succession as Godfather is confirmed by a demonic ritual of words and deeds. Although *The Godfather* seems at its beginning to establish Vito Corleone as its perspective, by putting us in his place as he listens to Bonasera's plea, it moves imperceptibly toward the clear implication of the final scene—that like Kay we may be outsiders to the family business, but not to the family.

More instructive even than these climactic sequences to *The Godfather* is the framing presence of religious ritual in each part of the trilogy. Though not, of course, the literal first and last shots in any of the films, rituals unquestionably give the actual opening and closing images their deep religious significance. Coppola, like the Godfathers he presents us, knows his Catholic ritual, its power to signify—and, hypocritically, to conceal.

The Godfather is framed by sacramental settings related to love and new life—the wedding of Connie and Carlo, and their son's christening. Marriage and baptism are sacraments inexorably linked in Christian faith inasmuch as through marriage children are procreated to become members of the church. *The Godfather, Part II* is framed by secondary rituals related to death. As if to sign the reductive tone of *Part II*, the film begins with a funeral procession and ends with a wake—Michael's grandfather's burial and his mother's wake. *The Godfather, Part III*, unlike its predecessors, juxtaposes rituals that are ironic inversions of the religious and the secular—a worldly honor conferred in church with a choral reenactment of the Passion Play in a production of *Cavalleria Rusticana*. If it is clear in *The Godfather* that Michael, while pledging to make the family's business legitimate, has pushed blood vengeance well beyond the limits his father had imposed, it is transparent in *The Godfather, Part II* that Michael's ruthlessness in consolidating his control over the mob has effectively destroyed his family. *The Godfather, Part III*, by contrast, is decidedly more affirmative in its worldview even as it explores the limits that fratricide imposes upon the possibility of redemption.

How then do the rituals illumine the actual opening and closing shots of the films? *The Godfather* opens with Bonasera shrouded in darkness, addressing Don Vito Corleone, as yet unseen, and closes with Kay in the light observing the obeisance being given to Michael as Godfather, till the door shuts in her face (leaving us in the darkness that enshrouds the new don). Marriage signals both a realignment and a reaffirmation of allegiances—new relationships, new business; the celebration initiates the events that effectively prepare the way for Michael's assumption of power in the Corleone clan, his most heartless act the murder of his godson's father that Kay confronts him with. The transfer of power within the Corleone family that occurs during and after the baptism yields, ironically, only the illusion of rebirth—the exclusion of Kay is the beginning of the end for the Corleone family. The sequence of rituals suggests the recurring cycle of union and new life; in reality, chaos and death have strengthened their hold.

The first scene of *The Godfather, Part II*, up to the title, shifts from Michael, standing in his office with hand extended for the ritual kiss of respect from one of his lieutenants, to the Godfather's empty chair, the blood-red seat of power; the last shot shows Michael seated alone, brooding and isolated, facing the waters of Lake Tahoe that have just received the body of his slain brother, but with his gaze obviously turned upon the emptiness inside himself. Within these framing images are the sacramental rituals of death that confirm the film's revelation of Michael's hardened heart and the consequent demise of his family. Unlike the Michael of *The Godfather*, who grows with events into his succession as don, the Michael of *The Godfather, Part II* undergoes no change at all save the exposure of his own spiritual death. Death, in fact, reigns in *Part II;* its most stunning revelation is Kay's admission that it was not a miscarriage, but an abortion that ended her pregnancy. She too has become a partner in the Corleone blood feud.

Thus, just as surely as the Corleone family is a metaphor for capitalist America, it is an avatar of the first family in the Bible. The Genesis story is the most primitive mythic locus for another religious truth that is central to our Jewish-Christian tradition: namely, if you presume to consider yourself above the known moral order, you—and those associated with you—will pay the consequences. The obvious implication of the redaction of the Genesis narrative that places the story of Cain, the first fratricide, immediately after the expulsion of Adam and Eve from the garden is that sin breeds sin. *The Godfather, Part II* as a sequel to *The Godfather* produces an analogous effect, as does its juxtaposition of the stories of the younger Vito Corleone and the mature Michael. *The Godfather, Part III*, with its proleptic appeal to the heart of the Christian myth, reveals the disintegration of Michael's nuclear family in a totally new light, focusing on his vain attempt to save it and himself by good deeds alone.

Whereas the intercutting in *The Godfather* and *The Godfather, Part III* is spatial (and climactic), the intercutting in *The Godfather, Part II* is temporal (and pervasive). The second film tells two stories: Vito Corleone's flight from Sicily to America at the turn of the century through to his triumphant return to Sicily, as a young don, to take vengeance on the senile Don Ciccio for the deaths of his mother, father, and older brother; and in the film's present time Michael's efforts to maintain control of his position as dominant Mafia chieftain during the turbulent years of the late 1950s. The design of the intercutting is concerned less with the immediate comment that juxtaposed segments of the two stories make on one another than it is with the overriding implications about the inexorable effects of a history of bloodletting. The two generations of the Corleone family recall pointedly the tragic world of Agamemnon and Orestes in Aeschylus's *Oresteia*. "Far from others I hold my own mind," the chorus laments over the curse on the House of Atreus, "only the act of evil breeds others to follow, young sins in its own likeness."[10]

In every respect, the focus in the second film is on the family and on the effects that the passage of time has had upon it. Structurally, as we have noted, the film begins and ends with family rituals related to death, the first from Vito's story, the last from Michael's, as if to imply that the Corleone family history from beginning to end is shaped by death. Michael's story, in the present time, is also framed by rituals that contain within themselves the impetus and resolution of the plot.[11] Thus, at the end of the day-long celebration of Anthony's first communion,[12] an attempt is made on Michael's life as he and Kay retire. Michael knows that someone within the family was necessarily involved: his plan to go undercover to investigate his suspicions sets in motion the principal sequence of events. And, at the film's end, long after Michael knows that Fredo arranged the attempt on his life, he takes advantage of his brother's presence at their mother's wake to have him killed.

There is, moreover, an implied ritual at the heart of the main story that complements the unity of beginning and end.[13] The climactic recognition scene follows the completion of yet another family celebration—Christmas—that we see only the trappings of, but that provides nonetheless the ironic counterpoint in Christian mythology to the events that transpire. Commemorating the birth of the divine child to Mary and Joseph, Christmas is, of course, the ultimate memorial to the sanctity of the family. When Michael returns home to the Tahoe compound after the New Year's revolution in Cuba, thinking, as Tom has informed him in Miami, that Kay has had a miscarriage, the survival of the nuclear family is on his mind. On his way into the house, he passes Anthony's red car half covered with snow—a Christmas present given without his knowledge, and therefore no gift at all, but a painful reminder to Michael of his absence from home. In subdued tones Michael questions his mother, and because she cannot fathom the depths of his doubt, he provides his own answer. "What did Papa think deep in his heart? . . . By being strong for his family, could he lose it?" Thinking Michael is grieving for his lost child, Mama Corleone comforts him by saying that he can have another. No, the family, not the child, is what concerns him, he explains. "But you can never lose your family," she reassures him. Eyes cast down, pensive, Michael, sensing differently, says simply: "Times

are changing." Michael has, of course, returned home with the knowledge that his own brother Fredo was the traitor within, and he will
discover shortly that the real reason there will be no infant in his crib is
that Kay has had an abortion. The mother of his children has taken blood
vengeance in order, she thinks, to put an end to the "Sicilian thing." Her
indictment of Michael is the film's climactic judgment: "Michael, you are
blind," she cries out. "It wasn't a miscarriage. It was an abortion—like
our marriage. It was a son and I had him killed because this must all end."

If we would understand the true horror of sin's consequences, however, it is not to the revelation of Kay's abortion that we must look. In *The
Godfather, Part II* as in the Genesis story, it is to an act even more
appalling—Michael's taking his own brother's life. Mama Corleone's
wake, the last ritual the family gathers for, is patently a wake for the
whole family. On the occasion of the gathering, Michael plots and exe-
cutes his complete revenge. To Tom Hagen's query, "Do you want to
wipe everybody out?" Michael responds, "No, just my enemies." The
final vendetta unfolds with the usual threefold solemnity: Hyman Roth is
gunned down in the Miami airport, Frankie Pentangeli commits suicide
(on instructions from Tom and, pathetically, according to ancient Roman imperial custom), and Fredo is shot in the back as he fishes in the
lake, reciting the "Hail Mary" for good luck.

The editing of this final sequence reinforces the film's variation on
Genesis. As Fredo says, "Pray for us sinners," the film cuts to Michael,
staring out at the lake through the boathouse window. With Michael, we
hear the shot, but do not see the treacherous act. A quick cut back to the
boat, showing the body of Fredo humped forward, a gull crying overhead
amid threatening clouds, is followed by a cut again to Michael slumping
into a chair in his study, his head thrown back. Then there is a slow fade,
presumably in Michael's thoughts, to the day of his father's surprise
birthday party in 1941 as Sonny is introducing Carlo to the assembled
family. There are, typically, three surprises in all. The Japanese have just
bombed Pearl Harbor, and the innocent young Michael announces to his
stunned and irritated brothers that he has joined the Marines. What will
happen to their father's plans for Michael's future? Tom asks. When
Michael demurs with "*My* future?" we are reminded that, though Michael is a member of the Corleone family, he is—and will always be—responsible for his own decisions; but as a consequence of the family's
business, it will be a future bathed in blood.

The interdependence of father and son is confirmed by the editing
of the film's last three brief shots. Slow fades underscore the causality.
The shot of the young Michael alone in the Corleone dining room, after
the rest of the family has left him to greet the old don, yields to Vito's

departure from Corleone on the train, waving his infant son's tiny hand in farewell; then back to Michael in the present time, brooding over his brother's murder and the dissolution of his family. Michael Corleone's inner corruption is mirrored in the destruction of his family, the inevitable consequence of his own demonic ruthlessness. The film's apocalyptic intention is patent: We choose freely to sin in the likeness of our parents, and the result of sin's baleful history is death. Like Michael, we are each of us, whether we care to admit it or not, descendants of Cain.

The Godfather, Part III, loosely structured on the pattern of *King Lear,* presents an older, seemingly wiser Michael Corleone, striving for fiscal legitimacy and personal acceptance. Seeking a reconciliation with his estranged children, he invites them and Kay to the papal ceremony for his investiture in the Order of St. Sebastian, honoring a gift of one hundred million dollars to the church of Sicily. The celebration that follows, no less brilliant in its intercut revelry and interviews with the don than the opening sequence of *The Godfather,* introduces the conflicts that carry the film to its tragic conclusion. Like Lear, Michael is rejected by his children, and his efforts to divest himself of his ill-earned fortune by settling accounts with the other "families" are ultimately futile, in part because of his fateful dalliance with Sonny's bastard son, Vinnie, who in Anthony's absence becomes heir to the family's criminal tradition.

The opening and closing shots of the film are of decay and death— the abandoned family compound at Lake Tahoe, symbol of the disintegration of the old Corleone alliances, and the passing of Michael Corleone, a feeble old man desolate and alone. The framing rituals, once again, provide the interpretation—purchased honor as an empty transition to propriety, the passion story as a reminder that redemption, if it comes at all, comes only through suffering. At the heart of the film, though, is the most uniquely Catholic sacramental ritual of all, Michael's faltering confession of his sins to the saintly Cardinal Lamberto. Convinced at first that he is "beyond redemption," Michael is reassured by his kindly confessor, who is about to become pope, that life *can* be redeemed by suffering.

Only on the superficial level of narrative is *The Godfather, Part III* the successor to the first two films. Its mythic dimension surpasses them the way salvation transcends the fall. The film's lengthy final sequence, a homage to the climactic baptismal sequence of *The Godfather,* intercuts the new Don Corleone's vendetta against the Mafia lords of international finance with a melodrama about doomed lovers, a reflector of Michael's failed love. Within the Easter production of *Cavalleria,* featuring Anthony's operatic debut, is a dramatic representation of the central drama of the Christian myth—the passion, death, and resurrection of Jesus.

Michael's reluctant capitulation to Vinnie's desire to revert to the former ways of family business has catastrophic consequences indeed. The assassin stalking Michael throughout the evening at the opera misses his mark and kills Michael's daughter instead. In a poignant inversion of the Pietà, Michael embraces Mary's lifeless body on the steps of Palermo's Opera Massima. His silent scream of anguish is one of the most moving moments in the history of cinema.

If it is easier to relate to the Michael Corleone of *Part III* than to either of his previous avatars—and it certainly seems to be—it is perhaps because we are no longer being asked simply to confront our own demonic hearts; rather, in its appeal to the passion narrative, it points beyond recognition to salvation itself, showing us the dark and painful path of redemption that each of us must take. In projecting the possibility of redemption, *Part III* is, therefore, less in the American Protestant Puritan tradition and more Catholic in its sensibility, at least in lower case. Its fusion of ritual and myth subtly suggests that the ravages of sin as well as the possibility of forgiveness are fully illumined only by Jesus' self-sacrificing death. There is no merciful end to Michael's suffering— only the agonizing daily remembrance of the effects of his sins and the long, slow, lonely passage to his own death.

Coppola's achievement with *The Godfather* films is, I think, singular. The casting alone is close to perfection, down to the very minor roles. And to have created a trilogy of films that are not only not an embarrassment but actually in many ways the artistic match for one another is without parallel in the history of American cinema.[14] Even though *The Godfather* is, in my estimation, the most fully integrated artistically and *Part III* the most powerful emotionally, there are some critics who consider *Part II* the best of the trilogy. In subtlety of allusion and richness of imagery and design, *The Godfather* films stand among the finest achievements of the American religious imagination.

PART III

Movement and Rebirth

The Wizard of Oz

(1939, Victor Fleming)

The Wizard of Oz, a.k.a. Professor Marvel (Frank Morgan), stripped of his aura of mystery, offers Dorothy (Judy Garland) a ride back to Kansas in the balloon that he has saved for an emergency. When this last enchanted avenue of "return" proves ineffectual—and unnecessary—Dorothy is reminded by Glinda that she has always possessed the power to return home on her own.

The Wizard of Oz and Other Mythic Rites of Passage

J. Scott Cochrane

In the relatively short but rich history of film, we find works which stand out not only as examples of extraordinary filmmaking, but also as cultural artifacts that have transcended the world of filmmaking itself. Recurringly, a single film emerges to evoke and define an entirely new way of knowing and speaking to the question of human identity and ultimately to articulate the religious self-understanding of a given period. In so doing, it anticipates, accentuates and expresses a coherent world-view, not simply based upon the way things are, but on the way things could be. The film functions to dredge up the deepest unconscious aspirations, dreams and fears of the collective attitudes of a given epoch; we witness the emergence of a contemporary religious mythos.[1] Such a remarkable film is MGM's 1939 version of *The Wizard of Oz*, based on L. Frank Baum's popular novel *The Wonderful Wizard of Oz*, published in August of 1900.

Myths are not, however, in any superficial sense created, but rather bring to expression the deepest values present in the collective human psyche. *The Wizard of Oz* offers an excellent example of how this functions in the arena of cinematic narrative. During its eighteen month production period, the film had ten writers, four directors, a variety of actors, and dozens of disparate creative inputs. No auteur theory which locates the creative process in a single source could deal adequately with the collective energies which coalesced into the final film. If one were to identify an auteur, that unifying vision would have to be given to Baum himself, but the film is far from a simple retelling of Baum's original narrative. Rather, the film must be regarded as a significant transformation of the story into an original cinematic entity which both extends and resignifies the narrative myth through a fresh and powerful contemporary visual form.

The key structural device and most significant religious motif of

The Wizard of Oz is the journey. From *The Iliad* and *The Odyssey* through father Abraham of the biblical mythos, Arjuna of *The Mahabharata* and *The Bhagavad-Gita*, to Buster Keaton's *The General* and *The Wizard of Oz*, the pattern of "journey" functions symbolically, religiously and mythically to give purpose, energy and motivation to the various heroes as they explore their environment and their own humanity. Mythically speaking, we know who we are, in part, by where we have been, through our experiences of venturing out and returning to tell about it.

In his book *The Hero With a Thousand Faces*,[2] Joseph Campbell offers a comprehensive study of the archetypal imagery of the epic myth, which builds on the treatment of myth found in Sir James Frazier's classic work *The Golden Bough*.[3] Campbell finds in the most culturally diverse storytelling and mythmaking a single, unifying narrative structure which he has called the "monomyth" or "the hero journey." For Campbell, the concept of "hero journey" functions in an all-encompassing way to trace the rhythms and the principal patterns of the "rites of passage"—"separation, initiation and return, which might be named the nuclear unit of the monomyth."[4] When we compare Campbell's full paradigm of the myth with the structure of *The Wizard of Oz*, striking similarities emerge.[5]

Campbell's first three categories are already evident in the opening sequence of *The Wizard of Oz*. Dorothy's sense of alienation (separation) from the Kansas farm is apparent when she discovers that no one will listen to her concerns. Her song "Somewhere, Over the Rainbow" expresses her sense of the lure of the beyond, a "call to adventure." And her decision to set off finds visual punctuation in a Chaplinesque, "down the road alone" image, with her back to the Kansas farm. "The familiar life horizon has been outgrown," Campbell explains, "the old concepts, ideals and patterns no longer fit; the time for the passing of a threshold is at hand."[6]

A penetration symbol is often required to connect the two worlds of the monomyth. Frequently a commonplace image becomes the symbol connecting the heights and the depths, as for instance the mountain in the Jewish story of Moses receiving the law, or the tree/cross of the Christian redemption story. Bridges too function as symbols joining the familiar with the other side, as in the tradition of the Buddhist Bodhisattva, where the ferryman comes to have a central place in Buddhist mythology.

In *The Wizard of Oz*, the cyclone is the penetration symbol connecting Kansas with the far-away land of Oz. The crossing of the first threshold via "the belly of the cyclone"[7] is signaled in the film by the spectacular transformation from sepia tones to technicolor and confirmed by the repeated narrative line, "Toto, I've a feeling we're not in Kansas any-

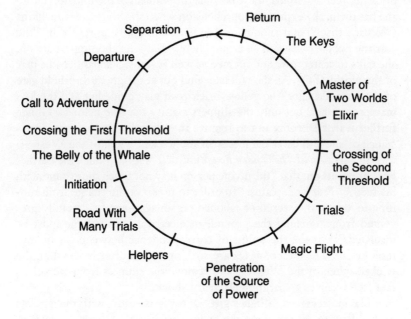

more." The now familiar tune "Over the Rainbow" is structurally re-stated and accompanies Dorothy as she steps out into Munchkinland. She has arrived and so awaits "initiation."

Dorothy not only has a feeling she's not in Kansas anymore, but also repeats the line, "Now I *know* we're not in Kansas," when she meets the good witch of the North. Campbell observes that the hero, having crossed the threshold, "moves in a dream landscape of curiously fluid ambiguous forms where he must survive a succession of trials."[8] The hero is "aided by the advice, amulets and secret agents of the supernatural helper,"[9] in this case provided by Glinda, the good witch of the North.

Dorothy becomes part of Oz only when she has the slippers placed upon her feet by Glinda; these become the emblem of the initiate. Before she has them, she expresses apprehension when she hears the munchkins ("What's that?") and announces her sense of confusion regarding "the way the people come and go around here." But after the slippers are on, she talks to scarecrows and tin men as well as lions. She has become part of the world of Oz. As she will later find out at the grand threshold gate of the Emerald City, the yellow brick road may guide her and the kiss may protect her, but only the slippers signify that she belongs. Glinda further warns Dorothy not to remove the ruby slippers in any circum-stance or she will be at the mercy of the wicked witch of the West.

In a section of *The Golden Bough* entitled "Not to Touch the Earth," Frazier points out that "the divine person may not touch the ground with his feet."[10] Frazier explains: "In order to preserve the charge from run-ning to waste, the sacred or tabooed personage must be carefully pre-vented from touching the ground; in electrical language, he must be insulated."[11] Again, the points of correspondence between classic my-thology and *The Wizard of Oz* are striking: when, later in the film, the wicked witch of the West tries to remove the slippers from Dorothy's feet, she receives a sparkling electrical shock.

Having received Glinda's gift, Dorothy is ready, with the amulets on her feet, to set out upon the yellow brick road. Glinda suggests to Dorothy that she and the other witches are only localized deities, again noted when Glinda reminds the wicked witch of the West that "you have no power here—begone before someone drops a house on you." If Dor-othy wants help beyond Glinda's abilities, as for instance in recrossing the threshold to get back to Kansas, she will have to journey on to the center of the land of Oz—the Emerald City. Here she will encounter the great and wonderful, but mysterious Wizard of Oz.

The image of "pilgrim" recurs repeatedly in the world's major re-ligious traditions, especially in Judaism and Christianity. But the pilgrim requires a way, a path.[12] It is the yellow brick road which originates in Munchkinland and terminates in the Emerald City[13] that enables Dorothy to find her way to her destination and provides much of the structure of the cinematic action. It is also along this path, this "road with many trials," that she establishes significant relationships which transform her aspirations and self-understanding.

The trials that befall Dorothy are usually a result of various digressions from the path. The first trial, with an animated apple tree, occurs when Dorothy steps off the path to pick an apple. But through trials she also encounters her most significant relationships. The scarecrow, the tin man, and the lion all bring new strength to Dorothy, and she to them; together, they have capabilities beyond any one of them to pursue their path, and face and survive the challenges that lie ahead. We are left with the sense that though one may not face pain or danger in the security of the predetermined "way," one is not likely to encounter anything new or significant either.

Surely one of the most beautiful and mythically evocative images of the film follows the escape from the deadly poppy field. Dorothy and her friends set out again upon the yellow brick road, and now the Emerald City looms large in the background of the cinematic frame. The shot is carefully composed so that the road itself connects the pilgrims with the city—a penetration symbol—while the city itself, its towers linking the depths and heights, suggests yet another. It is in this mythic city that we first encounter the source of power, the center of the universe,[14] and the wizard himself.

The path of the pilgrims leads through the outer walls, the inner city, and finally to the *sanctum sanctorum* itself as they penetrate the source of power. Each of these regions of the Emerald City is protected by doors and doorkeepers, and each presents itself to the pilgrims as another threshold to be crossed. Indeed, the entry to the Holy of Holies is imagined as a long hall of doorways, a rich image in the history of religions. Just as the pilgrims think they have reached the ultimate source of power, they are told by the wizard that there is yet another source that they must penetrate as well. This demand sends them on what Campbell has called "the magic flight"[15]—to obtain the broomstick of the witch of the West.

The image of the wizard we are given to contemplate is a fascinating combination of visual, mythic and theological conceptions. The cerebral image of the all-powerful male Oz shows every indication of having been influenced by the concept of the *mysterium tremendum* of nineteenth century piety.[16] "No one can look directly at him," the doorkeepers tell us. What we do see in the film, however, is a talking head, the divine logos, the disembodied mind of the Greek philosophical tradition and German idealism.[17]

However, this deity is a god of works, not of righteousness. He demands of Dorothy and her friends that they *do* something for him in return for his granting their wishes. This is the demand of the god of classical theism that the pilgrim party must take to the road in search of the holy grail. In humility and awe, and in fear and trembling, they obey—an equally classical response to the object of theistic faith. There are several other traditional theistic elements worth noting as well: the fire that does not consume, the image and voice of the stoic passionless absolute, the male image of patriarchal religion possessing all-controlling power, and the Divine Sanctioner of the status quo, all fused together to form the image of Oz, now evoked in the cinematic narrative as "enemy" —the final threshold.

It is during the trials of the magic flight that the pilgrims most clearly come to terms with their environment, their identity and their potential. Where they were once incompetent, they become competent. Where they were once weak, they discover strength. In seeking to prove themselves worthy in the sight of the wizard, they learn who they really are. The destruction of the witch's evil power confirms this and is evident even to the witch's guards, who willingly give Dorothy their allegiance. It is also confirmed by the structure of the film itself—at this point, its climax and moment of greatest excitement.

Dorothy and her friends are now free to encounter the Wizard of Oz once again, confident, centered in purpose, and strong in character. They have passed over into what the existentialists call "authentic selfhood," a product of conscious decisions, free choices, and responsibility to self. In the most contemporary sense, they are in control, free to demand of the wizard the fulfillment of his promise. Baum's narrative provided the sojourners with a free return flight via flying monkeys, but the film immediately places them before the throne of the wizard. The scene which follows becomes the occasion for the return crossing of the second threshold. Oddly enough, this crossing is initiated without the full awareness of the participants. It is Toto who reveals the humbug at work behind a curtain, showing that Oz, the Great and Terrible, is in reality a fake and, worse yet, a joke. It was this kind of existential awareness which Baum had suggested was the experience of authentic human liberation.[18] The film itself, as we shall see, suggests that belief in a magical wonderworker is an obstacle to religious maturity.

Baum's sense of the inconsistencies inherent in classical theism led him to articulate the death of an image of God for "a people come of age," as had Nietzsche before him, not as a carefully formulated philosophical statement, but in the form of a kindly tale.[19] Yet, whatever else it may be, Baum's "fantasy" has its feet planted firmly in the rich earth of modern experience.

The film, however, omits the return crossing of this second threshold and instead redirects our attention to the more superficial theme of bestowing gifts. Through sleight-of-hand and the semantic skill of a medieval nominalist, the wizard calls into being the sought-after entities simply by naming them. The recipients, seemingly quite content, graciously receive their symbolic gifts, Dorothy alone despairing: "I don't think you have anything in the little black bag for me."

Although such tricks had won the wizard his position, he had taken the precaution of retaining his balloon against the need of a quick getaway. Typically, even this strategy fails, and the wizard departs alone, although not without another revealing line: "You've ruined my exit!" Now for a moment there seems no help left in the Emerald City for Dorothy, only empty sky and existential predicament, hopelessness, and despair.

Prompted by Glinda, Dorothy begins to grasp the full import of her return crossing. "You don't need to be helped any longer; you've always had the power to go back to Kansas." The now-brainy scarecrow exclaims, "Why it's so simple—I should have thought of it myself!" But Glinda responds, "She had to learn it for herself." Then, suddenly, the film seems to lose its confidence, and turns toward its own special didacticism: "There's no place like home." There is of course a strong strain in eastern and western mysticism suggesting that, in matters of the heart, the goal of every quest is discovered finally within oneself.

The boon that Dorothy has to bestow upon her family and friends in Kansas is her newly-found knowledge, earned and brought back from the "far side." All that she humanly requires is within her. The contemporary myth of existentialism proclaims the death of a particular inherited notion of God and the self-sufficiency and power of human imagination and ability. Judaism and Christianity, though, have more venerable traditions for iconoclasm, surely reflected in *The Wizard of Oz,* which takes as its idol needing to be smashed a certain nineteenth century image of God as a divine magician capriciously responding to our needs.

This becomes the narrative "key" which liberates the hero from the inherited religious illusions of tradition, the elixir which functions to empower Dorothy's return from Oz. In the novel, the slippers, which could also have functioned as the elixir and proof that she had been there, fell off in the desert on her way back to Kansas.[20] In the film, the ruby slippers are psychologized away; they simply disappear, as does Dorothy's sense of confidence, the knowledge of where she has been. Dorothy is forced to give in to the Kansas conception of the real world, now presented again in dull sepia tones. Her understanding and appreciation for the technicolor life of the imagination is crushed under the monotone weight of Kansas. In Baum's novel, Dorothy may actually become the hero by mastering both worlds—the world of illusion (Kansas) and of reality (Oz). In the film, she seems to master neither. She simply ends up back where she started, with no journey and with no story. The audience, however, knows better. She will see people differently, just as we are inspired to see others and their potential in the best possible light.

Campbell argues that the experience of myth must transform those who participate in it, creating radically new ways of perceiving self. The conclusion of the film, however, offers only the re-establishment of an old order with its traditional rhythms and patterns, with Aunt Em securely in charge. Baum's novel apparently would have us believe that Dorothy, having ventured out and returned, had something fresh to tell, capable of introducing new options and transforming the existing order of the familiar Kansas terrain. In the film, Dorothy is silenced about her dream experience—if not about its effect on her vision.[21] Inadvertently, the film blunts the potential power of monomyth and its ability to tell a totally transformational tale. If the story the film tells is less transformational in character, it is also perhaps less confrontational and therefore easier to accept. It is surely one that is safer for a mass medium—one among many of Hollywood's less confrontative endings. Nonetheless, it is clear that for Campbell's hero, having ventured out and returned from the edge, there is no going back to the way it was before. The hero is transformed and must live authentically in terms of his new self-understanding.

MGM's production has clearly done a remarkable thing: it has extended Baum's novel into a cinematic world event, if not a global monomyth—an inspiring event to which we return at least once a year. And we are reminded again that the stories we tell, in the final analysis, also say something about us who tell them. *The Wizard of Oz* offers a compelling contemporary exemplification of this principle in the context of the study of religion and film.

The Treasure of the Sierra Madre: Spiritual Quest and Studio Patriarchy

Peter Valenti

"Perhaps a stable order can only be established," writes Gabriel Marcel, "if man is acutely aware of his condition as a traveller, that is to say, if he perpetually reminds himself that he is required to cut himself a dangerous path across the unsteady blocks of a universe which has collapsed and seems to be crumbling in every direction."[1] Some people lose sight of the condition of traveler and the process of life and literature as a quest. Narrative in particular possesses this sense of an objective, even if an unstated or dimly perceived one, behind human activity. Seemingly the most conventional of popular tales or fables, from *Jack and the Beanstalk* through the *Odyssey,* share this quality with such obviously spiritual meditations as Dante's *Divine Comedy.*

Joseph Campbell describes the ways in which a previously unknown figure or traveler can emerge from obscurity to lead a group to a higher state: "Whether the hero be ridiculous or sublime, Greek or barbarian, gentile or Jew, his journey varies little in essential plan. Popular tales represent the heroic action as physical; the higher religions show the deed to be moral; nevertheless, there will be found astonishingly little variation in the morphology of the adventure, the character roles involved, the victories gained."[2] Even in such an ostensible action/adventure melodrama as the 1948 Warner Bros. release *The Treasure of the Sierra Madre,* elements of this pattern elucidate our mythic search first to understand the self, and then to come to terms with others. The three men who venture forth for the gold demonstrate various aspects of the motif of journey so that the movie becomes as much a quest to determine and demonstrate what constitutes the "noble brotherhood" as it is a search for wealth. The unconscious sexism of studio patriarchy accepts and privileges such a masculine universe.

87

With its three principal roles well acted by Humphrey Bogart as Dobbs, Walter Huston as Howard, and Tim Holt as Curtin, and directed resourcefully by John Huston, the film has survived successfully as popular entertainment. But even more interestingly, in the final analysis, than the film's dramatic qualities is a certain numinous property: consideration of how the film achieves its spirituality suggests the reasons for its sustained popularity. Human relationships regardless of time or place, the film suggests, are constructed along similar lines and are subject to similar stresses. *Treasure*'s particular enunciation of mythic structures, its nature as a product of the studio system operating at Warner Bros., and its characteristic cinematic rhetoric provide solid means of understanding its potential spirituality.

The basic theme of *The Treasure of the Sierra Madre* is clear enough: greed for gold leads to loss of life and compromise of spirit. Almost as readily apparent is the mythic nature of the film as a version of the quest motif, here clearly one spiritual in nature, presented in a manner parallel to the despair and loss characteristic of the late 1940s *film noir*. As "down-and-outers," the men experience a universal human condition inasmuch as they demonstrate the making of friendship, the establishment of "brotherhood," against contrasting backgrounds of the poverty of life on the bum and the riches promised by discovery of a mother lode. Instead of a bleak urban landscape, however, in this film the rugged mountains of Mexico provide the setting against which the worst of human emotions are played out. The "treasure" of the Sierra Madre is indicated in the translation of the name as "mother mountain," especially in the sense of mother-ing or protective mountain, a role which it takes on as the major female force in the film. Initially, only Howard understands this dimension; it becomes the measure against which other men can be assessed. The storyline thus offers a secular version of the Grail myth even if the principal characters are unaware of their true objective, and parallels the quest-for-eternal-life pattern in other myths. Like the far-ranging adventures of Theseus and Heracles, the three prospectors accept the rigorous challenges of a hostilely arid, inaccessible environment in order to complete the quest. Like so many quests, however, what is sought is not what is found; instead, the physical search becomes a search into self which results in unexpected knowledge and fundamental self-awareness. The treasure differs for each of the three: the patriarch Howard, the successful adventurer Curtin, and the unsuccessful adventurer Dobbs.

Relationships among the principals in the film—the way in which character is constructed—offer one means of exploring the different meanings of "treasure." As the old man Howard says in the Oso Negro, the rundown flophouse, the "noble brotherhood" exists even there and by extension everywhere on earth until a pile of gold is involved; at that point, "brotherhood" breaks down and becomes something more selfish and brutish.[3] This more fundamental relationship, he suggests, is a natural state of humankind, achieved through respect both for others and for oneself. One way in which the film demonstrates the emergence of a new relationship is to show how the old man encourages transpersonal values in one adventurer, in effect converting him, and how his lessons fail with another whose values are more fixed on the material: the gold "for the fingers and necks of swell dames," as Dobbs says. Curtin's understanding of human relationships is more broadly based than that of his friend Dobbs, as is evident in his reading of the letter from Cody's widow. Curtin takes over the reading from Howard, just as he evidently takes over the spreading of the sense of "brotherhood" articulated by the old man. He reads aloud Mrs. Cody's comments on "life's real treasure," which is not gold but rather a lasting relationship with other humans.[4]

The notion of the female as antidote to male provides a clue to the real treasure of this film. Mrs. Cody intimates that she and her husband know what the ultimate treasure of life is; Howard consistently explains the need to coax the mountain, specified as female, to relinquish its treasure ("tickle it so it'll come out laughin' "). Even Dobbs in his foolishly masculine manner ("Fred C. Dobbs ain't a guy likes bein' taken advantage of") does have to admit in his response to Howard's request that they put the mountain back together that "she's been better to me than any woman I ever knew." Dobbs' sexism—a clear, if unwitting, parallel to the destructive properties of the masculine-centered studio system—seems to be repudiated in his fate. The relation between the feminine and spirituality explored in the film clearly extends far beyond the suggestions provided in this essay.

Through the explicit story of an adventurous search for gold in the rugged mountains of central Mexico, the ideology of the studio era is conveyed implicitly. That ideology is itself often difficult to pin down with confidence, but certain themes regarding "brotherhood" and the establishing of human relationships characterize many Warner Bros. productions of the 1940s. Values of patriotism, hard work, ethnic pride, familial devotion, and acceptance of the hegemony of existing power structures—which are *sui generis* patriarchal—are relentlessly uttered in such quasi-historical projects as *Knute Rockne—All American, They Died with Their Boots On,* and *Yankee Doodle Dandy.* Heroic male actions are turned toward perpetuation of institutions beyond the family and family traditions such as the educational/clerical/sport complex connoted by Notre Dame, the nostalgic western myth and militarism of the Custer legend, and popular arts as patriotic endeavor for George M. Cohan and his co-performers. Here in *Treasure*, though, male posturing is confined to Dobbs. He asserts his full name in opposition to the lack of identity of the old man; he asserts himself vigorously in opposition to the old man's complacent willingness to be a part of the larger group. The old man's recognition of the need for transpersonal value is indicated in the crane shots in the first Mexican village sequence where he revives the boy who nearly drowned: the camera perches high above the scene, showing the old man in the crowd of other small figures. What makes *Treasure* unique, however, is the manner in which the mythically religious material is presented: the film develops a cinematic point of view to articulate its religious universe.

Height of shots and relation between figures frequently use the rhetoric of predictable classic studio camera setups, but the film's departures from predictable rhetorical modes are even more illustrative of its particular viewpoint. The film does not, expressly, either align us with the consciousness of a central character or follow through to the development of a recognition or reversal in that central character. Instead, in a manner well-conceived by director Huston to catch the cynical morbidity of the B. Traven novel from which the movie is adapted, the narrative rhetoric places the audience in a unique position with regard to the film text. These slight departures from what could normally be expected in a studio production indicate the significant suggestions regarding the nature of spirituality and patriarchy the movie makes. Here revealed is not only the fundamental patriarchal bias of the studios, but also the smooth and apparently effortless style of classical Hollywood production which masks the subtler tones in which the message is conveyed. Eyeline matches are rare; much more characteristic of the film is the grouping of characters to indicate what they are learning.

First, the opening shot of the film orients the viewer into a world of random chance by fading in the numbers on a large board announcing the prizes in the *Lotteria Nacional* (for "public assistance"!) on February 14, 1925, thus establishing both a temporal universe and a filmic world determined by chance. The camera dollies out to a shot of a hand holding a ticket, then tearing up that ticket and throwing it away. Human activity is established through its actions: destruction, a failed opportunity, an emphasis on the work of hands through shots of hands. The first cut is to the face of Fred J. Dobbs as he looks down at the torn ticket, then up at the board, disconsolately. The full, tight shot of his face emphasizes the despair he feels; his particular sense of loss is underscored by his forlorn appearance and the crumpled newspaper he holds under his arm. In the opening moments of the film as the camera traces Dobbs' movement, two qualities are constant: Dobbs is imprisoned in self, giving nothing of himself and, in begging, asks only that someone give him something so that he can eat.

In order to understand the suggestive power of Dobbs' begging in the opening sequence, it helps to note the natural divisions of the film. Like many other epic quests, such as the paradigmatic story about Troy, the center of which is the heroic Homeric adventuring, the structure of this film story is threefold: preparation, quest, and return. *Treasure*'s version of this structure indicates the potential for the medium of film to bring about modifications in the basic structure. Each of the three major sections presents a violent encounter early on, and then mitigates that violence through further action. The first is the preparation, which includes the abortive trip under Pat McCormack to rig the camp. The transition from the first to the second stage—that of the actual quest itself—is the working out of the details for financing the trip. Dobbs' grandest gesture—his offer to help Curtin pay for the last of the shares—occurs as motivating action which empowers or enables the film to proceed. The second section introduces the bandits' raid on the train to establish the main danger of the quest, a danger present throughout this section and into the next. The third and final sequence presents the return: the outcome of the quest. The transition between the second and the third part is provided by the old man's generosity as he offers to repair the mountain and help the sick boy. His generosity is very different from Dobbs' because he knows the value not of money as assistance to others but of the giving of oneself, of one's own labors, to others.

No sooner does the old man perform his generous action, however, than the foolish Dobbs betrays this ideal. Without the kindly presence of the old man, Dobbs becomes the fearful and vicious man who attempts to execute his partner. Once down from the mountain, he is evidently unable to sustain even the marginal ability he demonstrated there to establish trust with others. Left alone with Curtin, the man who demonstrated only honesty and straightforwardness toward him, Dobbs demonstrates the validity of the old man's assertions that the "noble brotherhood" would dissolve under the influence of a pile of gold. The savagery of Dobbs' attack on Curtin is paralleled a few minutes later when the bandits attack Dobbs and kill him from behind; the visual parallel between Dobbs and the bandits as killers is reinforced when the bandits try on Dobbs' hat and boots, thereby looking as well as acting like him.

Camerawork reinforces other important themes in the film. Cinematically, the relation of Dobbs to other humans is articulated by positioning within the frame and by point-of-view shots. After his initial failure to get money for food from a passerby, a tall man in a white suit

The Treasure of the Sierra Madre
(1948, John Huston)

The film's singular instance of a subjective alliance between a character and the implied spectator occurs when Howard (Walter Huston) acknowledges he has found a treasure infinitely more satisfying than gold. The perfect bliss he enjoys at having his face stroked by the young native woman is conveyed by his long, direct look at the camera, confirming our suspicion that his values constitute the film's ideology.

gives him a peso. Significantly, Dobbs does not look up; the dramatic contrast between Dobbs' gray and rumpled clothes and the impressive linen of the taller man invests the man—who is played by director John Huston—with obvious importance. A cut from the shot of Dobbs' hand with the peso in it to his hands finishing up the meal he has secured emphasizes again Dobbs' reluctance to look either at others or at the camera and thereby establish a relationship with the implied spectator. When the child attempts to sell him a lottery ticket, Dobbs not only refuses to buy one, but also tells the boy he doesn't want to see him. When he finally does relent and buy a ticket, he tells the child to leave because he doesn't want to look at his "ugly face." Soon after this episode, Dobbs again begs from the man in the white suit, and again the composition emphasizes Dobbs' looking down and away as the man expansively puffs on a great cigar and reads his newspaper. The shot of the peso reaching the hand concludes the act of begging. But instead of using the money for a meal and a lottery ticket, Dobbs now pays for a shave and haircut. Thus nattily groomed, he asks the tall man for a handout a third time, but this time the man is incensed. Dobbs apologizes, saying, "I never looked at your face—I just looked at your hands and the money you gave me." Swearing that these final pesos are the last that Dobbs will get from him, the tall man ends his speech to Dobbs by saying: "From now on, you have to make your way through life without my assistance."

Coming as they do from the director of the film, these words are strangely prophetic and indicate much about the position of Huston in relation to the film. He functions as its "god" in the sense that he is the ultimate authority figure, the person who decides what is to be done. But in a much less dramatic sense, he is something else. He is the expansive white-coated American in a third world country beneficently handing out pesos; he represents the complex of American values upon which Dobbs can no longer count. As if to indicate this shift, the cut following this sequence plunges us into the world of darkness as Dobbs asks Pat McCormack for a handout in the doorway of a rundown dive. McCormack tells Dobbs he won't give him a red cent, but he will give him a job. Thus is Dobbs introduced to what to him constitutes the world of human action, at least for this film: Dobbs sees himself as an honest guy who can't even shine shoes in Tampico, yet is exploited by another who steals his labor. The shot of the two walking away from the camera down a dark alley toward a lighted store window with tuxedoed and gowned mannequins contrasts with the first shot following the disappointment of Curtin and Dobbs at being cheated of their wages; in the Oso Negro they walk down the dark alleyway of cots toward the camera and toward the voice of Howard, who talks about how the value of gold is derived: not from the inconsequential jewelry or dentures that are made from it, but rather from the human effort that went into finding it. The value of the labor of all the men who sought but did not find gold is added to the labor of those few who actually do find it, and so the substance acquires its final value. In this way, the monetary and spiritual values are conflated: the quest for the physical becomes as well an effort to understand the metaphysical nature of work, of labor. Rather than a vain effort to find material satisfaction, the effort should be to recognize the more lasting value of certain qualities. Curtin and Dobbs feel morally outraged that McCormack would steal their labor as he does, yet they participate in the profit from others' quests—at least in Howard's sense—as they mine the gold hundreds of other prospectors failed to find. Indeed, this is a complex universe in which the characters exist and through which they must pass as they attempt to articulate a code for living.

The film makes clear what these values should be in the relationships among the three principals. Dobbs, fixated on baubles and sensual gratification, loses the vision of the quest to which he subscribed so vehemently at the outset of the story: he falls victim to the gold and forgets his vow to the "noble brotherhood." Curtin, inspired by the text of the letter from Cody's widow, vows to go to visit her at the height of the harvest: the film makes clear the assumption that he will stay and help Mrs. Cody through the harvest. Indeed, the viewer feels that he may even remain with her longer and thus realize the dream he confessed during the evening when the three mused on what each would do with the profit from the mine. The picture of ripe fruit bursting forth is paralleled by the organic nature of the community he remembered in the San Joaquin Valley, a true experience of the transpersonal value of human relationships. Howard's picture of a small store and an easy life is given a slight twist, but is similar to his future as shaman to the Indian village. Interestingly, the one instance of a truly subjective alliance between a character in the film and the implied spectator occurs at the point when Howard realizes that he has found the dream he set out to find: the perfect bliss he enjoys at having his face stroked by a pretty young lady is conveyed in his long look directly at the camera/spectator. This is the most dramatic directorial comment on the film's action and values; it privileges the position of Howard beyond the text, since his knowing wink confirms the audience's previous suspicion that his set of values is, in the final analysis, the one that constitutes the ideology of the film.

An observation by the Christian existentialist Gabriel Marcel, suggesting the unity of both the quest and the goal of the quest, helps to sum up the spiritual potential of *The Treasure of the Sierra Madre*. Marcel's metaphor of the path supports both our human attempt to find the mode of life that will bring knowledge and our attempt as secular pilgrims to come to knowledge beyond the self:

> This path leads to a world more firmly established in Being, a world whose changing and uncertain gleams are all that we can discern here below. Does not everything happen as though this ruined universe turned relentlessly upon whomever [sic] claimed that he could settle down in it to the extent of erecting a permanent dwelling there for himself?[5]

The three travelers in the film come to such knowledge, even if Dobbs does so only by indirection. Because he is the central character for the greater part of the film, his position within the narrative leads the spectator to see clearly the working out of the values preached by Howard. And because Dobbs' example is a negative one, his point of view is studiously avoided by the camera, thus forcing the spectator to suspend identification with him. Instead, the religious potential for sharing with others is indicated cinematically by the crane and high angle shots introducing the sequences of Howard in the Indian village and by Curtin's decision to visit the widow Cody. Sadly, Howard's premonition about the failure of the "noble brotherhood" is realized as the Curtin-Dobbs alliance is broken by the partner who claimed to be above such temptations.

On the Waterfront:
Rebirth of a "Contenduh"
Neil P. Hurley, S.J.

The most compelling actor to appear in Hollywood after World War II, Marlon Brando brought an original posture to screen rebelliousness—not as defiant as James Cagney, nor as terminally fatalistic as John Garfield, nor as self-possessed and cool as Humphrey Bogart. With his tilted pelvis and hooded eyes, he spoke gutterally. The subtext of his character was potential violence, a latent sexuality that later would become text in *Last Tango in Paris* (1972). Brando starred as Terry Malloy, the central figure in *On the Waterfront;* otherwise, Budd Schulberg's grim screenplay about corruption on the New York/New Jersey waterfronts would have never reached the screen. One of eight Hollywood studios that had rejected the script, Columbia Pictures produced this film because of Brando. Elia Kazan had directed the moody actor in two previous hits—Tennessee Williams' *A Streetcar Named Desire* (1951) and *Viva Zapata!* (1953), in which Brando played a mustachioed Mexican rebel.

Budd Schulberg was attracted to the story when the wildcat strike of 1951 broke out on the docks of New York as a protest by disgruntled longshoremen over the abuses of mob-controlled union locals that were, in collusion with shipping interests, exploiting the workers by loan-sharking, shape-ups, and kick-backs, and stifling dissidents by contract murders and beatings. Schulberg became aware of a crusading "waterfront priest," the Jesuit Father John Corridan, through the Pulitzer Prize-winning series by Malcolm Johnson in *The New York Sun*—"Crime on the Waterfront." Schulberg was impressed by the labor "Padre." In a later tribute he described their first meeting: "I found a tall, gangling, energetic, ruddy-faced Irishman whose speech was a fascinating blend of Hell's Kitchen's jargon, baseball slang, the facts and figures of a master of economics and the undeniable humanity of Christ."[1] Karl Malden was given the role of the priest in the film. Called Father

"Pete" Barry, Malden gave the performance of his career, winning an Oscar.[2]

Besides Brando and Malden, the film boasts other inspired players: Eva Marie Saint as Edie, a convent-bred college girl, whose father was a rebel dockworker and whose brother is the victim of a contract "hit"; Lee J. Cobb as the calloused and corrupt union leader, Johnny Friendly (based on the real-life Joe Ryan, the president of the International Longshoremen's Association, later convicted by the tri-state Waterfront Crime Commission); and Rod Steiger as Charlie Malloy, brother of the ex-pugilist Terry and lawyer for the union which enjoyed a "sweetheart" relationship with the shipping interests. The motion picture refers obliquely to a shadowy magnate, a "Mr. Big," who is identified by journalist Raymond Allen in his book *Waterfront Priest* as William "Big Bill" McCormack, the powerful "waterfront czar" who was never indicted by the Commission. The picture never implicates "Mr. Big." He is shown in a cameo scene as the master puppeteer pulling the invisible strings that orchestrated the vast network of trucking, cargo-loading and shipping in the harbor of New York. Again he is seen briefly at the trial, but never convicted on or off screen.

Obviously, *On the Waterfront* could not encompass the entire story of how, under Father Corridan's leadership, the ILA was seriously challenged by a reform union created by the AFL-CIO, missing a victory by 493 votes in a hastily-held election prior to Christmas 1953. Nevertheless, the Schulberg/Kazan film manages to blend fact with fiction to create a Hollywood classic that elevates entertainment to the level of art while raising the consciousness of worldwide audiences regarding the injustice that prevailed in, at that time, the world's greatest port.

In the opening sequence of the film, there is a brooding nighttime scene: on the street, Terry Malloy calls up to a dockworker, a "pigeon-fancier" too and the brother of Edie, the girl Malloy will fall in love with. The viewer does not know that Terry is setting up a "hit," that he is a tool of union mobster Johnny Friendly and his own brother, Charlie, the union's accommodating lawyer. (Malloy thinks that the rebel longshoreman will be roughed up, not thrown to his death from the rooftop.) This establishing shot contains the seeds of the film's plot which is, basically, a tale of Terry Malloy's passage from a moral sleepwalker to an awakened mature man no longer willing to take orders from others. The early scenes of the film portray Malloy as sensuous, slow-witted and indolent. He is paid for "feather-bedding" and never swings a cargo hook. There is more than a faint resemblance between Marlon Brando's Terry Malloy and Victor McLaglen's Gypo Nolan in John Ford's *The Informer*. Both actors won Academy Awards playing physically strong men with low intellectual wattage who later undergo a change of heart. The difference is that, as an informer, Brando's Malloy helps the cause of the "underdog," whereas McLaglen's betrayal serves the British "Black and Tan" in the time of "the troubles" in Ireland. Malloy's conversion, unlike Gypo Nolan's, is a more gradual one and takes place with the help of a pretty young woman and a prophetic clergyman. Both are clearly "Christfigures"—McLaglen kneeling before a crucifix with arms outstretched, Brando punished physically for violating vested interests.

Elia Kazan has a decided penchant for betrayal scenes (e.g. *Viva Zapata!* and *Face in the Crowd*). Some critics feel that Kazan rationalized his own willingness to name names in the Hollywood witchhunt. Recall that the House Un-American Activities Committee solicited testimony from friendly witnesses who would implicate those suspected of being communists or, at least, fellow travelers.[3] Certainly, Kazan's interpretation of the informer is ambiguous, even apologetic. Terry Malloy's turning away from the mob, especially through his ties to his brother, Charlie, is a masterful treatment of motivation, perfectly plausible and totally convincing.

Karl Malden's Father Barry is an attractive man of the cloth—zealous for justice and the welfare of the men in his non-territorial parish, oppressed workers whom he considers as "sacred cargo." When a dissident stevedore is killed in a deliberate accident, in effect a mob "hit," Father Barry arrives and, brimming with righteous indignation, preaches a sermon right in the ship's hold at the site of the crime. The scene, Malden's most dramatic sequence, is based on an actual sermon which Father Corridan had delivered to the Knights of Columbus in 1948 (prior to the wildcat strike). Corridan's prophetic homily was called "Christ Looks at the Waterfront," reminding his hearers that Christ "carried carpenter's tools in His hands and earned His bread and butter by the sweat of His brow." Malden's sermon alludes to the Catholic doctrine of the Mystical Body of Christ (Paul's letter to the Ephesians, 4:1–16) by linking Good Friday to the injustice and indignities of the stevedores. For dramatic heightening, Schulberg adds an incident that had never happened to the actual waterfront priest. As Father Barry emboldens the men not to cower before intimidating threats, a "goon" in Johnny Friendly's employ throws a missile which strikes the priest on the side of the head. Although he begins to bleed, he does not halt in his impassioned plea for justice and reform of working conditions on the New York/New Jersey piers.[4]

True, Terry Malloy is motivated to change by the manly courage and religious conviction of Father Barry, but Edie's romantic and religious nature touches a deep chord in Terry. His attraction to purity in the form of an ideal somewhat like Dante's Beatrice is beautifully portrayed in a scene of creative serendipity; that is to say, the action flows in an unscripted way as a spontaneous chemistry develops between the two stars. Known in Hollywood as a "non-story" episode, the scene does not move the plot line along in any thematic way, but anchors the interest of the audience in the relationship between the man and the woman so that what happens to them in the future carries a greater emotional charge than if the scene had not been included.

The scene shows Terry and Edie enjoying an afternoon stroll amid the industrial environment of wire fences, cranes, crates and cargo (Kazan makes us feel alienation and oppression). Nevertheless the mood is romantic. Relaxed and free of care, the couple banter back and forth, getting to know one another. While they talk, Terry takes one of Edie's gloves and occupies himself with it in a playful manner. Before long, he begins to try to fit his fingers into the petite glove, obviously not made to accommodate his oversized, somewhat gnarled fingers. The charm of the scene lies in the fact that the gesture is completely unconscious: it is an eloquent plea arising from his deep self. The symbolism is both immediate and disarming: she (and we the audience with her) realizes that the gruff, uneducated former "pug" wants to fit into her life and that this wish will not be easy to fulfill.[5]

Despite this moving scene, Brando's Terry Malloy reverts to his explosive type-cast self later when he forces entry into Edie's apartment. His role in staging the death of her brother threatens to destroy their developing relationship. Of course, she feels deeply for him and knows his potential for growth. Nonetheless, he has not broken with the mob that ordered the murder of her brother. My personal conviction is that the film lapses with this scene of forced entry as Malloy crashes through the door and subdues Edie by the strength of his arms. While highly melodramatic, it contrasts too sharply with the daytime walk scene. He brings her down to earth in terms of his animal magnetism; she by contrast will elevate his animalism above its habitual level of physical need. I feel, however, that the psychological leap is too swift.

It is important to understand the central contribution of Brando to the immortality of *On the Waterfront*. His character symbolized latent violence and brimming sexuality (e.g. *The Men* and *The Wild One*). To see a Brando's untamed traits surrender to the refinements of romance and religion is a *volte-face* which could have failed except for the script, the direction and Brando's new-found range of performance. Inner remorse and spiritual regeneration are not part and parcel of the histrionic lessons taught in the school of Method Acting. Thus the power of *On the Waterfront* rests on mood, a fast-paced script and bravura acting—but especially on the evolution of Terry Malloy from an accomplice in rack-eteering and murder toward a spiritually agitated man looking for moral maturity. Love for a virginal well-bred woman, the example of a crusad-ing activist priest and a sudden awareness of his brother's manipulation of his promising fight career—all move him toward conversion.

The turning point in the film, prepared for by the uplifting influ-ence of Edie and Father Barry, is certainly the pathetic rendezvous scene in the taxi between Terry and his brother. The latter had cared for him when their mother died. Later Charlie is employed as the legal mind for Johnny Friendly, studying the thickets of the law for loopholes and cultivating the judges and politicians who could help prevent any interfer-ence with the rackets. In a sense he is an intellectual "goon," but as a professional he carries himself with dignity, aware of what he is about. Like many white collar criminals he has two sides—one, the Machiavel-lian manipulator; the other, a civilized and caring family man. For Charlie loves Terry and, indeed, risks his life in order to warn him that his involvement with Father Barry and Edie will only lead to trouble because of Johnny Friendly's decision to have him killed. Charlie does not sus-pect the moral and romantic development that has taken place in his brother. In order to be alone, Charlie and Terry meet in a taxi—its ominous destination, the local's headquarters. It is night; the setting is captured in expressionistic lighting with shadows predominating.

The scene is a "two shot" with the brothers facing one another in the back seat. The audience sees Charlie more in profile, Terry more frontally. An exception to the film's long and medium shots, the scene unerringly opts for the close-up. Charlie warns Terry not to squeal un-less he wants to die. However, his brother is not the docile, over-trusting "toadie" from before. His conscience has been pricked; his mental hori-zons have been expanded. An ex-pugilist, he confronts Charlie with the fixed fight in which he was asked by Johnny Friendly—through Charlie —to take a "dive" so that the mob and its associates could take advantage of the betting odds. The expression of lament, disappointment and fra-ternal betrayal remains one of the most touching moments ever filmed. The shot-reverse shot technique and the close-ups help the audience to witness an epiphany of rebirth, a passage from darkness into the light, and demonstrate sublimely how, at its best, motion photography can picture e-*motion*, indeed a spiritual conversion. With unwavering voice, Terry recounts the rare opportunity he had in the old Madison Square Garden to score a victory leading to a chance at the heavyweight cham-pionship of the world. But, no!—the "sure bet" temptation was too irresistible, Terry intimates. By throwing the fight to please his brother, he ended his promising career. As Terry phrases it colloquially, he got "a one-way ticket to Palookaville" instead. With his characteristic husky voice, Malloy holds up the mirror for himself and his brother to look at unflinchingly and utters the immortal line: "I could 'uv been a contenduh instead of a bum, which is what I am." Up to that point, Terry Malloy has lived in the present, the indicative mood, a pragmatist "taking the cash and letting the credit go." Now he speaks in the conditional mood—of what might have been.

If there is any quarrel in assessing the merits of the film, it is that the front-office decision-makers seemed to have been afraid of the realistic tragic ending that Budd Schulberg saved for his later novel, sparing Terry Malloy for the sake of the habitual "Hurrah" of the Hollywood happy ending. Why did the filmmakers shy away from the inner momentum of the plot? It was Aristotle who taught that plot predominates over character. In classic Hollywood, plot was all too often subordinate to the image of a star. As Parker Tyler suggests in *The Hollywood Hallucination*, the wisdom of too many Hollywood films resides more in profitability than in profundity.[6] Hitchcock could not make Cary Grant a murderer in *Suspicion;* Frank Capra could not have Gary Cooper jump to his death in *Meet John Doe.* Nor could Kazan-Schulberg kill Brando to end the film honestly.

Having decided that Terry Malloy would not die, the architects of the film—producer Sam Spiegel, director Elia Kazan and writer Budd Schulberg—decided to have him beaten to a bloody pulp. Budd Schulberg has put the scene into focus:

> The film mounted to a battle royal between conscience-troubled Terry Malloy (Marlon Brando) and his old *patron,* dock boss Johnny Friendly (Lee J. Cobb), ending with Father Barry (Karl Malden) urging the battered, now redeemed Terry to lead intimidated dockers into the pier, thereby breaking the hold of the "pistol local." Even though Johnny screams from behind them: "I'll be back—and I'll remember every last one of yus!" his dialogue was lost in the sweeping upbeat power of the camera.[7]

In the film Terry Malloy lives, intimating a resurrection, a second chance, a new life as an upright citizen in love with a beautiful refined woman, Edie. The finale is, to my mind, a waterfront crucifixion without the nails and the last gasp of "It is consummated!" Shades of Victor McLaglen's Gypo Nolan in John Ford's *The Informer!*

Despite the "false ending," the fulcrum of believability throughout the picture is Brando's presence—tough but tender, self-indulgent but

On the Waterfront
(1954, Elia Kazan)

After a battle royal with the dock boss Johnny Friendly, Terry Malloy (Marlon Brando) lies beaten to a pulp, but in no way defeated. Supported by Father Barry (Karl Malden) and his girlfriend Edie (Eva Marie Saint)—a variation on the *Pietà*—he will rise from his muted crucifixion and lead the intimidated dockworkers onto the pier in revolt against the "pistol local."

with an eventual "sticking point." One of the century's most electrifying actors, Marlon Brando overturned the inexorable logic of the plot, both historically and psychologically. Thanks to a refined love, an inspiring cleric, and a remorseful brother-martyr, Brando's Malloy rises from being a bum to a spiritual rebirth, a "contenduh" as a moral champion.

On the Waterfront bristles with the "sacred discontent" of the Bible.[8] Part of the scriptural patrimony of the Jewish-Christian tradition is transcendence, that driving impulse not merely "to be," but "to become." This restless aspiration to ascend informs Brando's portrayal of Terry Malloy. Note the biblical subtext. Terry avoids the work-sweat assigned to Adam as a penalty for original sin. He also sees woman as pleasure-object, not soul-mate—that is, until he meets the pure Edie. She will complement him, refurbishing the faded image of God latent within his boorish personality. A shadow falls across the family unity the Bible upholds. Terry's brother Charlie needs to learn that lesson of divine revelation. If priestly mediation is a constant thread of both Testaments, Father Pete Barry is such a bridge-builder, reconciling fallen man to a forgiving God.

We must not overlook betrayal and infidelity, core themes of the Bible. In the Kazan/Schulberg film we have both—the union bosses "selling out" the "rank-and-file," the remote "Mr. Big" muscling the city and pulling wires to control others; Charlie compromising his boxer-brother; and, finally, Terry turning state's evidence for the sake of justice and his own future. He does this through ritual sacrifice, echoing the pattern of the Bible. When he runs the gauntlet of hateful violence, we have the martyrdom themes of the Jewish and Christian scriptures, a veritable *via crucis* which, in Schulberg's later novel, ends with a contract murder in the Jersey swamps, but which in the film provides an uplifting resurrection motif.[9] In either case, we have a biblical concordance, whatever the short-term intentions of the commercial filmmakers.

On the Waterfront is a classic. The major actors, to my mind, have never surpassed their respective roles—not even Brando. For this reason alone it is eminently reseeable and ultimately unforgettable.

The Art of "Seeing": Classical Paintings and *Ben-Hur*

Diane Apostolos-Cappadona

The primacy of sight is undeniable. Seeing is that human experience which precedes speech. The visual allows for the development of knowledge and of memory. Through the use of images,[1] sight is constitutive of "the world" as we come to know it. Seeing is believing.

Sight is developed and nurtured by the discipline of *seeing*.[2] In this sense, to *see* means more than to look. *Seeing* demands and challenges the viewer. Careful attention to images, to their purposes and to their meaning, is part of the discipline of *seeing*. Viewers become totally engaged when they *see* as the total sense of self is integrated and transformed. In this way, the viewer becomes a *seer* for whom a whole new world opens up through every image and every visual symbol encountered. A person trained in the discipline of *seeing* is transformed and made new through a visual encounter.

The images of classical paintings form and shape a viewer's subliminal and conscious way of seeing. As an example of this "shaping" of a viewer's perception, consider Sören Kierkegaard's testimony:

> Once upon a time, there was a man. As a boy he was strictly brought up in the Christian religion. He had not heard much about that which other children commonly hear, about the little child Jesus, about the angels, and suchlike. On the other hand, they showed him all the more frequently the Crucified, so that this picture was the only one he had, the only impression of the Saviour. Although only a child, he was already an old man.[3]

Impressions made upon a viewer's subconscious and conscious mind by images have long-lasting and profound implications. Studies have indicated that the most successful magazine advertisements and television commercials are dependent upon a visual presentation that is based upon a classical painting. What the purchaser is buying, then, is not simply the product and what it promises you will become by using it, but also the aura of cultural and social status that accompanies both the classical painting and the privileged class of its original owner.[4]

In a similar fashion, classical paintings have influenced the set and costume designs, character portrayals, and atmosphere of authenticity of those films recognized as "classics." A series of visual connectors registers in the viewers' subliminal and conscious minds as they watch these films. The assimilation of the images from classical paintings has a dual result: first, they present the viewer with a sense of cultural ambience and authenticity; second, they allow for the principles of a painting masterpiece to be employed in a film.

The most powerful expression of the image's ability to form and shape the conscious and unconscious mind of the viewer is found in the vital symbols of religious traditions. Such symbols embody shared memories that are the ground for social and political community identity.[5] From its earliest centuries, Christianity was cognizant of the power and importance of sight.[6]

Such references by a filmmaker allow him the opportunity to participate through the viewer's eyes in that history of shared memory and communal identity. In the case of a film with a biblical theme, that "shared history" has a double meaning: both the religious history and the cultural history are the sources of association. Further, visual analogies lend an aura of both authenticity and reality to the film—by contributing to a *real* presentation of the story that is unfolding before the viewer's eyes. Inevitable audience associations may transcend or enhance the intended visual analogies made between classical painting and film classics. In many cases even the unintentional associations to classical religious art affect the informed viewer's experience of a film classic; such is the case with William Wyler's *Ben-Hur*.

The credits for *Ben-Hur* are projected against a backdrop of Michelangelo's *Creation of Adam*—an indication of Wyler's intentional visual analogies to classical paintings. To further emphasize his interest in this artistic masterpiece, Wyler focuses on one of its themes, the touch of new life, which is visually imitated in the two scenes in which Judah Ben-Hur encounters Jesus of Nazareth. Wyler has the image of the *Creation of Adam* slowly reduced through the frames of the credits. Ultimately, the viewer sees clearly the detail of the "touch of new life" extended by God to Adam. The religious and thematic implications play upon the viewer's subconscious memory.

Two of Wyler's visual analogies have a more secular origin: Thomas Cole's *The Course of Empire: Consummation of Empire* (see il-

The Course of Empire: Consummation of Empire
(1836, Thomas Cole)

Ben-Hur's scene of Quintus Arrius' triumphant entry into Rome is strongly reminiscent of this panel from Cole's serial panorama *The Course of Empire*. Following Cole's depiction of massive structures ornately decorated, William Wyler too makes a visual argument against the power and wealth that corrupt.

lustration) and the scenes of Quintus Arrius' triumphant entry into Rome; and the genre of sea paintings exemplified by Aelbert Cuyp's *The Mass at Dordrecht* and the film sequence on the Mediterranean Sea.[7]

One of America's first romantic painters, Cole has a place in American art because of the fame and popularity of his panoramic series, best-known of which is *The Course of Empire*. Although overtly secular, *The Course of Empire* is typical of Cole's paintings. Its theme is effectively sacred. In fact, *The Course of Empire* is avowedly evangelical in its visual Christian rhetoric. Cole's analogy is between the rise and fall of the Roman empire and the industrialization and secularization of his contemporary American society.

The Course of Empire was a serial panorama designed and executed for public exhibition. Serial panoramas provided the American public with "a genuine theatrical experience, calculated to please and instruct a wide audience, much like the popular epic movies of the twentieth century."[8] In fact, the 1836 exhibition of *The Course of Empire* netted Cole almost $1,000. Spectators in the 1830s lined up to see exhibitions of serial panoramas just as spectators in the 1950s lined up to see biblical epics like *Ben-Hur* and *The Ten Commandments*. A further analogy could be drawn between the evangelical Christian rhetoric of the 1830s and that of the 1950s. Serial panoramas like Cole's *The Course of Empire* were the nineteenth century American forebears of the cinematic blockbusters of the 1950s.

Cole himself plays upon a tradition of visual analogies in *The Course of Empire: Consummation of Empire*. Like all artists who have studied the works of great masters, Cole reflects in his works a convergence of their influences and his own personal interpretation. The influences of Claude Lorraine, Turner, and Piranesi are the most obvious in this particular instance. Cole's scrupulous and exacting concern for archaeological and architectural accuracy is evident in the careful detail work of this painting. Although his vision of the *Consummation of Empire* was based as much on known sources as on his own artistic vision, Cole adds his own identifiable "touch" to *The Course of Empire*.

Like Wyler's scene of Quintus Arrius' triumphant entry into Rome, Cole's *The Course of Empire: Consummation of Empire* shows a victorious army and its general entering Rome in a triumphant procession. The anticipation and the excitement of the moment are made known to us through the artistic details of garlands and festoons draped on the architectural sites, such as the lavender festoon on the Triumphal Arch. The myriad activities from the revelries of the crowd to the movement of the triumphant procession to the ships in the lagoon express the energy and vitality that was Rome.

The grandeur and architectural splendor of Rome are attested to in the careful detail work on the pediment and columns of the Temple to Diana on the left hand side of the painting. The opposite side of the painting is under the aegis of the statue of Minerva, goddess of wisdom and war, who blesses her triumphant general and army with her outstretched right hand. The glorified buildings, triumphant presence of the army, revelries of the crowd, and anticipated presence of the emperor all come to symbolize the power and the glory that *was* Rome.

Wyler's scenes of imperial Rome, which are based on paintings like Cole's, offer a symbolic contrast to the sparser and simpler sets that dominate the scenes in Jerusalem. Like Cole, Wyler has made a visual argument against the power and the wealth that corrupts. For it would appear that the Romans can never surround themselves with either sufficient luxury or enough elegant architecture. By contrast those who believe in the one God, i.e. followers of the Jewish-Christian tradition, are satisfied with the basic necessities and with simpler environs.

The more obvious visual relationships between *Ben-Hur* and classi-

The Adoration of the Shepherds: With the Lamp
(c. 1654, Rembrandt van Rijn)

The visual parallels between this work of Rembrandt and *Ben-Hur*'s nativity sequence are striking in both composition and design; both situate the Virgin and Child on the right, the Magi on the left. Rembrandt's suffused light foreshadows the film's thematic emphasis on the intimacy of the touch of new life.

cal paintings are found in Christian art. Since the story of Judah Ben-Hur is subtitled *A Tale of the Christ*, we naturally anticipate interconnections between the film and biblical narratives. But analogies to Christian art also abound. The film opens with the Christmas story, and classical visual analogies are found for the artistic representations of such episodes as the adoration of the kings, the adoration of the shepherds, and the flight into Egypt. Further visual analogies can be found by comparing the film sequence of Jesus of Nazareth teaching on the hillside to artistic renderings of the sermon on the mount, and the film sequences of the valley of the lepers to artistic interpretations of the miracle of the raising of Lazarus.

Two obvious but important visual analogies occur in the nativity scene itself and in the crucifixion scene. In both cases, the "collective" images of these religious themes have been original works of art as well as reproductions on Christmas cards, in prints and in engravings since the sixteenth century. Readily available as an additional source of inspiration are the ubiquitous illustrated Bibles, especially those featuring drawings, engravings, and prints by Rembrandt.

The importance of prints and engravings cannot be underestimated. This form of artistic expression allowed an artist to make more than one copy of a work of art for a minimal effort. In turn, the lower cost of prints and engravings made it possible for "average" people to find "real" works of art affordable and therefore have them accessible in their homes. There is probably much credibility to the art historical argument for the importance of Albrecht Dürer's prints to the spread of Protestantism in the early sixteenth century.

No artist made the print his vehicle of artistic expression or of popular recognition to a greater degree, though, than did Rembrandt. For example, we can consider the visual parallels between his print *The Adoration of the Shepherds* (see illustration) and the film's nativity sequence. The similarities in composition and design in both the print and the film are obvious as both situate the Virgin and Child on the right and the magi on the left. Further, the basic composition of the ambience of a poor stable is both authentic to the scriptural story and common to its artistic representation.

Light is a crucial element in works of both art and the cinema. Light has effective and affective qualities. An effective and insightful use of light can result in leading the viewer's eye in the path appropriate to the artist's [or filmmaker's] interpretation. The softness of light in this film sequence indicates the tenderness between the mother and her newborn child, while the wonder of the shepherds and the homage of the magi are reflected in the glowing light. Thus, the theme of the "touch of new life" is doubly present in this sequence. It is seen first in the tactile engagement between the mother and her newborn infant son—the reality of the touch of new life! Secondly, the symbolism of light which bathes the magi and the shepherds represents the "new life" into which all are born who accept Jesus as the Christ. Rembrandt employs a similar use of light in his print.

A comparison of Rembrandt's print *Christ Crucified Between Two Thieves* (see illustration) to the crucifixion scene would provide similar visual and symbolic parallels. Consider the form of the body of Jesus of Nazareth nailed to the cross, or the internal relationships among the mourners and Roman soldiers. In both cases, the "form" is pyramidal, or triangular. In fact, if we look closely at either Rembrandt's print or a film still, we notice that the composition of the entire scene is a large pyramid

Christ Crucified between the Two Thieves (The Three Crosses)
(1653, Rembrandt van Rijn)

Like Rembrandt's crucifixion scene, Wyler's in *Ben-Hur* is pyramidal in form, perhaps the most effective and harmonious design in the visual arts. This appeal to the classic masterpieces of western painting adds aesthetic subtlety to the emotional depths of the drama enacted as well as a sense of commonality with the history of sacred art.

composed of a series of smaller internal pyramids, e.g. the groups of mourners, the groups of soldiers. Even the body of Jesus of Nazareth as it is nailed on the cross forms an upside down pyramid, while simultaneously being the top of the larger pyramid.

Pyramidal composition is the most effective and most harmonious form of visual design. Leonardo da Vinci retrieved and popularized the practice of pyramidal composition in Renaissance painting. A careful study of the classic masterpieces of western painting reveals an amazing fact: the majority of these paintings are based upon pyramidal composition. Recall da Vinci's *Last Supper*, Raphael's *Transfiguration of Christ*, and Rembrandt's *The Night Watch*.

Wyler employs this compositional device to great advantage in the depiction of the crucifixion of Jesus of Nazareth in *Ben-Hur*. First, the design empowers the emotional and situational drama with aesthetic subtleties. Second, the commonality of the pyramidal composition grants a sense of familiarity to the film sequence. Finally, Wyler's use of visual analogies to classical paintings of this scene gives his depiction of the crucifixion an aura of historical accuracy and of the sacrality conferred by Christian tradition.

One of the great masterpieces of western art is Mathias Grünewald's *Isenheim Altarpiece*. The central panel of the altarpiece, the *Crucifixion* (see illustration), is one of the earliest representations of the dead and tortured body of Jesus of Nazareth on the cross found in western Christian art. Such a depiction of the crucified Christ is as much a result of theological understandings of the sacrificial nature of the suffering and death of Jesus of Nazareth as it is a symbol for his compassion for human suffering.

Consider the visual evidence of the body of Jesus of Nazareth. Most viewers notice first either the unnatural greenish tone to the skin, the pricked and open sores on the body, or the enormous size of that figure in comparison to the others. Just above the right hand of St. John the Baptist in the dark background of the sky, Grünewald has inscribed the scriptural phrase, "So shall He increase, so shall I decrease."

Consider now the action surrounding the crucifixion scene in *Ben-Hur*. The three female characters, Esther, Miriam and Tirzah, are returning to the valley of the lepers after witnessing part of Jesus' walk toward Calvary. Ben-Hur's mother, Miriam, and sister, Tirzah, were infected with leprosy during their confinement by the Roman tribune, Messala. They believe that they have lost their chance of being healed by this charismatic young teacher. Suddenly a strange and terrible storm comes upon them and they take shelter in a cave. The skies darken (as in Grünewald's painting) and torrents of wind-driven rain descend upon the earth.

Wyler's sense of visual analogies and his directorial genius take over in the next sequence of shots, intercut between the crucifixion scene proper and the three women in the cave. We see the mother and daughter slowly being healed of their ailment as their open sores and disfigurement are washed away by the torrential rains. Simultaneously, we notice that the body of Jesus of Nazareth becomes distorted in a fashion similar to Grünewald's Christ as he takes on "all the sins [physical ailments] of the world." Wyler's most dramatic portrayal of these miraculous activities comes in the close-up of the distorted and diseased hands of Jesus, and in the shot where Esther *touches* the healed hands of Miriam.

The symbolism is strengthened by the visual analogies. The mother

Crucifixion (from the Isenheim Altarpiece)
(1515, Mathias Grünewald)

Wyler intercuts the gradual distortion of Jesus' body on the cross with the scene from the cave of lepers, as Ben-Hur's mother and sister are healed of their disease, their deformed hands reminiscent of Grünewald's Jesus. Although they had despaired of seeing the charismatic young teacher again, his death miraculously effects their cure.

and sister of Judah Ben-Hur are afflicted with the deformities and surface lacerations associated with leprosy. At the moment of his sacrificial death, Jesus of Nazareth takes on more than the sins of the world; he also takes on the physical ailments of the world. His body becomes contorted and disfigured by the pain and deformity associated with leprosy. The symbolic and thematic connections to Grünewald's Christ empower the visual referent.

Furthermore, the theme of the entire film is reprised in this crucial climactic episode. We are reminded of the variations on the theme of the "touch of new life": Judah Ben-Hur's encounters with Jesus of Nazareth, the healings by Jesus of Nazareth that were witnessed by Esther, and the bond of father and adopted son formed between Judah Ben-Hur and Quintus Arrius, which is sealed by the gift of a familial ring and a clasping of hands.

The retreat of the three women from the storm into a cave symbolizes perhaps the entombment and resurrection of Jesus of Nazareth. The Christian scriptures recount that *three* women go to the tomb on Easter morning to attend the body of the crucified, only to find that the tomb is empty and to hear that Jesus as the Christ has been raised from the dead. In *Ben-Hur,* however, the three women who enter the tomb are not the same three who depart from it. Two of them have been healed and physically reborn, while the third has had her waning faith restored and is spiritually reborn. Of course, the principal visual analogue for his "touch of new life" is found in the opening and closing credits of *Ben-Hur,* the projection of Michelangelo's *Creation of Adam.*

One final example of *Ben-Hur's* appeal to classical paintings is in the portrayal of the heroine, Esther. Beautiful women have always been the subject of artistic masterpieces since the beginning of western art. The beautiful heroine as projected by Wyler's presentation of Esther is delicate in demeanor but strong in character, passive in the outside world but active in the domestic arena. Physically, Esther could be best described as soft, sweet, and implicitly sensual. In other words, she is Raphaelesque.

In America from the colonial period to the middle of the twentieth century, Raphael was considered to be the greatest of all artistic geniuses.[9] His work was highly prized by collectors, museums, art historians, and the general public. Most American homes owned at least one reproduction of a Raphael painting, usually the *Madonna of the Chair.* Even Thomas Jefferson hung replicas of Raphael paintings in Monticello. When P.A.B. Widener purchased the most sought-after prize of all American collectors, a Raphael Madonna, the purchase was the headline story in *The New York Times.*[10]

Works by Raphael were to be found in illustrated Bibles, prints, replica paintings, reproductions, church bulletins, and the ubiquitous Christmas card. One of the major appeals of Raphael's paintings, especially his paintings of "the dear sweet madonnas," was his ability to present a sentimental, soft, delicate, young woman whose gaze radiated an aura of strength and sensuality. The characteristics of a Raphael Madonna such as *The Small Cowper Madonna* were ingrained in the American consciousness from the colonial period.

If we compare Wyler's Esther to a Raphael *Madonna* (see illustration), we notice the common characteristics of delicacy, strength, softness and sensuality. Like Leonardo's portraits of women which Raphael admired (as evidenced by *The Small Cowper Madonna*), Wyler's Esther is

The Alba Madonna
(c. 1510, Raphael)

There is little doubt that Wyler appealed to Raphael's Madonna for the portrayal of *Ben-Hur*'s heroine, Esther. As played by Haya Harareet, she is soft, sweet, and implicitly sensual. Like Raphael's Madonna—an image ingrained in the American consciousness from the Colonial period onward—Esther also shows an unmistakable inner strength.

regularly seen with an aloof but sentimental gaze. Like *The Small Cowper Madonna* and Leonardo's *Mona Lisa*, Esther says more with her quiet smile and sad eyes than all the other characters in *Ben-Hur* say with words. After all, a picture is worth a thousand words.

The works of art examined here as visual references in *Ben-Hur* were familiar to the average American in the 1950s, usually from reproductions or replicas. Art historical training is not necessary either to study or to be influenced by the style of visual analogies employed in

Ben-Hur. Examination of the cultural context in which a film is produced and the audience for whom it is intended helps to define the role of religion in that society. In those instances where both the film and the work of art share a religious worldview, as is the case in question, an in-depth interpretation of the iconographic, symbolic, and theological aspects of both the film and the visual analogies is warranted and helpful.

William Wyler's 1959 production of *Ben-Hur* followed an American tradition for serial panoramas and biblical epics. The American of the late 1950s reflected the conservatism and restraint of the Eisenhower administration. Charles Sanford has identified Eisenhower's chief appeal as president of the most prosperous nation of the free world as "a naive simplicity which recalls America's preindustrial past."[11] This nostalgia for a simpler America, joined with a reaffirmation of such basic and identifiable Jewish-Christian values as the family, trust in God, and personal honor as central to the sermons preached by American religious leaders, parallels the basic moral stance taken by Judah Ben-Hur. The projection of the Jewish-Christian worldview throughout Wyler's *Ben-Hur*—despite the millennia that separated modern America from ancient Rome—made the film as familiar and acceptable to the average American as the fundamental "American" values of God, mother, and apple pie.

The visual allusions in *Ben-Hur* not only led to its acceptance by the film audience, but also contributed to its status as a classic American film. Surely Kenneth Clark's two major characteristics of an artistic masterpiece are applicable to Wyler's film: "A confluence of memories and emotions forming a single idea, and a power of recreating traditional forms so that they become expressive of the artist's own epoch and yet keep a relationship with the past."[12] In this way, classic films, like classic paintings, become simultaneously symbolic of culture *and* spirituality. Seeing is believing.

PART IV

Montage and Transforming Love

Casablanca
(1942, Michael Curtiz)

In an unforgettable scene of parting and love, Rick (Humphrey Bogart) bids farewell to his beloved Ilsa (Ingrid Bergman) as she prepares to join her husband on the plane for Lisbon—and freedom. In sacrificing love to duty, Rick embodies the biblical virtue of altruism as the redemptive antidote to narcissism.

Love and Duty in *Casablanca*

Mara E. Donaldson

Who has not wept at the nobility of the final words of Rick (Humphrey Bogart) to Ilsa (Ingrid Bergman) as he sends her off with Victor (Paul Henreid) at the end of *Casablanca?* "Here's looking at you, kid," he says. And when Rick walks into the fog with Renault (Claude Rains), the audience knows that in sacrificing love to duty, Rick has made the moral, indeed the righteous, decision.[1]

Casablanca, the 1942 Michael Curtiz film, epitomizes the Jewish-Christian virtue of altruism—self-denying, sacrificial love. Both the theme of sacrificial love and the nostalgic mood created by the cinematography have combined to make *Casablanca* an enduring, and virtually irresistible, piece of American cinema—in short, a classic. Such altruism, as well as the longing for a mythic past, seems to be endemic to western religious identity.[2]

This essay seeks to place *Casablanca* in its historical and cultural context and argues that a tension between private love and public duty is the key to the film's enduring appeal, and that Rick's transformation from a self-centered, narcissistic character to one who chooses the welfare of others over his own self-interest resolves that tension. The nostalgic mood created by the film's visual effects reinforces the ultimate triumph of Rick's altruism. Taken together, the love-duty theme and the nostalgic longing of the cinematography are what open *Casablanca* to the need for further theological scrutiny centered upon the character of Ilsa, curiously the most forgotten major character in critical appraisals of *Casablanca*, and upon the theme of sacrificial love and of the seductive power of the film's nostalgia.

If in film, as in life, timing is everything, then the release of *Casablanca* for Thanksgiving of 1942 was timely indeed. The opening of *Casablanca* coincided with three Allied landings in North Africa.[3] By only a few months, it predated the Casablanca Conference, which demanded the unconditional surrender of the Axis states. The war was on everyone's mind and, as the declaration signed by the allies at the Casablanca Conference (January 14–24, 1943) guaranteed, would be for some time.

The New York Times on November 27, 1942, carried both the first review of *Casablanca* and a report of a prayer service conducted by President Roosevelt at the White House. While thousands of moviegoers were watching Humphrey Bogart leave Ingrid Bergman to "do his duty," Roosevelt was praying to God for the Allied forces, that "being filled with wisdom and girded with strength [they] may do their duty to Thy honor and glory."[4]

The first reviews of *Casablanca* emphasized the connection between the film's themes and the national preoccupation with the war. In his first *New York Times* review of *Casablanca,* Bosley Crowther wrote that "once more, as in recent Bogart pictures, they have turned the incisive trick of draping a tender love story within the folds of a tight topical theme"—the war in North Africa.[5] It was Crowther, in fact, who first recognized that the "stunning performance of Humphrey Bogart as Rick" was centered upon "his beautiful demonstration of cold conflict between his *love* for a woman and his *sense of what is right*"—his *duty.*[6]

Although *Casablanca* was a "timely" film, both in its release to the public and in its themes, its "timelessness" as a classic was not anticipated. When the film won the Academy Award for best picture, best director (the only Oscar for Michael Curtiz) and best film script (to Julius and Philip Epstein and Howard Koch) for 1943, *Newsweek* was not alone in calling *Casablanca* "a dark horse to the sweepstakes."[7]

Still, most recent discussions of *Casablanca* have attended to the "timelessness," rather than the "timeliness" of the film as the key to the interpretation of the love-duty theme. Robert B. Ray in *A Certain Tendency of the Hollywood Cinema, 1930–1980* has gone so far as to call *Casablanca* "the culmination of Classic Hollywood."[8] He focuses on the theme of Rick's *duty,* seeing in Rick's conflict with Laszlo the tension between "divergent strains of American mythology." For Ray, Rick embodies the *narcissistic* "outlaw hero" while Laszlo represents the *altruistic* "official hero." Sidney Rosenzweig goes even further, calling the central conflict in the film the one between *private* feelings and *public* duties, a common theme in other Curtiz films: "[Rick] is an irresistible identification figure for that urge in all of us for a splendid and noble martyrdom. What could be more satisfying than the image of ourselves *sacrificing* all that we *love* for a virtuous ideal, ending up utterly but heroically alone?"[9] Barbara Deming's provocative study *Running Away*

From Myself interprets the tension between love and duty as masking an underlying crisis of faith. Rick's excessive self-preoccupation, or narcissism, is endearing for the war-weary moviegoer because it is transformed into a truly lovable self-denial, or altruism. As Deming puts it, the movie is seductive precisely because, although "[Rick] wears the aspect of utter cynicism, one can be sure that he is the real man of faith."[10]

In these and other discussions of *Casablanca*, critics have rightly identified aspects of both the "timely" and "timeless" character of the film which have made it a classic. Love, duty, sacrifice, and faith are all part of the American myth of the frontier hero. But Rick's sacrifice of his love for Ilsa to his duty to defend his country is not simply a reworking or extension of the American frontier myth, as Ray argues. Nor are love and duty to be reduced to private feelings and public responsibilities, as Rosenzweig has wished to claim.

Of all the standard interpretations of *Casablanca*, Deming has come the closest to capturing what is really at stake in what she has described as Rick's transition from cynicism to faith. Yet, not to push on to a distinctly *theological* interpretation of this transition is to miss a more foundational, distinctly Jewish-Christian subtext in the film. It is to miss seeing that the transition from love to duty in *Casablanca* begs to be seen in the religious cultural context in which it was created. Rick's development from self-love to self-denying duty needs to be interpreted in its theological context, as the redemptive transformation of Rick's sinful narcissism (his egoism) into altruism—the salvific sacrifice of his selfishness for the welfare of others.

Rick's narcissism is best shown by examining three scenes in particular. Bogart's character is first presented to us as a self-centered, autonomous individual with a hidden past. He is a person whose only allegiance appears to be to himself. Before we ever meet him directly, we are told that Rick, owner of the Café Américain, meeting place for exiles waiting for exit visas to America, never drinks with customers; the camera allows us to see only a disembodied hand signing a check. When he finally appears on screen, he is a figure alone, "no expression in his eyes."[11]

This first glimpse of Rick, aloof and mysterious, is reinforced by his early exchange with Renault, the French prefect of police. Renault provides some background on Rick. "I know your record," he says. "In 1935 you ran guns for Ethiopia, in 1936 you fought in Spain on the Loyalist side." Not letting Renault make him a hero, Rick responds: "And got well paid for it on both occasions." Whatever he did in the past that might be construed as involvement in patriotic activities, Rick is unapproachable, detached, and indifferent now. When Renault warns him not to interfere with the arrest of Ugarte, the petty thief who has stolen the letters of transit from two German couriers, Rick replies sharply: "I stick my neck out for nobody."

In the way that Rick is introduced to us visually, we not only encounter him center stage, but also know that he is "centered" on himself. We see him from the chest up. Half his face is in shadow; his head is down, the persistent cigarette in his mouth. He sits alone, but is clearly in control of himself and his cafe.

Our introduction to Rick, as Ray demonstrates, makes it clear that *Casablanca* is his story, a story about Rick's preoccupation with himself and his impact upon the other lives which he encounters. It is significant that we see this first evidence of Rick's narcissism in a conversation he has with Renault. For Renault is also narcissistic. He abuses his position as prefect of police to get Annina, a young Bulgarian, to sleep with him. He refuses to get involved in the French resistance movement. He might as well be Rick when he says late in the film, "I have no convictions. I blow with the wind."[12]

The second key scene that sharpens our awareness of Rick's narcissism concerns another major character in the film, Victor Laszlo. Laszlo goes to Rick when he finds out that Rick has the valued letters of transit out of Casablanca. Rick refuses to give or sell them to him. With apparent indifference to Laszlo's needs, Rick concludes: "The problems of the world are not my department. I'm a saloon keeper."

If the character of Renault reinforces Rick's narcissism, then Laszlo's character presents an alternative altruism. A major underground leader who has just escaped from a concentration camp, Laszlo has devoted his whole life to "doing his duty." He arrived in Casablanca trying to get visas so that he and his wife could leave. But when the Nazi Major Strasser offered free passage in exchange for the names of the resistance leaders, Laszlo of course refused. Clearly he is a man of honor and integrity whose concern for others is above reproach.

Ray makes much of the contrast between Rick and Laszlo, seeing in their juxtaposition the thematic and formal paradigm of classic Hollywood. According to Ray, "the narrative traced Rick's progress from self-centered detachment to active involvement in the Allied cause, with the plot turning on whether he would choose to help Laszlo"—the turn from narcissism to altruism.[13]

What is most relevant in Ray's treatment of the conflict between Rick (as the outlaw hero) and Laszlo (as the official hero) is his discussion of the film's dominant formal strategy, the shot-reverse shot. "With fully 50 percent of [*Casablanca's*] transitions employing the reverse field structure," the shot-reverse shot supports the tension, Ray claims, between "self-centered detachment" represented by Rick and "active involvement" typical of Laszlo.[14]

Finally, Rick's narcissism is shown climactically in a third key scene. This time he is with Ilsa, who is not only Victor's wife, but also Rick's former lover. After Laszlo's failure to obtain the letters of transit, Ilsa herself goes to Rick to demand his assistance. When she reminds him that he, like Victor, had once fought for the underground cause, he retorts: "Well, I'm not fighting for anything anymore, except myself. I'm the only Cause I'm interested in now."

Rick's relationship with Ilsa is more significant to Rick's conversion than is his relationship with either Renault or Laszlo. For it is this relationship which provides the key to Rick's transformation from narcissism to altruism. Indeed, Rick does not begin to relinquish his self-centeredness until Ilsa tells him what really happened when she suddenly left him in Paris. She was married at that time to Victor, she says, but she thought him dead. On the day Rick and Ilsa were to leave Paris together, she found out that Victor was alive. She chose to go to him because she believed in him and in the cause for which he was fighting.

Ilsa's confession to Rick enables him to begin to commit himself again to something beyond himself. Without telling Ilsa, Rick devises a scheme to get Victor and Ilsa out of Casablanca. At the airport, when he surprises everyone (perhaps even himself?) by giving the letters of transit to Victor and Ilsa, Rick shows his transformation to be complete. When Ilsa protests Rick's decision to send her away with Victor while Rick remains in Casablanca, he is able to say: "But I've got a job to do, too, Ilsa. I'm no good at being noble, but it doesn't take much to see that the problems of three little people don't amount to a hill of beans in this crazy world."

The altruism here is redemptive, a transformation of one kind of love (which is self-absorbed) and duty (only to oneself) to another. We are reminded of the commandment in Leviticus, "You shall love your neighbor as yourself" (19:18), which Jesus claims is the second commandment (Matthew 22:39; Mark 12:31; Luke 10:27). The film's portrayal of Rick's final act of altruism also reflects the words of the Gospel of John: "Greater love has no man than this, that a man lay down his life for his friends" (15:13). This is the "greater love" (directed toward another person) and "the greater duty" (to a cause beyond self-interest) that Rick comes to know and act upon. Such a model of redemption is presented to us by the film as good and true and right.

The triumph of altruism over narcissism is reinforced visually throughout by the film's nostalgic mood, created by the lighting, the music, and the flashback sequence. Most of the scenes are shot at night.

Rarely are figures filmed in full light. The darkness, the fog, the play of shadows reveal a mythic past—a time of love in Paris, a world that is simpler, truer than the world-at-war surrounding Casablanca.

The theme of self-sacrifice, in particular, is reinforced visually by the use of low-key lighting on Rick and high-key lighting on Ilsa. When we first see Ilsa and Rick alone together in the cafe, Ilsa appears on the right hand of the screen, the place of nobility. The shot is a low angle shot with a slight soft focus. The result of this lighting is to present Ilsa to us as an angelic or Madonna figure.

The music, too, triggers the theme of nostalgia. When Ilsa first enters the Café Américain, she spots Sam, the black piano player, and she urges him to play a particular tune. "Play it once, for old times' sake. Play it, Sam. Play 'As Time Goes By.' " It was Ilsa's and Rick's love song in Paris. As Sam starts to play, Rick appears suddenly, admonishing Sam, saying, "I thought I told you never. . . ." And then he sees Ilsa, and Paris is renewed in the midst of Casablanca.

The flashback scene, too, is crucial. It is used to set up the past as the time, Rick says later, "when faith was all in one piece." Paris is where and when, in the words of their theme song, "the fundamental things apply, as time goes by. Woman needs man, and man must have his mate, that nobody can deny." The nostalgic longing for a lost past is epitomized in Rick's reminder to Ilsa, "We'll always have Paris." Rick's transformation is made possible in the film because of the rediscovery of his love for Ilsa and her love for him. Indeed, Ilsa has often been discussed precisely as such a "mediating" character.[15] It seems to me, though, that Ilsa's story must be investigated in its own right. She is not a minor character but a major one, and her own development deepens our understanding of the narcissism-altruism theme in the film as a whole.

From the flashback sequence in Paris, we learn that Ilsa started out by acting altruistically, by giving up her love for Rick to do her duty to her husband Victor. This was her own decision, though she made it within the boundaries of her particular cultural situation. The basis for her decision, Ilsa explains to Rick, was not her love for Victor, but her sense of duty to him and to his cause.

Once Ilsa and Victor are in Casablanca, her altruism is apparent in two scenes in particular. First, when she and Victor are speaking with Ferrari, the owner of the Blue Parrot, Ferrari offers her an exit visa, but Ilsa refuses to go without Victor, even though remaining with him in Casablanca is increasingly dangerous for her. When Ilsa, acting on behalf of Victor, goes to Rick's apartment, she is willing to shoot Rick, the man she really loves, if that is necessary to obtain the letters of transit. In both scenes, duty appears to weigh more heavily than Ilsa's self-interest.

At the crucial point when Ilsa realizes that she cannot shoot Rick, she chooses love over duty. Ilsa attempts to overcome her culturally defined female altruism in a way that is not really narcissistic, but a genuine act of self-affirmation. Torn by these two conflicting emotions —love and duty—she says, "I can't fight it anymore. I don't know what's right any longer." The "it," here, is her love for Rick, a love which though genuine is nonetheless adulterous and sinful by Jewish-Christian standards of morality. And so she leaves his apartment, thinking that Rick, too, has made the decision to be with her.

Thus, when Ilsa finds out at the airport that Rick has chosen duty rather than her love, Ilsa's surprise reflects ours too. Sacrificial love once again is shown to be a higher, nobler love than either Rick's selfish, narcissistic love or Ilsa's self-affirming love. Rick not only calls Ilsa back to her duty, but also eases Victor's ego by telling him that Ilsa tried to get the letters of transit by pretending that she was still in love with Rick.

Increasingly, some women question the way in which both narcissism and altruism have been understood within Judaism and Christianity.[16] Narcissism, the emphasis on one's own self rather than upon others, has been dismissed as hubris, or pride; it has been denounced as the basis of "sin." The religious antidote to such narcissism has characteristically been altruism. Self-sacrifice or self-denial has been at the heart of what Christianity at least has called "redemption." In her decision to stay with Rick, Ilsa attempts to find a way of claiming self-affirming love, rather than self-denying duty. Her decision is not to be understood as narcissistic. To the contrary, it is an effort to transcend the limits of altruism as our shared religious culture has defined it.

Rick reinvokes the traditional patriarchal model, overriding her decision, reminding her that her duty is to her husband and to his cause. He thus subverts her freedom to decide, as well as her efforts at self-affirmation. She acquiesces, having been reminded of her own "sacrifice" in Paris and of the seductiveness of the nostalgic, ideal past.

Still, as we watch Ilsa walk off with Victor to the plane which will take them to Lisbon, we have to wonder, in the light of recent developments in feminist theology, what the fate of *Casablanca* would have been if Curtiz had used the alternate ending and had Ilsa stay with Rick. Can the traditional paradigm itself have the last word in any life that has tasted of the forbidden fruit of the knowledge of authentic self-affirmation, beyond love and duty, beyond narcissism and altruism?

Notorious: Penance as a Paradigm of Redemption

Harold Hatt

Notorious was released in 1946, a year after World War II had come to an end. Frank Nugent comments that with *Notorious* Alfred Hitchcock was bringing to an end the cycle of spy films that began with *The 39 Steps.* But, says Nugent, Hitchcock found another war "which has few truces and never an armistice, which drips with intrigue and double dealing and not infrequently with human gore. Hitch has discovered the Battle of the Sexes."[1] Hitchcock himself always insisted that *Notorious* was more a love story than a spy story.[2] But what kind of love story is it?

Notorious is a story of redemptive love, of love as a means to new life. Alicia Huberman (Ingrid Bergman) has dissipated her life through excessive drinking. Her sense of self-worth is dealt a further blow when her father is convicted of treason. The opening scene is the sentencing of Huberman as a Nazi spy. We first see a close-up of a press camera. As we see the reporters, they are clearly anxious to get a story. But it is Alicia's reaction they want and not her father's. As she walks past the cameras, her head is down and her lips are silent. When she first lets her guard down, it is at a party she gives to drown her sorrows. At that party she meets Devlin (Cary Grant), a government agent. We first see his back, basically a silhouette of his suitcoat and head. But he is to become prominent, for he comes to offer Alicia an opportunity to do an unspecified job for her country, which will assuage the guilt she feels for her own wasted life and the shame she feels for her father's treason. Devlin also offers an opportunity for love, a relationship which will redeem her wasted life.

However, the very person who brings this opportunity cannot believe her. This is partly because Devlin cannot believe she can change and partly because, as he confesses to her, he is afraid of women. Thus, even when Devlin develops a love for Alicia, he cannot confess it.

Moreover, this story of the frustrated potential for renewal through love is unfolded against the foil of death. On the plane to Rio, where she

126

will receive her assignment, Alicia learns that her father has committed suicide in his cell. Her task is to get information from Sebastian (Claude Rains), a colleague of her father, and their first conversation concerns death. The Nazi group at Sebastian's home kills one of their number who was weak. When Sebastian discovers that Alicia is a counterspy, he plots her death. But Alicia's last minute rescue by Devlin leaves Sebastian to face his own death. *Notorious* is the story of the potential of new life through love set against the foil of the actuality of death.

On a deeper level, though, *Notorious* deals with the same human situation that is addressed through the sacrament of penance. The Catholic doctrine and practice of penance would, in fact, seem to be the dominant religious influence on *Notorious*. Keep in mind that Hitchcock had a strict Catholic upbringing which was reinforced at St. Ignatius College, a Jesuit prep school in Stamford Hill, London. Furthermore, it may be mere coincidence, but it is at least worth noting that Pope Pius XII, in his encyclical on the Mystical Body,[3] commended the practice of frequent confession in 1943, just three years prior to the 1946 release of *Notorious*.

Paul Anciaux opens his chapter on "The History of Penance in the Church" by identifying two complementary aspects of the sacrament of penance—the "inward-individual" and the "ritual-community."[4] Later he refers to these as "the remedy offered to the sinner" and the "ecclesiastical reality." For Anciaux these are the "two essential and inseparable aspects of ecclesiastical penance."[5] Anciaux may well be correct in his insistence that we cannot properly understand theological treatments of penance without keeping both aspects in mind. Indeed, Bernard Häring makes a similar point by stressing the importance of focusing attention not on the sins of the penitent but on the proclamation of the good news of the peace of God.[6] But a film is not a theological treatise. Thus, more often than not, if a film appeals to the dynamics of penance, it will deal with the inward-individual or the remedy aspect of the sacrament. Although a valid sacrament requires the context of the church and the agency of the priest, the dynamics of penance can occur in other contexts with other agents. There are no priests in *Notorious*, so we have to begin and end with the penitent. The doctrine of penance recognizes three actions of the penitent: contrition, confession and satisfaction.

Contrition, or interior penance, is genuine sorrow for sin and a firm resolve to change. An act of the will is fundamental. Since the problem stems from an act of will which creates guilt, the resolution involves another act which redirects the will.

Confession, or external penance, is specific, although not dwelling on minor details.[7] A sense of responsibility is fundamental. Confession is

Notorious

(1946, Alfred Hitchcock)

Just after her father has been convicted of treason, Alicia Huberman (Ingrid Bergman) meets Devlin (Cary Grant), who offers her the opportunity for a new life while disbelieving her capacity for change. In this story of frustrated, though potentially redemptive love, the bottle is symbolic of everything that holds them apart.

an act of revealing to another something for which we take responsibility. And in this sense, confession is not solely of our sins, but also of our faith.

Satisfaction is compensation for injury inflicted, especially to God, but sometimes also to another person. It involves the performance of religious and righteous work as a way of validating and strengthening one's penance. Resolve is fundamental here.

To discern contrition, confession, and satisfaction in a film such as *Notorious* it will be necessary, of course, to look for their secular analogues. As an expression of *contrition*, we will be alert for a state of sorrow and act of will; of *confession*, for a state of self-examination and an act of responsibility; of *satisfaction*, for a state of self-discipline and an act of resolve. And of course, human nature being what it is, we are looking for these in their failed as well as in their successful forms. In the failed forms, the result will be lack of reconciliation and absence of peace and serenity.

The plot of *Notorious*, on which Ben Hecht collaborated with Hitchcock, is a straightforward chronological development, with no flash-backs or flash-forwards. The narrative has two centers, with Alicia common to both of them—namely, her developing relationships with Devlin and with Sebastian.[8] Drinking is the visual metaphor that links the centers. A focus on this motif, which runs throughout, will help to keep our analysis sober, so to speak.

At the party following her father's conviction, where she meets Devlin, Alicia is clearly a dipsomaniac. She tipsily says, "The important drinking hasn't started yet." Later, when she asks the other guests to leave, the camera tracks so that we can see Devlin's face, and he holds up a bottle between them. The bottle is symbolic of the things that hold them apart. Later, when Alicia awakens with a hangover, a glass dominates the foreground of the screen, perhaps containing orange juice with a raw egg. When she looks at Devlin, there are tilt shots, and even an upside-down shot. It's going to take more than orange juice and a raw egg to cure this hangover.

After arriving in Rio, Alicia and Devlin are at an outdoor restaurant. Alicia complains that Devlin thinks once a tramp always a tramp. She asks him to hold her hand, adding an assurance that she won't blackmail him for it. This is when Devlin admits that he has always been scared of women. Alicia tries to move from the general to the particular, asking, "Why won't you believe in me, Devlin? [long pause] Just a little." Devlin says nothing; he simply takes another sip of his drink.

In the extended but intermittent (for the sake of the censors) kissing sequence, we get a sense of Devlin's ambiguous feelings. His mind is on business, which is to take advantage of Sebastian's attraction for Alicia to deploy her as a counterspy. This disturbs Devlin as a person, but as a professional he finds himself unable to express his uneasiness. When he leaves the office, we see a close-up of the bottle of wine Alicia had asked him to bring on his return, but which he leaves behind. The professional has won out over the personal in his internal struggle. Giving up on trying to persuade Devlin that she is a new person, Alicia takes a drink and asks, "When do I go to work for Uncle Sam?"

Devlin helps Alicia make "accidental" contact with Sebastian while horseback riding. Unlike Devlin, Sebastian is able to express his feelings for Alicia. In a variation on the drinking motif, he tells her that she always affects him like a tonic. Pursuing Alicia, Sebastian invites her to dinner at his home where Emil, one of his Nazi cohorts, becomes visibly upset about a particular wine bottle. After dinner, the other Nazis confer, deciding that Emil's loss of composure threatened to expose their operation and that such weakness demands death. Alicia does not comprehend all this (nor do we, because the secret of the wine bottles is withheld for a while), but she dutifully recounts Emil's "scene" to Devlin. When she reports that Sebastian has asked her to marry him, Devlin is personally upset but cannot bring himself to object, except for his professional concern that a honeymoon will slow down the government operation.

In setting up house as Sebastian's wife, Alicia learns that the wine cellar is locked and that Sebastian has the only key. She persuades Sebastian to throw a grand party and to invite Devlin, who can then investigate the wine cellar. Alicia removes the key from Sebastian's chain and is almost undone when he returns to their room while the key is still in her hand. He kisses the palm of her empty hand, but when he turns to the other hand she prevents exposure by throwing her arms around him. After throwing her arms around Sebastian, Alicia drops the key behind Sebastian and then kicks it out of sight—an implausible maneuver at best. The contortion involved would surely have called Sebastian's attention to the process. By editing from fragments, Hitchcock elicits feelings of relief rather than disbelief.

It is the excessive drinking of the party-goers that eventually leads to Sebastian's discovery that he has married a counterspy.[9] Alicia and Devlin have just discovered that some bottles contain a mysterious substance. When Sebastian and his steward arrive to get more champagne, Devlin tries to confuse Sebastian by giving Alicia a romantic kiss and the embarrassed Sebastian dismisses his steward. What Devlin found difficult to do as a personal expression of love he does easily as an espionage agent's technique of deception. Alicia aids and abets the deception by telling Sebastian: "I couldn't help what happened. He's been drinking." Thus Alicia reverses Devlin's speaking of her as an excessive drinker. Sebastian is not deceived for long, however, since he soon returns with his steward to the cellar for wine, only to discover that his key is missing.

The next morning, Sebastian notices that the key has been returned to his chain and goes immediately to the wine cellar. His suspicions are confirmed when he sees a spill on the floor, discovers a different wine bottle holding the uranium ore, and finds pieces of the broken bottle. Recalling the swift retaliation against Emil for merely showing concern when he saw a bottle with the uranium ore among those to be served, Sebastian goes to his mother for help. She becomes steely hard, a change reinforced by a striking image of her lighting a cigarette. She suggests poisoning as a way of disposing of Alicia slowly and inconspicuously.

Coffee is the medium for the poison. At first Alicia feels ill, but is able to get around. Devlin requests a transfer to Spain, believing that her illness is a recurrence of alcoholism. Just as one of the Nazis tells Alicia that she must see a doctor to find out what is wrong with her, there is a cut to Madame Sebastian pouring some coffee. She and her son discount the need for medical attention and suggest rest. There are three shots with the coffee cup in the foreground, occupying more screen space than Alicia's head. This sequence recalls the earlier shot of the glass containing the antidote for Alicia's hangover. When the Nazi doctor mistakenly picks up Alicia's cup, Sebastian and his mother stop him, but create a scene more obvious than Emil's earlier indiscretion over the wine bottle. As recognition dawns on Alicia, the camera dollies in to Sebastian and his mother. A subjective shot shows them blurred, as Alicia sees them, and the two images merge. The subjective camera continues to show her distorted perception; she faints and is taken to her room. Sebastian has the phone removed on the pretext that she needs rest.

Devlin, by now suspicious, decides to make a social call on Alicia. When he tells his boss of his determination, the latter is in bed, not ill (as Alicia is thought to be), but drinking wine with cheese and crackers. Devlin gains access to Alicia's room, and there is a sequence of shots with their faces close together, similar to the earlier kissing sequence. This time, though, he can tell her that he loves her. Devlin leaves with Alicia clinging to him. Earlier her unsteadiness was an effect of the excessive drinking; now it is an effect of the poison. Sebastian confronts them, but can say nothing, lest he divulge his failure. The Nazis are told that Devlin phoned the hospital and is taking Alicia there, but the deception is exposed when they recall that Sebastian had removed the phone from Alicia's room. Although Sebastian begs to be taken away in the car with

Devlin and Alicia, they leave him to his certain fate at the hand of his partners. The film closes, as it opens, with the pronouncement of a sentence behind a closed door.

Where, then, in *Notorious,* is to be found the triad of contrition, confession, and satisfaction in its secular analogues of acts of will, responsibility, and resolve?

Contrition, as we have noted, involves an exercise of will. Hitchcock commonly develops a theme of an ordinary person in an extraordinary situation, usually involved against his or her will. Here we can see a Jansenist influence overriding the Jesuit influence on Hitchcock. And yet in *Notorious* there is a significant degree to which Alicia can be said to be acting on her own will. She is sorry for what has happened to her life and her father's. When she tries to drown her sorrow, she is acting more according to habit than will. But the commitment that she makes early in the film and that guides her throughout the film is the will to make things right.

It is quite true that, having made her commitment, Alicia is not always free. At her first visit in Sebastian's home, Alicia has to meet all of his Nazi associates and convince them that she is sympathetic to their cause. And Hitchcock makes us feel the threat—the limitation of her freedom—by an eye-level shot, so that we see each of them as she sees them. In commenting on the intensity produced by this use of the subjective camera, Hitchcock responded: "I wanted to say visually, 'Here is Ingrid in the lions' den; now look at each lion!' "[10] Again, in the striking crane shot at the party which swoops down the grand staircase and moves in on the key in Alicia's hand, Hitchcock has not merely linked the general and particular, but pointedly contrasted the carefree context and the life and death drama being played out within it. Gene D. Phillips calls our attention not only to the movement of the shot, but also to the composition of the image. "The checkered pattern of the ballroom floor, when photographed from the high angle from which this shot begins, resembles a chessboard, implying Alicia's unenviable position as a pawn in the game of international intrigue."[11] She is a pawn, but only because she has chosen to be a pawn. And she so willed it because she was contrite. Later we see Sebastian walking across this same floor knowing that he has been betrayed in the game of international intrigue. Alicia faints on this floor when she is being poisoned. And Alicia, Devlin, Sebastian, and his mother look down on the Nazis standing on this floor as Devlin and Alicia start their escape.

For most of the film Devlin is not contrite. He may be sorry for the situation and most of all for himself, but there is no sense of resolve to change the situation. Indeed, toward the close of the film he wants to get away, asking for a transfer to Spain, on the pretext that for all practical purposes the job is done. Only at the last moment does he risk the government operation and himself to rescue Alicia.

In confession, we assume responsibility for our past and future by means of a clear and specific verbalization. In theological terms, confession is both of sin and of God. As was the case with contrition, Alicia is an example of the power of confession to focalize problems and resources, and Devlin is an example of failed confession—until the end.

Alicia confesses her own failure. She has wasted her life and now she wants to make something of it. She recognizes her father's failure, but that is not her confession of failure. Rather her recognition provides the opportunity or hope for redeeming the situation. She thinks of herself as the "new" Miss Huberman and is distressed that Devlin cannot acknowledge her regeneration.

Devlin, by contrast, cannot confess his love even when a very sultry and sensuous Alicia tempts him to take the sexual initiative. He goes along with the kissing, but not fully. Keeping his mind on the job is not so much a matter of putting public duty above private interest as it is a way of avoiding responsibility.[12]

Ambiguity and hesitation qualify Devlin's actions throughout. It is not until the very end that Devlin can see how his inability to confess his love has been harmful. And only then can he tell Alicia that he really requested a transfer because he loves her. Eric Rohmer and Claude Chabrol may be a little unfair to Alicia by speaking as if she and Devlin were developing at the same rate, but they are right on target in noting that *Notorious* portrays more than the classic "lovers' quarrel." "The misfortune of the two protagonists," they write, "comes from the fact that as victims of their mutual preconceptions, they refuse to pronounce the saving 'word.' They fail to appreciate the virtue of this confession, which is the key to all Hitchcock's films."[13]

Satisfaction involves an act of resolve—doing something to make things right. For Alicia satisfaction consists in risking her life for the sake of the secret mission she has accepted for her country. There is significant personal sacrifice when she flirts with and then marries Sebastian in order to spy on the activities of the Nazi cell in his home.

The most sacrificial act of resolve occurs when Alicia steals the key to the wine cellar. In reality this action would take only a moment, but its dramatic significance is such that Hitchcock edits the scene out of fragments, and thus extends the time involved. Normally, editing compresses time. Since Sebastian does not know what is going on, his arrival cannot be menacing in and of itself; the subdued lighting and eerie sound track create the appropriate mood to accompany the editing.

Devlin's risk is closely associated. Once he enters the wine cellar, he has placed himself in danger. Hitchcock heightens suspense by cross-cutting between Devlin's discovery in the wine cellar and the wine steward's recognition of the rapidly dwindling supply of champagne, which will necessitate a visit with Sebastian to the wine cellar. Devlin, for his part, seems quite calm and efficient and even thinks quickly when caught in the act. However, he is acting here in his role as an intelligence agent. So this is not really the act of resolve we are concerned with. That comes when, having convinced his reluctant boss that the operation will not be jeopardized by his placing a social call, he enters Sebastian's home to liberate Alicia. It is not just the operation but his own life that he is putting in jeopardy. Ironically, it is neither Alicia nor Devlin, but Sebastian who will pay with his life. Earlier in the film, Devlin disclosed his government position in order to save Alicia from arrest for drunk driving. Now he conceals it to save her from Sebastian. As Donald Spoto notes, "rank has yielded to humanity."[14]

In her condition Alicia could not possibly have saved herself. Who but Devlin could come to the rescue? And so the film ends with this final act of resolve. The hesitant Devlin has become the resolute Devlin. Alicia, on the other hand, as she walks out of Sebastian's home in the final scene, is less in control of herself than when she walked out of the courtroom in the opening scene. Nonetheless, her situation is more hopeful. She and Devlin manifested weaknesses that prolonged her notorious behavior, but they developed strengths that have overcome it. Love has transformed their lives. Thus, Spoto rightly says that the "serious" issue here "is one of common humanity—the possibility of love and trust redeeming two lives from fear, guilt and meaninglessness."[15] For both Alicia and Devlin there is such redemption, rather than destruction. In terms of the sacrament of penance, both are absolved.

It's a Wonderful Life: Divine Benevolence and Love of Neighbor

Robert E. Lauder

If the ultimate test of a classic is the test of time, then Frank Capra's favorite artistic creation *It's a Wonderful Life* more than qualifies. When the story of small town good Samaritan George Bailey (James Stewart) opened in December 1946, it was met with less than raves from some eminent critics.[1] But over the last forty years the film has touched deeply the audience for whom Capra made the film, the average moviegoers he judged needed a testimonial.[2]

What distinguishes George Bailey from previous Capra Quixotes is that his battle is primarily within himself. In a sense, George Bailey is in the opposite position from St. Paul (Rom 7:14–16): the good that George Bailey does not want to do he does, the evil he wants to do he does not do; yet he is not happy with himself, his choices or their consequences. *It's a Wonderful Life* depicts a spiritual journey, the passion-death-resurrection odyssey of a modern-day "everyman." That Capra includes an angel named Clarence who moves the film toward its supra-happy ending does not detract, surprisingly, from either the power or the realism of the film, but rather underlines, albeit humorously, half of Capra's theme—namely that a divine benevolence rules the universe and loves each and every person. The other half of Capra's theme, that we imitate that divine benevolence by loving our neighbor, is articulated in the closing seconds of the film in the inscription that Clarence has written for George in the frontispiece of *The Adventures of Tom Sawyer:* "Remember no man is a failure who has friends." Capra's title refers to both truths: a human life can be wonderful because of God's love for each of us and also because of our love for one another.

It's a Wonderful Life was the first film Frank Capra made after returning from service in the Second World War. In a marvelous sum-mary statement of his vision that had begun to be evident in earlier films, Capra years later articulated what he had wanted to do as he thought about the first film he would make after the war.

> My films will explore the heart not with logic, but with com-
> passion. . . . I will deal with the little man's doubts, his curses,
> his loss of faith in himself, in his neighbor, in his God. And I
> will show the overcoming of doubts, the courageous renewal of
> faith. . . . And I will remind the little man that his mission on
> earth is to advance spiritually. . . .
>   And finally, my films must let every man, woman, and child
> know that God loves them, and that I love them, and that peace
> and salvation will become a reality only when they all learn to
> love each other.[3]

After reading Philip Van Doren Stern's short story "The Greatest Gift,"[4] Capra was so excited about the idea at the heart of the story that he believed it was the "kind of idea that when [he] got old and sick and scared and ready to die—they'd still say 'He made *The Greatest Gift.*' "[5]

To compare "The Greatest Gift" with the film masterpiece that was created from it is to see that *It's a Wonderful Life* is one of the best examples of a piece of literature that is almost totally transformed in its journey from the written page to the silver screen. Though more people worked on the screenplay than on any other Capra project, the finished product is Capra's most personal film.[6] In fact George Bailey's life has striking parallels to Frank Capra's.[7]

In *It's a Wonderful Life*, Capra explores the inner struggles that George Bailey has with his desire to love and help his neighbor and the strong attraction that wealth, travel and adventure have for him. In every instance when it is a matter of choosing for self or for others, George chooses for others. However, the war within George does not stop. Each time he chooses for others he is not completely content with his choice and is even resentful about it. That throughout the film we can believe George's altruism but also accept his anger at not being able to fulfill his dreams is a tribute both to Capra's direction and to James Stewart's exceptional acting. The suggestion that all the actors and actresses do the best work of their careers in this film is not so far-fetched;[8] certainly Stewart does. George Bailey has a wonderful life, but for most of the film he does not fully realize how blessed he is—that is, until he sees what the world would be like without him.

A careful analysis of *It's a Wonderful Life* reveals how integrated its technique is to the development of the theme. Capra's clever but unobtrusive use of the camera, his editing, his use of lighting and music, not to mention his direction of actors, is extraordinary. In discussing Capra's artistic accomplishment in *It's a Wonderful Life*, it helps greatly to break the film down into five segments:[9] (1) the present—Christmas Eve, 1945 at about 9:45 in the evening, (2) extended flashback—1919 to Christmas Eve, 1945, 9:45 P.M., (3) the present—Christmas Eve, 1945 at about 10:45 P.M., (4) fantasy sequence, and (5) the present—Christmas Eve about 10:45 P.M. Each of the five segments is well constructed and cinematically effective and this contributes enormously to the artistic success of the film. In fact the five segments are essential to Capra's theme: taken together they reveal Capra's theme, and each considered individually visually highlights the theme from a particular angle or perspective. The first, third and fifth segments highlight the involvement of a divine benevolence in human affairs; the second and fourth in contrasting ways highlight the importance of love of neighbor.

The first segment's structure enables Capra to dramatize visually a central theme of the Jewish-Christian tradition: God's loving presence to us calls us to love one another. Some consideration of each of the five segments may illuminate why *It's a Wonderful Life* has such a powerful effect on viewers.

In the opening sequence, much of the structure of the film is set and the theme is introduced. The shots are of various streets and buildings in the town of Bedford Falls, somewhere in New York State. As shots of homes appear, we hear voices praying. The voices are those of Gower the druggist (H.B. Warner), Martini the restaurant owner (William Edmunds), George's mother (Beulah Bondi), Bert the policeman (Ward Bond), Ernie the cab driver (Frank Faylen), George's wife Mary (Donna Reed), his daughter Jane (Carol Coomes), and his youngest child Zuzu (Carolyn Grimes). Each person prays for George, and the tone and words of their prayers reveal that George is in serious trouble. While Mary's, Jane's and Zuzu's voices are heard, the camera is on the Bailey home. The camera then swoops up and travels through the sky until it focuses on a firmament full of stars. We hear heavenly voices, and as each voice speaks a star twinkles brightly. A conversation takes place between an angel called Joseph and another celestial power who in the film is referred to simply as "Sir." The conversation between the heavenly powers reveals that George Bailey is in such dire straits that in about an hour he will consider suicide. An angel named Clarence (Henry Travers) is summoned to go to earth to help George in his crisis. To prepare Clarence for his work, Joseph provides an overview of George's life— hence the extended flashback.

Several important points are established in the opening moments of the film. Knowing that our hero will soon consider suicide colors the whole extended flashback. Everything we see George doing we see against this truth: this is the past life of a man who is about to consider suicide. From the opening prayers and the heavenly conversation, we can infer that George is loved, that those who love him have asked for God's help, and that God is responding to the prayers of those who love George. Later in the film we will discover that God responds also to George's prayers.

It's a Wonderful Life illustrates Capra's uncanny ability to interpose the most serious dramatic moments with marvelous humor.[10] No sooner have we heard the prayers than the introduction of an angel named Clarence, who has "the I.Q. of a rabbit" but "the faith of a child" and who is trying to win his wings, has us smiling. Throughout his film Capra will interpose comedy and drama successfully until in the final moments of his film he has us crying tears of joy. Capra wrote:

> Comedy is fulfillment, accomplishment, overcoming. It is victory over odds, a triumph of good over evil. . . .
> Comedy is good news. . . . The Gospels are comedies; a triumph of spirit over matter. The Resurrection is the happiest of all endings: man's triumph over death. The Mass is a 'celebration' of that event. Priests and parishioners 'celebrate' a Mass. It is a divine comedy.[11]

In *It's a Wonderful Life*, Capra most successfully realizes this theory of comedy.[12]

Not only is Capra able to interpose serious moments with moments of comedy, but throughout the film he juxtaposes, as Robert B. Ray ably demonstrates,[13] images of self-centeredness and unselfishness and so keeps his theme visually before us. The first scene of the flashback shows George at the age of twelve (Bobbie Anderson) saving his younger brother from drowning by risking his own life. The image of George's nearness to drowning is carried throughout the film:[14] when the bank rush threatens the Building and Loan, George runs through a torrential downpour; drowning is the form of suicide he chooses; significantly George is the first to fall into the pool in the humorous scene in the gymnasium; moments before George falls, he is described as standing directly over the opening and the image of George over an abyss in danger of drowning is a fitting image for the interior battle that engages him throughout his life. The paradox of course is that George feels he is losing himself by helping others and would have lost himself by being self-centered as the fantasy sequence reveals. (The most horrible experience for George within the fantasy sequence is when he realizes that he has no identity in Pottersville, that even Mary does not recognize him.)

In the second scene of the extended flashback, the conflict that will plague George throughout the review of his personal history is introduced through a juxtaposition of images. After viewing Potter in his hearse-like carriage and hearing him described by celestial power Joseph as "the richest and meanest man in the country," we see George enter Mr. Gower's drugstore and pause at the old-fashioned lighter to say, "Wish I had a million dollars." While waiting for young Mary (Jean Gale) to give her order, George shows her his copy of the *National Geographic* and tells her that he is going to travel around the world and have a harem of wives. As George is describing his imagined fulfillment, Capra shoots Mary's face in soft focus, foreshadowing his shot of grown-up Mary on George's wedding night. In George's life of unselfish love, the central role of Mary is suggested by these shots as well as by George's mother's comment made to George about Mary when he is deeply saddened that he may be stuck in the Building and Loan for the rest of his life: "Nice girl, Mary . . . kind that will help you find the answers."

After telling Mary about his harem, young George discovers that Mr. Gower has inadvertently put poison in a prescription that George is about to deliver. Seeing the pharmacy poster "Ask Dad, *he* knows," George goes to his father's office to seek advice. Capra's ironic juxtaposition of the sign with the harried and seemingly exhausted Mr. Bailey (Samuel S. Hinds) may imply that more than a human father will be needed in George's life. The scene in Mr. Bailey's office is the only time in the film that George, his father, and Mr. Potter (Lionel Barrymore) are on screen together. The older men represent diametrically opposed desires in George, and the tension divides him throughout the film. The battle that goes on within him could be represented through several of his relationships,[15] but I think his relationship with his father and with Mr. Potter is especially revelatory of George's struggle. Reflection on some key scenes makes this evident.

In the scene in Mr. Bailey's office in the Building and Loan, George's father and Mr. Potter are arguing about how to treat people who need financial help. In the midst of this discussion, Capra shoots young George between the two men as Potter calls Mr. Bailey a failure. The shot is significant because, though George angrily responds that his father is not a failure, he will be torn between the two sets of values that the men represent and, though he always opts for those of his father, he will not become totally convinced that following them will not make him a failure until the final moments of the film.

The first time we see George as an adult he is looking at a piece of luggage given him by Mr. Gower in preparation for a trip to Europe. As he enters Mr. Gower's store, he again strikes the lighter and wishes for a million dollars. Later, in one of the most important scenes in the film, George, excited about his trip, is having dinner with his father, who admits being tired of his battles with Potter. Trying to explain Potter, Mr. Bailey says that Potter is frustrated and sick and hates everybody who has anything he can't have. Mr. Bailey knows that George has yet to learn fully that loving and being loved are the secret to human fulfillment. There is a touching interchange between father and son. After half-jokingly asking George if he is still hoping to make a million before he is thirty, Mr. Bailey inquires if after college George might consider coming back to the Building and Loan. George is stunned and embarrassed because the question and the fact his father asks it touch the nerve of his conflict. As George tries to answer, his face goes in and out of the shadow cast by the lamp hanging over the dinner table, and the contrast between shadow and light provides a fit image for the two sides of George's character.

Having canceled his trip to Europe in order to help at the Building and Loan after his father's death, George is ready to leave for college. At what should be his final meeting at the Building and Loan, he hears Potter criticize his father and suggest that the Building and Loan should be closed. George attacks Potter and powerfully eulogizes his father's love for people. As George moves around the table, we see his face alongside the photograph of his father on the wall until finally George's face is superimposed over the photograph. George concludes, "People were human beings to him, but to you, a warped frustrated old man, they're cattle. Well, in my book he died a much richer man than you'll ever be!" Moments later George learns that the board of trustees has voted to keep the Building and Loan open, but only if George runs it. Surrendering his chance to go to college and agreeing to run the business for four years while his brother Harry (Todd Karns) goes to college, George once again opts for the spiritual riches his father lived for, yet he is resentful. The closeup of George's face, which reflects his anger at having to accept responsibility for the Building and Loan, provides a powerful visual conclusion to the scene in which the board of trustees tells George of its decision. George is resentful again four years later when he allows Harry as a college graduate to take a promising job out of town, which means George may be trapped at home permanently. Again Capra uses a closeup to accent George's anger and frustration at the train when he learns that Harry wants to take a job out of town. The two other times that Capra effectively uses a closeup of George is when George is tearfully praying in the barroom and when in the fantasy sequence he discovers Mary does not recognize him.

Besides the scene at the Building and Loan when he criticizes Potter, there are three other key scenes in which Potter clearly represents for George the allurement of wealth against a life of relative poverty due to the unselfish service of others. On George's wedding day there is a rush on the bank. Though he is on his way to his honeymoon with $2,000 in wedding gifts, he goes back to the office to persuade people not to panic. When Potter in a phone call offers to pay off all customers, George sees the opportunity to throw off his burden, to flee with his wife and allow the townspeople to be exploited by Potter, but instead of thinking of himself George stays to help others. Immediately after hanging up on Potter, George stands next to his father's portrait beneath which is the motto "All you can take with you is that which you've given away." Afterward, George is seen behind the counter's high screen, with the panicky customers on the other side—a striking visual metaphor for his experience of life as a cage because of his commitment to people.

Years later, in order to rid himself of the Building and Loan and of George's influence in the town, Potter offers George a job with a huge salary and opportunities for travel. The scene is shot in Potter's office with its large bust of Napoleon (Mr. Bailey's office had a picture of Woodrow Wilson). Potter, having opted for possessions over people, knows very well the conflict George experiences. He prefaces his offer by sketching George's life, reminding him that he is extraordinarily talented and intelligent, that he hates the Building and Loan almost as much as Potter does, and thus that he is "frittering his life away playing nursemaid to a lot of garlic-eaters." George does not disagree; though he acts unselfishly, he clearly feels that he is being cheated by life. George, settling into a low plush chair so that he is below Potter, is stunned by Potter's offer and can hardly believe that his dream is being offered to him. Almost ready to accept, George stands in order to shake hands, placing Potter beneath him. George suddenly sees through the seduction and angrily rejects Potter's offer saying, "In the whole vast configuration of things . . . I'd say you were nothing but a scurvy little spider." Because of his selfishness Potter has lost his identity as a person as George in the fantasy sequence in Pottersville discovers he would have if he had not lived a life of loving concern for others. However, that Potter has touched a sore nerve is revealed in the following scene when George, late at night, enters his bedroom. Potter's voice making the offer is heard on the soundtrack and George's facial expression reveals his discouragement. But again Capra juxtaposes a hopeful image with soft-faced framing as Mary tells George she is pregnant.

It's a Wonderful Life
(1946, Frank Capra)

His prayers and those of his family and friends answered, George Bailey (James Stewart), realizing that he is not dead, experiences rebirth into a "wonderful" life. Dead-center frame are his daughter's rose petals—an obvious symbol of new life—that he shows to Bert (Ward Bond); the precious, gemlike quality of his gift appears in contrast with the chilling snow and the impersonal structure of the bridge.

In the third scene with Potter, George, in danger of going to jail because Uncle Billy (Thomas Mitchell) has lost $8,000 of the company's money, comes to Mr. Potter for help. Potter ridicules him, saying, "Why don't you go to the riffraff you love so much and ask them to let you have eight thousand dollars? You know why? Because they'd run you out of town on a rail." George's face suggests that he believes Potter. When the old man, referring to George's insurance policy, tells him that he is worth more dead than alive, George believes him.

George's prayer in Martini's restaurant, which George thinks is unanswered, is the crucial moment in the third segment of the film.[16] Capra and Stewart make the scene exceptionally poignant. Desperate, George asks God for help. This prayer and the one at the end of the fantasy sequence he realizes have been answered only when the fantasy sequence ends and he is reunited with his family and friends. The prayers at the beginning of the film, George's prayers in Martini's restaurant and his prayer ending the fantasy sequence emphasize that Capra's film is about God's love for us as well as our love for one another.[17] It is God's love and the love of his friends that help George Bailey through his suffering and "death" to his "resurrection" and return to his wonderful life. The victory of that love makes *It's a Wonderful Life* a divine comedy.

The fantasy sequence is Capra's cinematic *tour de force;* he uncannily uses the presence of Clarence for humor while filming most of the sequence in the techniques of *film noir*. During the fantasy sequence, places and people we had seen in the extended flashback are transformed to become a disturbing revelation of what the world would be like if love and unselfishness were absent. As we revisit Martini's bar, the house of George's youth, the home he and Mary lived in, and the streets of Bedford Falls now called Pottersville, Capra's use of low-keyed and high-contrast lighting[18] and Dimitri Tiomkin's musical accompaniment create a world radically different from the one in which George Bailey's life was a redeeming presence. In the extended flashback, Violet (Gloria Grahame), as she was leaving George's office, had said, "I'm glad I know you, George Bailey." In the fantasy sequence, we realize the same line could have been spoken by Martini, his bartender Nick (Sheldon Leonard), Mr. Gower, Ernie the cab driver, Uncle Billy, Harry, George's mother, Mary and the many families George helped through the Building and Loan. Especially well-filmed is the scene at the cemetery when George sees the grave of his brother Harry who died at the age of eight because George was not there to save him. Clarence, noting that men on a destroyer were killed because Harry was not there to save them, says, "You see, George, you really had a wonderful life." The final blow for George occurs when Mary does not recognize him and indeed screams when he embraces her. This is literally unbearable for George, so he races back to the bridge, begging, "Please, God, let me live." This prayer ends the fantasy sequence and initiates George's resurrection-return to his wonderful life.

The final moments of the film are among the finest in film history. Leaving the bridge and racing through the streets of Bedford Falls shouting "Merry Christmas" to everyone, even to Mr. Potter, George arrives home. He rejoices with the sheriff that there is a warrant for his arrest, kisses the knob on the bannister that had always annoyed him, and passionately hugs his children and Mary. As he and his family stand in front of their Christmas tree, the townspeople enter with gifts of money because they had heard he was in trouble. This scene, inter-cutting from the faces of George and Mary to the faces of the people George has loved and who had loved him, is as close to perfect as a scene can be. George's daughter Janie plays "Hark the Herald Angels Sing" on the piano, and everyone starts singing first the hymn and later "Auld Lang Syne." The hymn proclaims divine benevolence, the song the importance of love of neighbor. The climax of the scene is the entrance of Harry Bailey, who because he heard his brother was in trouble has left a dinner in Washington honoring him as a war hero. Taking a glass of wine he says, "A toast . . . to my big brother, George. The richest man in town!" The light of recognition in George's eyes reveals that he has finally resolved his conflict. Reading Clarence's inscription that no man who has friends is a failure, George knows its truth immediately. George is at peace with himself and grateful to God for the gift of life.

Frank Capra wrote that he wanted to make films that would let people "know that God loves them and that I love them."[19] He certainly made one such film. In his autobiography Capra claims that, when he finished *It's a Wonderful Life,* he considered it the best film he had ever made. It is. He goes on to say that he thought it was the best film anybody ever made.[20] I wouldn't argue with him.

One Flew Over the Cuckoo's Nest: A Salvific Drama of Liberation

Charles B. Ketcham

How could a film, rich in religious symbolism, which evokes tension, anger, sympathy, despair, and triumph, which raises the most profound human questions about dignity, suffering, and freedom, be classified as comedy? Ridiculous—yet that is often where the film is catalogued in our cassette rental stores, not under "Drama" as one might expect.

The classification confusion is all the more extraordinary because of the attention the film has received and continues to attract. Released in 1975, the film is directed by the Czech/American Milos Forman who had previously given us such dark comedies as *Loves of a Blonde*, *The Firemen's Ball* and *Taking Off*. It is based upon Ken Kesey's 1962, establishment-busting novel of the same name. With such an all-American preoccupation and with a superb cast headed by Jack Nicholson and Louise Fletcher, *One Flew Over the Cuckoo's Nest* won all five major Oscars: Best Picture, Best Director, Best Screenplay, Best Actor, and Best Actress. That was an achievement which had not happened since Frank Capra's *It Happened One Night*. With this much attention, why does there seem to be such confusion about whether the film is "comedy" or "drama"?

Re-viewing the film has convinced me that the classification error is plausible if not laudable. Superficially, the film is funny. There are some wonderful bits of irreverence, slapstick, distortion, exaggeration—what David Denby in his film review called an appeal to the "emotions of late adolescence"[1]—but classification on the basis of this observation alone would be to miss the power and significance of the film. Even Vincent Canby's review, prejudiced, I believe, by the Forman films noted above, is entitled " 'Cuckoo's Nest'—A Sane Comedy About Psychotics."[2] However, we are much closer to the humorous heart of this film and the intent of its director, Milos Forman, if we recall Sören Kierkegaard's

145

admonition that "humor is always a concealed pain." For Kierkegaard all conditions, all activity, all conversation, all relationships which occur within the context of absurdity become absurd and, consequently, material for comedy; it is the absurd itself which is truly tragic. The paradox persists: minor pains are transformed into humor at the cost of finally exposing a more profound pain—the agony of our human lostness.

To counter such a profound spiritual *angst* while respecting the paradox, one must find an appropriate affirmation of redemption. Forman does this by adopting and adapting Ken Kesey's symbolism in *One Flew Over the Cuckoo's Nest*. Like Kesey, Forman introduces an unlikely, even irreverent, messianic figure, Randle P. McMurphy (Jack Nicholson), in whose life, suffering, and death he finds an analogue to the Jewish-Christian figure of the Suffering Servant.

As in the Kesey novel, the story takes place in a mental institution to which McMurphy is being sent for evaluation. Assigned to a prison farm to work off his sentence for statutory rape ("she was fifteen, goin' on thirty-five, Doc"), McMurphy decides that serving his time in a mental institution would be preferable to his present circumstances, so he fakes insanity to secure his transfer. He is no sooner escorted through the state hospital door than he realizes his possible error. Nicholson gives us this apprehensive assessment with one quick, cold, calculating look, an eye encounter with a "real" psychotic. Too late to change his mind, McMurphy throws himself into the act, kisses his cigar-chomping guard, and literally waltzes into the ward. Both acts are so contrived that they could only be the products of a sane mind ineptly faking insanity.

When the doors clang shut, we are suddenly aware that we and the camera are locked into the environs which director Forman has prepared for us. So long as we are within the regulated world of the mental institution, all patient actions, by definition, lack normal significance and consequently become the ground for the comic. As McMurphy makes us increasingly aware of this dislocation—this immutable disjunction which deprives the patient by bureaucratic decree of any rationality, sensitivity, integrity, or depth of feeling—what we had accepted as comic is subverted into the tragic. This transformation of the comic gradually colors our interpretation of the action and message of the film. It becomes evident to us that Milos Forman and his screenwriters Lawrence Hauben and Bo Goldman are using the mental institution not as the insane "asylum," a refuge from the world, but as a metaphor for contemporary society itself. If we identify ourselves at all with McMurphy, we find ourselves in a world in which our ability to control our lives or to effect our own destiny is being arbitrarily denied us.

In the novel Kesey sees the hospital, i.e. the World-Establishment, as the Evil Empire which, if we are to be saved, must be challenged and reformed by the forces of the Good. In this titanic and religious struggle, the forces of evil are manifested in Nurse Ratched, the infamous "Big Nurse," and the forces of good in the Christ-figure R.P. McMurphy. It is McMurphy's self-sacrifice which alone will save the inmates and, hence, the world. The messianic parallels are pointed enough that McMurphy, about to be subjected to shock therapy, asks, "Do I get a crown of thorns?" Forman uses the same theme, but his treatment is more sophisticated, more convincing.

Forman sets the mood at the beginning of the film by giving us a visual motif to which he returns at the end, a motif that symbolizes the spiritual trauma through which he is about to take us. As the credits roll across the screen, we are viewing a stunning wilderness scene in the Pacific northwest. Illumined by early morning light—lots of warm browns and blacks in the foreground—a sunlit snow-covered peak dominates the background but is reflected in water in the foreground. Everything radiates beauty, stability, order, majesty, and peace. Simultaneously, the sound track is giving us a plaintive song played on a saw, accompanied by the sound of Indian leg bells and tom-toms thumping out an unmistakable heartbeat. The cut from this sylvan scene to the ward at the Oregon State Hospital at Salem is visually and conceptually jarring, and immediately sets up the dialectical tensions for the thematic development of the film.

Randle P. McMurphy virtually explodes upon a scene of enforced tranquility. He is assigned to a sterile white ward supervised by the sterile white-uniformed Nurse Ratched. It is surely no accident that it takes several "introductions" to know whether staff and patients are saying "Nurse Wretched," "Nurse Ratchet" (or was it "Hatchet?"), or "Nurse Ratched." All three variations seem to apply. Louise Fletcher's Nurse Ratched runs a very tight ward with three tough orderlies to enforce her control. She presides above it all—incontestably in charge, insufferably pleasant, and inquisitionally right. She conducts the group therapy sessions with the same imperious manner that she enforces the rules of the ward. In such a context, the rights of the individual are always subordinate to the efficient ordering of the institution.

A contest of wills between Nurse Ratched and McMurphy is inevitable, and in this "land of the free and home of the brave" there is no doubt where the sentiments of the audience lie. The lines are so clearly drawn by Forman that cheers and clapping continually interrupt the film as McMurphy challenges Ratched's authority. When McMurphy suggests that the ward be permitted to watch the World Series, Nurse Ratched argues against the suggestion because it would be "changing a very care-

One Flew Over the Cuckoo's Nest
(1975, Milos Forman)

R.P. McMurphy (Jack Nicholson) confronts the intractable, self-righteous, moralistic Nurse Ratched (Louise Fletcher). Although his plea for freedom is here subverted by the guarded glass partition, nothing is sufficient finally to keep these ambivalent adversaries apart. Their last confrontation, which effects McMurphy's symbolic liberation of the ward, is subtly climactic in more senses than one.

fully worked out schedule." McMurphy argues exception for an extraordinary event. "Even in the cooler they let you watch the World Series. There'd be a riot." Denial would be "un-American." Nurse Ratched, convinced of her own authority to dominate—intimidate, really—permits a vote to settle the matter "democratically." McMurphy loses five to three. The vote is repeated the next afternoon, but by this time McMurphy has convinced his ward-mates to vote with him. Ratched is out-voted nine to nothing. She then changes the rules; the vote has to represent a majority of the whole ward, not just the marginal patients but also the "vegetables." As McMurphy struggles to find one more vote, Ratched closes the meeting. One more vote is found—Chief Bromden, a deaf and dumb Indian—but Ratched keeps to schedule by claiming that the vote came too late. Organizationally legal but morally reprehensible. Sitting in front of a black TV screen, McMurphy creates his own game which soon has the whole ward cheering. Ratched can only try to drown him out with Muzak. It is clear who has won the hearts, and even the minds, of this company.

McMurphy is convinced that the System and even its rigid adherence to Laingian therapy is causing more problems than it's solving. Discovering one day that most of his fellow inmates have voluntarily committed themselves for treatment, he tries to jar them loose with a dose of early "reality-therapy." "Are you crazy or somthin'? Well, you're not. You're no crazier than the average asshole out walking around the street." Gradually he instills in them a sense of identity, worth, and even courage to challenge Nurse Ratched. The clash of System vs. personal freedom which inevitably follows results in a melee in the ward, and McMurphy, Chief Bromden, and the riot's unwitting initiator, Cheswick, are all given shock therapy, ostensibly to settle them down, but more obviously to punish them.

The trauma brings McMurphy and Chief Bromden together. The Chief is a character of mythic proportions. Physically, he stands at six-foot seven; symbolically he stands for the "noble savage" buried deep within us all. However, Chief Bromden, like McMurphy, has been faking it all along. He confides to McMurphy that he can both hear and speak. McMurphy responds, "What are we doing here, Chief, you and me?"

McMurphy knows that the time has come; he has either to escape or submit to becoming a vegetable himself. Late one night, with the aid of Candy, his beyond-walls girlfriend, he smuggles in whiskey and a second woman, to throw a final party for the Ward. McMurphy fails to leave in time because he decides to indulge his inhibited, stuttering, mother-smothered friend Billy Bibbit. He asks the unbelievably compliant Candy to have sex with the enamored Billy even though it puts them all at risk by being discovered. The dreaded and seemingly inevitable occurs. Nurse Ratched and the orderlies return, which sets in motion a series of violent encounters between patients and staff. Billy is discovered with Candy, but he has been transformed by his experience of making love. Publicly he defends his action without stuttering. Only when Ratched savages Billy by threatening to inform his domineering and censorious mother does Billy break down and confess that McMurphy is behind it all. This public castration leads directly to Billy's suicide, and to McMurphy's attempt to strangle Nurse Ratched. Forman has made the scenes vivid enough that audiences actually cheer McMurphy on when he finally attacks Ratched.

Pulled back by the orderlies just in time to save Ratched's wretched neck, McMurphy is taken away. The next time we see him, he has been lobotomized—a real vegetable. It is enough to enrage Chief Bromden, who suffocates McMurphy rather than "leave" his friend to be the humiliated and exploited exhibit of failed revolt. Then, using a water basin as a battering ram, the Chief smashes his way through a caged window and runs to freedom amidst the cheers of the inmates—and theater audiences.

It is obvious that the Forman/Kesey theme has struck a deep responsive chord in the American audience. If freedom and dignity must be bought at the price of rebellion, murder, or euthanasia, so be it. It is hard not to see such actions as justified in the larger scheme of things. The socio-political parallels in our culture are everywhere: the civil disobedience and confrontations of the civil rights movement, the often violent opposition to the war in Vietnam, the organized refusal to pay taxes; or, on the other side, the popular support for Nixon's Christmas bombing of Cambodia in violation of international law, or for the arbitrary and illegal operations of an Oliver North and John Poindexter.

To Forman's great credit, the film's presentation of these conflicts reflects the complexity we know to be there rather than Kesey's simplistic formulas. It's often not easy to tell who the "good guys" are. In Kesey's novel, Big Nurse is malevolently evil; there is no question that she is the Darth Vader of the Ward. In Forman's film, however, Nurse Ratched's "evil" is more classically present; it is the distortion of goodness. Forman symbolizes this by introducing us to Nurse Ratched wearing a black coat and hat over her white uniform. In one sense Forman's Ratched is much more dangerous than Big Nurse, because Ratched believes that she is right, that she is doing good, that she is transforming chaos into order. To be convinced that one has moral authority on one's side is a much stronger position than blatant, self-acknowledged savagery. This moral dimension becomes the locus of the disclosure of the religious symbolism of the film.

Both novelist and director employ the messianic Suffering Servant to convey the religious-mythic nature of the struggle for human dignity and freedom. Although Kesey does not go so far as to claim that R.P. McMurphy is Jesus Christ or even that McMurphy thinks he's Jesus Christ—which would actually be ironically antithetical to the point that Kesey is making—he does have McMurphy identify himself as a Christ-figure. It is he who brings to the patients their sense of worth and dignity, it is he who stands up against the Evil One who has tyrannized the "crazies," and it is he who suffers and dies so that they may be free. Kesey's treatment is a straightforward utilization of the Christus Victor theme in traditional Christian thought.

Forman utilizes the same messianic theme, but, as in the other levels of this discussion, his treatment is more sophisticated and, as a consequence, more universal. Our first view of the ward gives us the character of his thought. As soothing music plays in the background, the patients all line up to receive their medication. Each comes to the Nurse's station, receives his proper dosage followed by a small cup of water to wash it down. The parallel to the dispensation and purpose of the sacrament of the Eucharist cannot be missed. One patient even presents his tongue on which the nurse places a round, wafer-like pill. He does everything but say "Amen." Forman wants us to see that all orders, all claims to ultimate power, have their operative sacraments. In every case, the suppliants come forward to the source of authority and power to receive the holy oblation which will enable them to survive, to live in harmony and peace within their community. As such it is the key to their security, power and meaning in life.

Forman's implication is devastating. We live in a world which is doing its best to tranquilize us out of our minds, to make us robots unable to think or even care for ourselves, let alone others: the state which defines our patriotism and civic duty in the name of civil religion, the party which makes our political decisions, the club which dictates our social conformity, and the school which determines our education. All of this is in contrast to the Christian Eucharist in which the above should ideally be rooted to enhance the life of humankind rather than enchain it.

This sacramental parallel is not the only use Forman makes of the Christian tradition. By the use of disguised parallels to the life of Jesus Christ, Forman not only sharpens his objections to the dangers of adherence to a soulless establishment, but also, albeit subconsciously, calls upon the spiritual and cultural power of two thousand years of tradition. "Into a world of madness," writes David Graybeal of *The Christian*

Century, "comes the uncategorizable man McMurphy. . . . When the chief authority says, 'Tell me who you *really* are,' McMurphy points to his record and responds, 'What does it say there?' ('Who do men say that I am?').["3] McMurphy then proceeds to make disciples of the men in the ward and to defy the petty legalisms imposed by the authorities. Once, when he jumps over the barbed wire fence with the help of Chief Bromden, he does not try to escape but commandeers a hospital bus and takes his wardmates, scheduled for an outing, on a *real* outing; he takes them fishing. To one and all he says, "You're not a goddamn loony now, you're a fisherman!"

The tensions mount to the point that McMurphy knows he must go, so he throws a final, illegal, late-night party (a last supper) with illegally imported wine, women, and song—"That's right, Mr. Martini, there is an Easter bunny!" says McMurphy despite the fact that it is now the Christmas season and the ward is appropriately decorated. To accommodate Billy Bibbit, as noted earlier, McMurphy once again forgoes escape. Forman makes sure that we know McMurphy's decision is a conscious one. For sixty-five seconds, with no dialogue, the camera scrutinizes McMurphy's face so that we see the decision being made. Billy, discovered by the orderlies and unmercifully pressured by Ratched, betrays McMurphy as the instigator of it all. Then Billy, like Judas, destroys himself.

"Crucified" by lobotomy, McMurphy is returned to the ward amidst rumors that he had escaped and other reports that he was "upstairs, meek as a lamb." Chief Bromden, seeing the stigmata, holds McMurphy in a position reminiscent of the Pietà. Saying, "You're coming with me," the Chief suffocates the persecuted body, pulls the great marble stone water dispenser out of the floor releasing fountains of "living water," hurls it through a window and escapes. The jubilation in the ward has all the ringing affirmation of the shouts "He is risen!" The Chief, the camera, and we are all liberated from the enprisonment of the ward and returned to that freedom and beauty of the natural wilderness from which we started and of which we "know" ourselves to be a part.

"The history of Jesus Christ," writes Graybeal, "has taught us all that the nonconformist, the questioner of certified authority and established procedure, the lover of persons and of life, will be killed. God's story in Christ has also taught us that not even death will be able to stop the liberator's empowering effect. The audiences applaud because, once more, they have heard and seen the truth."[4]

PART V

Other Forms, Other Visions

It Happened One Night
(1935, Frank Capra)

Ellie Andrews (Claudette Colbert) and Peter Warne (Clark Gable), chance companions on Ellen's flight from her father up the east coast, get acquainted around the "walls of Jericho," Warne's name for the protective blanket he hangs between their beds. Falling in love is a process, the film refreshingly reminds us, that precedes falling into bed.

It Happened One Night (Frank Capra, 1934)

One of the great romantic comedies, and still one of only two films to have made a sweep of the major Oscars (best film, actor, actress, director, writer); the other was *One Flew Over the Cuckoo's Nest* (1975). Ellie Andrews (Claudette Colbert), fleeing her father's yacht to rejoin the flyer she had eloped with, tries to travel incognito from Miami to New York by night bus. Her chance companion is Peter Warne (Clark Gable), a newspaper reporter from New York, who recognizes her from her newspaper photos, but declines to turn her over to the pursuing authorities her father has unleashed. Their journey up the coast like all quests is fraught with setbacks; it takes four days, or rather four nights. The "it" of the title that happens "one night" is doubtlessly their realization, on the fourth night, that they have fallen in love. Twice during the trip when they share accommodations at Warne's insistence (pretending that they are married is her best protection), he hangs a blanket from a rope between their beds, calling it the "walls of Jericho." The innocence of the conceit is refreshing and reassuring, especially fifty years later when falling in bed invariably precedes falling in love, if the latter ever occurs. Falling in love is a process, unfolding in time and space, that has little if anything to do with what we have, and everything to do with who we are. Needless to say, the walls come tumbling down only when, further obstacles overcome, the two are married.

Stagecoach (John Ford, 1939)

The best of the metaphor-for-life movies, including *Grand Hotel, Lifeboat, The Hospital,* and *Ship of Fools* as well as Ford's other great western *The Searchers.* The group riding the Overland Express from Tonto to Lordsburg is emblematic of late nineteenth century America. From north, south, and west come representative types: a lawman (George Bancroft), a gunman (John Wayne), a prostitute (Claire Trevor), an alcoholic Yankee doctor (Thomas Mitchell), a southern gambler (John Carradine), a banker (Berton Churchill), a whiskey salesman (Donald Meek), the pregnant wife of an army officer (Louise Platt)—and an "everyman," clown driver (Andy Devine). The Apaches led by Geronimo provide the apocalyptic threat that reveals each person's true colors. Life does indeed proceed by stages, and even though Ford expects tolerance of all as the fundamental American virtue, his film maintains that only those who think of others ahead of themselves can provide a confident basis for lasting community. With Carradine's death Ford buries the Confederacy; the portrayal of the banker's greed ("What's good for the banks is good for the country," Churchill says, as he absconds with funds) is Ford's prophetic indictment of American capitalism's perennial sin. If this was, as many claim, the film that made John Wayne a star, it may also be his most genuine performance. At any rate, the country's future seems in the best of hands as the Ringo Kid (Wayne) and Dallas (Trevor) ride off in the night, away from "the blessings of civilization." The repeated establishing shots against the majestic background of Monument Valley are a symbolic reminder of the pettiness of human pretensions in contrast to life's grand designs.

Gone With the Wind (Victor Fleming, 1939)

Unquestionably the American film that deserves more superlatives than any other—the most popular, the best-remembered, the most-widely seen (even though, in the age of inflated ticket costs, many have made more money) and, arguably, Hollywood's greatest artistic achievement. Thanks to David O. Selznick's tight control of every phase of production, it stands among our most perfectly cast and flawlessly staged films. Victor Fleming got the final credit for directing though George Cukor began the project and at least three other directors had a hand in shaping it, including William Cameron Menzies, who helped design the stunning pull-back crane shot of Scarlett's passage through the sea of wounded and dying Confederate soldiers at the Atlanta train depot. Scarlett O'Hara (Vivien Leigh) survives the Civil War, the burning of Atlanta, and two short marriages before she finally succumbs to the charms of Rhett Butler (Clark Gable) as part of her plan to prevail over the Reconstruction of her shattered homeland. Scarlett and Rhett are the screen's most famous lovers; their on-again off-again relationship (because of Scarlett's lingering infatuation for her cousin Melanie's husband) is a poignant reminder of our unfinished human condition. If Scarlett's gritty determination typifies the new, pragmatic south, her instinct for survival amid adversity makes her also, ironically, a perfect avatar of Miss Liberty. The film's narrative rhythm of reversal and renewal, of setback and survival, sustains our assumption that this American classic is the quintessential cinematic representation of fundamental hope. "After all," Scarlett reminds us, in the film's final memorable line, "tomorrow is another day."

The Philadelphia Story (George Cukor, 1940)

A sophisticated comedy, superbly acted, based on Philip Barry's play. Tracy Lord (Katharine Hepburn), a Philadelphia socialite, is about to marry for the second time, this time "beneath her" to a prosperous young businessman. C.K. Dexter Haven (Cary Grant), her first husband, cuts a deal with the editor of *Spy* magazine, promising to get a writer and a photographer into the house for an intimate portrait of the wedding, in order to keep the story of Tracy's father's affair with a "dancer" out of the magazine. The writer, Macauley Connor (James Stewart), considers Tracy a "young rich, rapacious American female," but falls in love with her; she likes his short stories, particularly one that suggests that "with the rich and mighty, [one] always [needs] a little patience." The marriage, everyone seems to agree, is doomed because Tracy acts like a "virgin goddess" who finds "human imperfection intolerable." Her father tells her that she has "everything that it takes to be a lovely woman except the one thing essential, an understanding heart." Tracy's innocent dalliance with Connor, provoked by excessive drinking, shows her own frailty. "Regard for human frailty" is essential to true humanity, and experiencing one's own frailty may be the surest way to an understanding heart. A cameo shot of the delicate model of Dex's sailboat, afloat in the pool, is the film's emblem. Cukor's final freeze frame, converting the film into a *Spy* magazine cover story, cleverly accentuates the superficiality of the frozen moment.

All the King's Men (Robert Rossen, 1949)

From Robert Penn Warren's Pulitzer Prize novel about the rise and fall of an American demagogue, more than reminiscent of Louisiana's Huey Long. Robert Rossen is faulted consistently—surely in homage to Warren, but without justification—for making the film Willie Stark's story whereas the novel tells narrator Jack Burden's as well. In a tightly-crafted script, Rossen does make Willie the focus of climactic attention, but Jack remains the central intelligence. Aristocrat Burden (John Ireland), a journalist covering the political opportunism of rural populist Willie Stark (Broderick Crawford), is eventually drawn into the inner circles of power alongside Willie's mistress Sadie (Mercedes McCambridge), as events conspire with Willie's native shrewdness to catapult him into the state house. "Man is conceived in sin and born in corruption," Willie claims; find the secret sin in his past, and he becomes your pawn. True to the novel's images, Willie is act and dirt and harsh reality; Burden's Landing—the aristocrats' enclave and symbol of the past—is aloofness, pharisaical whiteness, and genteel illusion. Fatefully, when Willie orders Jack to discover "the dirt" on Judge Stanton, leader of the movement to have him impeached, the implied Humpty Dumpty of the title begins his fall from the wall of tyranny. About to be exposed, the judge takes his life; over his body, in a signature frame, stand Anne and Adam (his niece and nephew), Jack, and Willie—with all gazes on Willie. The dialogical focus of the film as of the novel is the knowledge that kills; the central image of both, the spider web (and wink) of complicity. In telling this tragic story of universal connivance in the abuse of power, Jack honors our human need to know when to break the pattern of killing confidences.

All About Eve (Joseph Mankiewicz, 1950)

The best film ever made about Hollywood's aristocratic eastern rival, the Broadway stage, but as the title itself suggests in using the Hebrew name for the mother of the race, it is also, and more fundamentally, all about the fall. The temptress of this theatrical Eden is Eve Harrington (Anne Baxter), an aspiring actress, who cons her way into the life and affections of Margo Channing (Bette Davis) with a view, we come to discover, of supplanting her on the stage. Eve's companion in evil is the theater critic and cynic Addison De Witt (George Sanders), whose name alone is a reminder that this is no heavy-handed version of the fall from grace, but a clever, witty tale of demonic connivance—in the American literary tradition of humorous apocalypse, with the loosing of satan as a con artist foreshadowing the end. Unwittingly drawn into Eve's scheme are the playwright Lloyd Richards (Hugh Marlowe) and his wife Karen (Celeste Holm), the director Bill Simpson (Gary Merrill), and the producer Max Fabian (Gregory Ratoff). Only Birdie (Thelma Ritter), Margo's dresser, remains skeptical of Eve throughout. There's plenty of "mendacity and hypocrisy" here, to borrow a phrase from Tennessee Williams, but then where isn't there? Center-film, as it were, is the unmistakable signal of the director's intentions—a marquee announcing "The Devil's Disciple," just behind the theater where Margo's current hit is playing. When the film's final scene shows the process starting anew as Eve, having achieved her goal, is conned by another young aspirant to the stage, we see her image multiplied tenfold in the mirrors she preens before. We are all the devil's disciples. In naming us "legion," the film clearly updates the biblical narrative.

The African Queen (John Huston, 1951)

The script itself is a masterpiece; credited to James Agee and Huston, it demonstrates throughout Agee's deft sense of dialogue, his awareness of the power and beauty of language. Set in German East Africa at the beginning of World War I, the film traces a journey with a mission down one of Africa's more treacherous waterways from a Methodist Mission compound to a lake at the river's mouth. Charlie Allnut (Humphrey Bogart), the Canadian captain of the riverboat *African Queen,* is zany enough until he comes under the guidance of the British spinster missionary Rosie Sayer (Katharine Hepburn), who seems to say all the right things. The mission—to destroy the German warship *Louise*—is Rosie's patriotic idea, no doubt in partial retribution for the Germans' destroying the Mission compound and causing the tragic death of her brother (Robert Morley). The film, whose central image for the quest is the river itself, exudes a feeling for a purposeful universe, the confidence that flows from trust in a benevolent deity. Things don't always work out, of course—far from it—but when they do, Charlie and especially Rosie seem aware of their partnership in a providential plan. The film is also, and perhaps more pointedly, about our need to aim high, to transcend the pull of our lower inclinations. Surely its best line is Rosie's response to Charlie's feeble defense of his occasional excesses in drinking, claiming that it's only human nature. Rosie retorts, "Nature, Mr. Allnut, is what we have been put in this world to rise above."

Singin' in the Rain (Gene Kelly and Stanley Donen, 1952)

Rightly considered the greatest of all the Hollywood musicals, but also much more than that. It may be the best movie ever made about the making of movies, especially since it is about the catastrophic passage from silent movies to talkies that saw many of the lustrous stars of the earlier era fall from the studio-made firmament. While basing much of its humor on cinema's capacity to fashion reality out of illusion, it is uncompromising about the evils of living a lie. Don Lockwood (Gene Kelly) and Lina Lamont (Jean Hagen) are studio-created stars both on and off the screen. But their romance is a sham and Lina, though pretty, has a raspy-coarse voice that resists the transition to sound. Debbie Reynolds as Kathy Selden is the talent of the moment, waiting to satisfy the demands of personal love and industry transition. The resolution of these tensions, the film's perennial pleasure, is worked out around a series of musical numbers (taken by Kelly from the best MGM musicals) that in Hollywood tradition have little or nothing to do with the story, but who cares? The title number, arguably the most famous scene in a Hollywood musical, is the film's visual-aural tribute to the joyous reaches of the human spirit. "I'm laughing at clouds, so dark up above," Lockwood sings, smitten with love for Kathy, "the sun's in my heart, and I'm ready for love." No wonder Stanley Kubrick appropriated this song for one of the most violent scenes in his adaptation of Anthony Burgess' futuristic novel *A Clockwork Orange*, a film that creates its sense of dystopia by reversing all noble human sentiments.

East of Eden (Elia Kazan, 1955)

Adam Trask (Raymond Massey), like his biblical eponym, has two sons —Cal (Cain) and Aron (Abel)—and, similar to the Genesis story, one son, Aron (Richard Davalos), is favored by his father, while Cal (James Dean) is rejected. The film focuses on Cal's quest for a sense of personal dignity, which leads him to travel back and forth between the Monterey of his mother (Jo Van Fleet) and the Salinas of his father, between the shrouded coastline of white slavery and the sunlit valley of righteousness. The title, taken from Genesis 4:16, indicates immediately that the dramatic action takes place "after the fall"; only the unfolding drama and the visual motifs of the film can tell us it also occurs "because of the fall." Cal's rejection by his father is repeatedly emphasized—short of the final scene—by a composition of frames that shows him in angular juxtaposition to the physical world around him. Although the film foreshortens considerably the three-generation, east-to-west sweep of John Steinbeck's novel, it nonetheless consciously strives to make the Trask family a paradigm of the American experience, which, Kazan suggests, following Steinbeck, is also lived "east of Eden." When Adam finally accepts Cal as he is—impetuous, unruly, but devoted—the film confirms our Jewish-Christian belief that each of us is a sad, but hope-filled mixture of good and evil. One accepts another despite the evil in him only if one acknowledges and transcends the evil in oneself. *East of Eden* is especially memorable as the occasion of James Dean's finest performance in his tragically short-lived career.

To Kill a Mockingbird (Robert Mulligan, 1962)
The excellent adaptation of Harper Lee's Pulitzer Prize novel about growing up in a small Alabama town in the 1930s. The film preserves, even enhances, the novel's viewpoint: the voice-over narrator is a grown woman fondly recalling two summers, and a fall, from her childhood. The sharply-contrasted light and shadow of the film's black and white cinematography capture perfectly that mixture of terror and surprise that dominate a child's impressions of the adult world. Although presented as a remembrance, the film is anything but nostalgic. It's about seeing through others' eyes until we can see for ourselves—and about remembering to be grateful for the way we are taught by our elders early on to read the world. For Scout (Mary Badham) and her slightly older brother, Jem (Phillip Alford), it's their wise, generous and gentle lawyer father, Atticus Finch (Gregory Peck), who shares with them, as the occasion warrants, the kinds of practical insights that we need in order to live with compassion, how "you didn't really get to know a man till you stood in his shoes and walked around in them." Two narrative strands are artfully interwoven—the children's determination to expose the mystery of their retarded neighbor, Boo Radley (Robert Duvall), and Atticus' doomed defense of a black man falsely accused of rape. If it's "a sin to kill a

mockingbird" because all they do is sing pretty songs, then it would be like killing a mockingbird to deprive Boo Radley of his privacy. Jem's box of simple treasures, the film's central symbol, serves as a memento of the real gift others give of themselves.

Who's Afraid of Virginia Woolf? (Mike Nichols, 1966)

A brilliantly acted, superbly directed, photographed and edited adaptation of Edward Albee's provocative play. Some of the language of the film, tame by contemporary standards, barely passed the censors in 1966. Although the unities of time and place are almost classical, and the setting is apparently realistic (a home and its immediate environs in a New England college town named New Carthage), almost nothing else about this film is realistic. The characters, the dialogue, the dramatic rhythms are pure cinematic expressionism. The title, an academic party parody of the Big Bad Wolf, is in its choice of "Woolf" a key to the film's postmodernist tone. It is about the power, abuse and limits of language. George (Richard Burton) and Martha (Elizabeth Taylor), the fruitless first parents of this end-time America, have created an imaginary son to fill the void in their lives. Martha, the daughter of the college's president, takes advantage of her connections and George's enduring love by testing the virility of new male appointees to the faculty. This late weekend night (2 A.M. Sunday), after one of her father's welcome parties, she invites a handsome biology teacher, Nick (George Segal), and his mousy wife, Honey (Sandy Dennis), over for drinks. The games played in succession are "Humiliate the Host," "Get the Guests," "Hump the Hostess," and "Bringing Up Baby." They are the games that people play with language, often mercilessly, to render others defenseless, to strip away their illusions. When the inebriated Honey calls attention to her peeling the label from a brandy bottle, George says, "We all peel labels, baby!" Although George and Martha both claim that we can't tell the difference between truth and illusion, but must proceed as if we do, the film's real point seems rather to be that we can tell the difference, but that the prospect of living without certain cherished illusions is frightening indeed—because they are our tenuous shield against the hazards of existence. To persevere without them may be love's greatest test.

Bonnie and Clyde (Arthur Penn, 1967)

Along with *The Graduate*, also released in 1967, this film altered forever the appearance and tone of American films, ushering in the era of detached irony. As portrayed by attractive stars, Clyde Barrow (Warren Beatty) and Bonnie Parker (Faye Dunaway) may seem like a latter-day Greek tragic hero and heroine, deprived by poverty compounded by the

Midnight Cowboy
(1969, John Schlesinger)

Before Joe Buck (Jon Voight) leaves rural Texas for New York City expecting to strike it rich as a stud, it is clear that his hopes of sexual conquest are grounded in illusion. The only complete image of him is of his narcissistic reflection in the mirror—less substantial even than the poster of Paul Newman because Joe's inflated likeness will vanish as soon as he moves.

Depression of the very knowledge that would save them—that one can't correct injustice by injustice. To migrants stripped of their property by banks foreclosing on loans, they boast, as if to assuage the anger of the people, "We rob banks." Robin Hoods they aren't though, only criminals foolishly seeking the privileges of wealth. Under Arthur Penn's direction and as drawn by David Newman and Robert Benton, Bonnie and Clyde are actually composite figures of Depression-era gangsters, including John Dillinger and "Pretty Boy" Floyd. Gene Hackman, Estelle Parsons, and Michael Pollard round out the gang. Despite the introductory historical references and the misunderstanding of some critics, this is neither film biography nor documentary, but fiction. If Bonnie and Clyde achieve a kind of mythic stature, the mythological rhythm of their escapades points to the inevitable tragedy of misguided intentions. Clyde, whose impotence is symbolic of the life they lead, can't even promise Bonnie sexual fulfillment, except finally as the little death that mirrors Death and that, in this film, closely precedes their violent dance of death—gunned down in slow motion by lawmen in a roadside ambush. Such sociopathic behavior inevitably isolates people from society, as we are reminded by the intermittent far shots of their flight from pursuers into the wide open countryside.

Midnight Cowboy (John Schlesinger, 1969)

John Schlesinger's adaptation of James Leo Herlihy's novel is a tribute to the power of fraternal love in the midst of, and despite, the perils of the impersonal city. The use of the zoom lens to identify important details underscores the depersonalizing effects of modern urban life: we repeatedly see the whole before the part, the masses before the individual, the feet before the person. Joe Buck (Jon Voight) leaves rural Texas for New York City expecting to strike it rich as a stud. Everything along the way—billboards, neon signs, radio talk-shows, TV—seems humorously to support his naive ambition; later the same media will comment ironically on the absurdity of his sexual odyssey. Joe's fortuitous encounter with Ratso Rizzo (Dustin Hoffman), a street-wise urban con man, introduces money, pure and simple, as an object of the American quest. Ratso's deformed and consumptive body is the visual reversal of Joe's attractive, though presumptuous packaging. A deep bond of friendship develops slowly but surely between the two men. Just as Joe seems finally at a mod party to make a successful sexual contact through Cass (Sylvia Miles), he abandons his empty ambitions in order to take Ratso south, hoping that the warm climate will cure Ratso's illness, but not realizing how close he is to death. Touching imagery of rebirth confirms the transforming power of their love and the sacrifice it has prompted. Joe finally calls Ratso "Rico" as he has always wanted, and as they approach Miami, Joe discards his cowboy outfit and buys them both new shirts. Rico's, with brightly painted palm trees on it, becomes a joyous shroud for his passage through death; Joe's plain shirt suggests the dawn for him of a more realistic new start in life.

The Last Picture Show (Peter Bogdanovich, 1971)

Another masterful movie about movies (based on Larry McMurtry's novel), not about making them, but about their almost sacred centrality in American life prior to the advent of television. The film begins and ends with shots of the Royal Theatre, the only movie house in a small, desolate Texas town named Anarene that, like so many stations on the American way west, is dying out. Sonny Crawford (Timothy Bottoms) and Duane Jackson (Jeff Bridges), seniors in the class of '51, spend most of their free time at one of the three public places—cafe, pool hall, and movie theater—owned by Sam the Lion (Ben Johnson), the town's principal father figure. Sam's ward Sonny goes from a painful experiment in sex with Ruth Popper (Cloris Leachman), the wife of the coach, to a brief unconsummated marriage with the local tease, Jacy Farrow (Cybill Shepherd), and finally to near seduction by Jacy's mother, Lois (Ellen Burstyn). Bogdanovich following McMurtry uses the pattern of sexual liaisons as a metaphor for the frantic attempts of the young to reach for solid moorings in the chaos of disintegrating structures. Only with Sam's untimely death do we discover the nature and extent of his wisdom. In fact, it is the challenge of wisdom gained through honest suffering, the film suggests, that is youth's last, best hope. Bogdanovich's gamble with black-white photography, unfamiliar faces in important roles, and a classical style of film narration borrowed from Ford and Hawkes is so successful that some considered this at the time of its release the most impressive film by a new American director since *Citizen Kane*.

Slaughterhouse-Five (George Roy Hill, 1972)

A darkly humorous anti-war film, vastly superior to its source—Kurt Vonnegut's cult novel about a space-age "everyman" who has come "unstuck in time"—that makes the fire-bombing of Dresden in World War II a symbol of apocalypse, the basis of its passionate plea for peace. The narrative's abrupt shifts in time, that in Vonnegut's telegrammatic prose are often clumsy, are rendered smoothly here through visual association, sound overlap, and the look of outer regard. In an encyclopedic way the film manages to level its sights at the excesses of an entire world, not unlike ours: against science and affluence, science fiction and middle America, patriotism and marriage, parenthood and free enterprise, fantasy and fascism. Billy (Michael Sacks), abducted by space travelers, spends his best moments on the planet Tralfamadore with the girl of his dreams, Montana Wildhack (Valerie Perrine). The Tralfamadorans claim that humans are "bugs in amber," that any attempt to change reality is futile. The structure of the film, however, runs counter to their wisdom. Inasmuch as Billy's ordeal as war prisoner from his capture behind German lines to the fire-bombing of Dresden (that Vonnegut himself survived as a POW) is presented as a straight-line though interrupted story, we are left with the clear impression that there are some atrocities against art and humanity that ought to be avoidable. The film's condemnation of human pretensions as well as its expression of hope is compellingly and tenderly conveyed in the warmth of the performances that Hill has drawn from his cast and in the affection with which Miroslav Ondricek's exquisite color photography records even the most bizarre of human tragedies.

Nashville (Robert Altman, 1975)

Robert Altman's grand contribution to our bicentennial celebration makes our country music capital a metaphor for America. Joan Tewkesbury wrote the intricately-plotted script for this tour de force in which twenty-four characters are introduced, developed and dispatched during a single busy weekend. Nashville is celebrating the return from a sanatorium of one of its high-strung stars, Barbara Jean (Ronee Blakley), as Hal Phillip Walker (unseen) prepares to inaugurate his Replacement Party presidential campaign with a rally at the Parthenon. Outsiders mix easily with insiders to provide "fun and games" in the name of patriotism, politics, sex and greed. No one dominates the superb cast that includes Lily Tomlin, Henry Gibson, Keith Carradine, Ned Beatty, Karen Black, Keenan Wynn, Scott Glenn, Geraldine Chaplin, and Shelley Duvall; each supports perfectly the convergences of the plot, which is itself the star. It is an extraordinary ensemble effort; the actors not only (reputedly) improvised lines, but also wrote songs for the film—including Gibson, Tomlin, Carradine, Blakley, and Black. A montage of Sunday morning church services at the heart of the film suggests Neibuhrian "musical" sources of denominationalism. Even those who are put off by the country-and-western sound will revel in this gently satirical tribute to our country's capacity for surviving its perennial political and cultural insanity. After the film's climactic assassination attempt, a would-be star calms the crowd at the rally with an improvised song, whose refrain is ironically emblematic of our national resilience in the face of catastrophe: "You may say that I ain't free, but it don't worry me." On a more self-laudatory note, Gibson's comical lead song contends: "We must be doing something right, to last two hundred years."

Close Encounters of the Third Kind (Steven Spielberg, 1977, 1980)

Of science fiction films, this is the most richly textured and religiously satisfying. Released the same year as *Star Wars*, it far surpasses its more popular rival in depth and artistry. Expanded, reedited, and rereleased in 1980 as *The Special Edition* (the version that's available on tape), it is a visual masterpiece of the rarest kind, especially if seen as it should be on the silver screen. Three groups converge upon a mesa in Wyoming, with varying degrees of assurance that there will be an encounter with aliens—scientists, the U.S. government, and simple people capable of wonder. Roy Neary (Richard Dreyfuss), a utility worker in Muncie, Indiana, and a child named Barry (Cary Guffey) from a nearby farmhouse are given special invitations. The team of scientists, headed by Claude Lacombe (François Truffaut), is collecting evidence of unexplained phenomena of disappearance and epiphany—World War II fighter planes in Mexico's Sonora Desert; a cargo ship in the Mongolian desert; and in India, natives pointing to the sky and chanting a five-note mantra. A pattern begins to emerge. The decoded musical notes point to a rendezvous with the extraterrestrial visitors at Devil's Tower, an allusion to the biblical high place where one encounters God. The plot is simple; the development of the visual-aural evidence is stunningly complex. In his vision of the kindly and intelligent aliens, who communicate through music and gesture, Spielberg has achieved cinema's most profound representation of the ultimate benevolence of the universe. The look of outer regard is the film's visual refrain for radical openness to mystery: as the space ship descends and its occupants emerge, the faces of those called to share the encounter show a mixture of fascination and awe. The film's structure suggests the biblical pattern of election and response; its visual splendor instills that sense of childlike trust that comes through the revelation of benevolent purpose.

Reds (Warren Beatty, 1981)

Ostensibly about the American Left's reaction to World War I and the Russian Revolution as seen through the lives of Jack Reed (Warren Beatty), the Oregonian journalist who wrote *Ten Days That Shook the World* and reputedly the only American to be buried in the Kremlin, and his wife Louise Bryant (Diane Keaton), feminist writer and fellow radical. The settings are principally American bohemian and Russian Bolshevik as the narrative follows Reed and Bryant from Portland to Greenwich Village and Provincetown, and then to and from Petrograd and Moscow. Despite appearances, the film praises neither revolutions nor revolutionaries, but rather the millennial spirit as an icon of fundamental hope, portraying our inevitable pursuit of ideals and their tragic inaccessibility. Its presentation of the ruthless Communist bureaucrat Zinoviev (Jerzy Kosinski) and of Emma Goldman (Maureen Stapleton) dissenting from the totalitarian policies of post-revolutionary Russian leaders leaves us with the clear impression that this revolution failed because it sacrificed the individual to the demands of party and state. Beatty's "witnesses"—friends, acquaintances and contemporaries of the Reeds (including Henry Miller, Rebecca West, Will Durant, and George Jessel), filmed in a limbo setting and commenting on the times—are at once Greek chorus and detached modernist commentators, challenging us to discover, if we can, our own sense of the heart of the matter. Beatty as director won a well-deserved Oscar, no doubt for the film's masterfully-rendered epic structure with haunting visual and aural refrains—Reed chasing after wagons shrouded in dust, the IWW flier with his love poem to Louise on the back, white lilies, and the songs "I Don't Want to Play in Your Yard (if you're not good to me)" and "I'll Be Home for Christmas." Among the film's dramatic encounters, the scenes between Louise and Eugene O'Neill (Jack Nicholson), her Provincetown lover, are particularly memorable; and the skillfully edited montage of the Revolution, at the end of the film's first half, intercutting the rising chorus of the masses singing "The Internationale" with a reconciliation of the estranged spouses is unrivaled in American cinema. The intent of the images is obvious: the pursuit of an ideal in the social order must be balanced, however precariously, by the demands of one's personal life and loves.

The Right Stuff (Philip Kaufman, 1983)

Following Tom Wolfe's fascinating account of the early years of the American space program, the film takes a detached, almost ironical, often wryly humorous view of the proceedings, pitting the gritty individualism of Chuck Yeager (Sam Shepard), the test pilot who broke the sound barrier but refused to be "Spam in a can," against the schoolboy competitiveness of the college-educated flyers who were packaged by NASA as America's Mercury astronauts—with special attention to John Glenn (Ed Harris), Alan Shepard (Scott Glenn), Gordon Cooper (Dennis Quaid) and Gus Grissom (Fred Ward), among the seven principals. It lampoons the government's showmanship in striving to overcome our setback in space after the Russians launched Sputnik, and the media's hype in covering it; the Hallelujah Chorus accompanies the astronauts' first press conference! Though unsuccessful at the box-office perhaps because of its length (192 min.) or, as some have suggested, because it was seen as promoting John Glenn's Democratic presidential aspirations, the film is exceptional; its other notable virtues aside, it has some of the most exciting special effects related to flying and space of any film to date, and Bill Conti's score is a marvelous musical complement. Its stunning climactic sequence intercuts Sally Rand's fandance at Vice-President Johnson's barbecue for the astronauts in the Astrodome with Yeager's attempt to surpass the Russian altitude record for a straight climb in a jet. Who has "the right stuff"? Individuals like Yeager, without a doubt, the film insists, but the astronauts too, because they also possess that mixture of courage and determination that societies depend on in forging new frontiers. The omnipresent minister who brings sad tidings to the widows of dead test pilots and sings at their desert burials is doubtlessly the film's visual *memento mori*, reminding us that there are definite limits to human endurance—and to our potential. Yet Kaufman's dramatization of the achievement of these pioneers in space leaves us with a clear sense of transcendent wonder, if not of the sacred, especially when sparks from an ancient aborigine's fire in Australia seem miraculously to engulf—and empower—Glenn's endangered Mercury capsule, and when Cooper, surprised by the brilliance of the sun in space, exclaims (in the film's last shot), "Oh Lord, what a heavenly light!"

Hannah and Her Sisters (Woody Allen, 1986)

Undoubtedly the best of Allen's comedy dramas about the American condition viewed through the distressed interpersonal relations of sophisticated, neurotic New Yorkers. There is a wonderfully naturalistic composition to the film, almost devoid of close-ups, its exteriors rich with Manhattanscapes. The sequences are neatly introduced by literate titles, white on black, and supported by some classic love songs like "Bewitched" and "Isn't It Romantic." Hannah and her sisters are the adult daughters of a has-been show-business couple, who alternate between studied sweetness and mutual confrontation over petty infidelities and lapses into alcoholism. Hannah (Mia Farrow) is the caring, composed, successful and dependable sister. Her second husband, Elliot (Michael Caine), has just discovered he's been smitten by Hannah's sister Lee (Barbara Hershey), who lives with a self-indulgent, depressive artist (Max von Sydow). Holly (Dianne Wiest), a neurotic, drug-dependent writer, and Mickey (Woody Allen), Hannah's first husband, a hypochondriacal TV producer, live tangentially to the family—until they're lucky enough to meet again. Mickey's bouts with Catholicism and Hare Krishna, as he tries to cope with death's certainty, are as funny as the episodes dealing with his groundless fear of brain cancer. Watching the Marx Brothers, he decides to hang his hope on the "slim reed" of "maybe," determining, as he puts it, "to stop ruining my life searching for answers I'm never gonna get, and just enjoy it while it lasts." The film is framed by three Thanksgiving dinners, the American family's ritual gathering—a reassuring signal of Allen's modest affirmation of the transcendent "maybe."

Hannah and Her Sisters

(1986, Woody Allen)

In this affirmative drama about the American condition, Woody Allen shows his genius for finding humor in the distressed interpersonal relations of sophisticated, neurotic New Yorkers. His cinematic alter ego Mickey obsessively seeks assurance from a doctor that his sudden loss of hearing in one ear is not caused by a brain tumor; rain and phone booth humorously accentuate his self-imposed isolation.

Appendix

Video Availability

Films Listed Alphabetically	*Distributor*
The African Queen	CBS/Fox Video
All About Eve	CBS/Fox Video
All the King's Men	RCA/Columbia Pictures Home Video
Ben-Hur	MGM/UA Home Video
Bonnie and Clyde	Warner Home Video
Casablanca	CBS/Fox Video
Citizen Kane	Nostalgia Merchant
City Lights	CBS/Fox Video
Close Encounters of the Third Kind	RCA/Columbia Pictures Home Video
East of Eden	Warner Home Video
The Godfather	Paramount Home Video
The Godfather, Part II	Paramount Home Video
The Godfather, Part III	Paramount Home Video
Gone With the Wind	MGM/UA Home Video
The Grapes of Wrath	CBS/Fox Video
Hannah and Her Sisters	HBO Cannon Video
High Noon	NTA Video
It Happened One Night	RCA/Columbia Pictures Home Video
It's a Wonderful Life	Nostalgia Merchant
Midnight Cowboy	MGM/UA Home Video
Nashville	Paramount Home Video
Notorious	CBS/Fox Video
On the Waterfront	RCA/Columbia Pictures Home Video

One Flew Over the Cuckoo's Nest	Thorn/EMI Video
The Philadelphia Story	MGM/UA Home Video
Reds	Paramount Home Video
The Right Stuff	Warner Home Video
Singin' in the Rain	MGM/UA Home Video
Slaughterhouse-Five	MCA Home Video
Stagecoach	Vestron Video
Sunset Boulevard	Paramount Home Video
The Last Picture Show	RCA/Columbia Pictures Home Video
To Kill a Mockingbird	MCA Home Video
The Treasure of the Sierra Madre	Key Video
2001: A Space Odyssey	MGM/UA Home Video
Who's Afraid of Virginia Woolf?	Warner Home Video
The Wizard of Oz	MGM/UA Home Video

Films by Director

ALLEN, Woody	*Hannah and Her Sisters*	1986
ALTMAN, Robert	*Nashville*	1975
BEATTY, Warren	*Reds*	1981
BOGDANOVICH, Peter	*The Last Picture Show*	1971
CAPRA, Frank	*It Happened One Night*	1934
	It's a Wonderful Life	1946
CHAPLIN, Charles	*City Lights*	1931
COPPOLA, Francis	*The Godfather*	1972
	The Godfather, Part II	1974
	The Godfather, Part III	1990
CUKOR, George	*The Philadelphia Story*	1940
CURTIZ, Michael	*Casablanca*	1942
FLEMING, Victor	*Gone With the Wind*	1939
	The Wizard of Oz	1939
FORD, John	*The Grapes of Wrath*	1940
	Stagecoach	1939
FORMAN, Milos	*One Flew Over the Cuckoo's Nest*	1975
HILL, George Roy	*Slaughterhouse-Five*	1972
HITCHCOCK, Alfred	*Notorious*	1946
HUSTON, John	*The African Queen*	1951
	The Treasure of the Sierra Madre	1948

KAUFMAN, Philip	*The Right Stuff*	1983
KAZAN, Elia	*East of Eden*	1955
	On the Waterfront	1954
KELLY, Gene and Stanley Donen	*Singin' in the Rain*	1952
KUBRICK, Stanley	*2001: A Space Odyssey*	1968
MANKIEWICZ, Joseph	*All About Eve*	1950
MULLIGAN, Robert	*To Kill a Mockingbird*	1962
NICHOLS, Mike	*Who's Afraid of Virginia Woolf?*	1966
PENN, Arthur	*Bonnie and Clyde*	1967
ROSSEN, Robert	*All the King's Men*	1949
SCHLESINGER, John	*Midnight Cowboy*	1969
SPIELBERG, Steven	*Close Encounters of the Third Kind*	1977
WELLES, Orson	*Citizen Kane*	1941
WILDER, Billy	*Sunset Boulevard*	1950
WYLER, William	*Ben-Hur*	1959
ZINNEMANN, Fred	*High Noon*	1952

Films by Year

1931   *City Lights* (Chaplin)

1934   *It Happened One Night* (Capra)

1939   *Stagecoach* (Ford)
         The Wizard of Oz (Fleming)
         Gone With the Wind (Fleming)

1940   *The Grapes of Wrath* (Ford)
         The Philadelphia Story (Cukor)

1941   *Citizen Kane* (Welles)

1942   *Casablanca* (Curtiz)

1946   *Notorious* (Hitchcock)
         It's a Wonderful Life (Capra)

1948   *The Treasure of the Sierra Madre* (Huston)

1949   *All the King's Men* (Rossen)

1950   *Sunset Boulevard* (Wilder)
             All About Eve (Mankiewicz)

1951   *The African Queen* (Huston)

1952   *Singin' in the Rain* (Kelly/Donen)
             High Noon (Zinnemann)

1954   *On the Waterfront* (Kazan)

1955   *East of Eden* (Kazan)

1959   *Ben-Hur* (Wyler)

1962   *To Kill a Mockingbird* (Mulligan)

1966   *Who's Afraid of Virginia Woolf?* (Nichols)

1967   *Bonnie and Clyde* (Penn)

1968   *2001: A Space Odyssey* (Kubrick)

1969   *Midnight Cowboy* (Schlesinger)

1971   *The Last Picture Show* (Bogdanovich)

1972   *The Godfather* (Coppola)
             Slaughterhouse-Five (Hill)

1974   *The Godfather, Part II* (Coppola)

1975   *Nashville* (Altman)
             One Flew Over the Cuckoo's Nest (Forman)

1977   *Close Encounters of the Third Kind* (Spielberg)

1981   *Reds* (Beatty)

1983   *The Right Stuff* (Kaufman)

1986   *Hannah and Her Sisters* (Allen)

1990   *The Godfather, Part III*

About the Contributors

DIANE APOSTOLOS-CAPPADONA is professorial lecturer in religion and the arts at Georgetown University. She is the editor of *Symbolism, the Sacred and the Arts* by Mircea Eliade (1985), *Art, Creativity and the Sacred* (1984), and *The Sacred Play of Children* (1983), and the co-translator of *A History of Religious Ideas, Volume III* by Mircea Eliade. With Douglas Adams, she edited a collection of methodological essays, *Art as Religious Studies* (Crossroad Publishing, 1987); they are currently editing a collection of historical and methodological essays, to be titled *Dance as Religious Studies,* also for Crossroad. Dr. Apostolos-Cappadona is the general editor of *The International Encyclopedia of Religious Art* (4 volumes), due from Crossroad in 1992.

J. SCOTT COCHRANE is the pastor at the Brownsville United Methodist Church in Bremerton, WA. While completing his M.A. and Ph.D. degrees in religion and film at the Claremont Graduate School, he taught film courses at the Claremont Colleges, the University of Puget Sound in Tacoma, WA, and the University of LaVerne in LaVerne, CA. He has written several articles on religion and film and is working on a theological text written from the perspective of religion and the arts, entitled *Comic Rhythm and Christian Existence.*

JACK COOGAN grew up just outside a little town called Hollywood and, despite formal training in theater and communications as well as film, seems fatally drawn to this newest and liveliest of the arts. In 1967 he helped to establish a program in religion and film at the School of Theology at Claremont, and in the early 1970s worked with Frances Flaherty, who with her husband, Robert Flaherty, created classic films like *Nanook of the North* and *Man of Aran,* to establish a study center at Claremont focused on the points of interaction between films in the Flaherty tradition, the arts, and religious studies. He is professor of communication arts at the School of Theology and at the Claremont Graduate School, and visiting professor of film studies at Pitzer College.

MARA E. DONALDSON has a B.A. from Wilson College, an M.A. from Vanderbilt, and a Ph.D. from Emory University. Donaldson is currently assistant professor of religion at Dickinson College. She uses films extensively in her courses, especially in religion and fantasy and in feminist theology, and has presented papers on religious themes in contemporary drama and film at professional meetings, including "Daring One to Believe: God According to Salieri, Agnes and Celie" at the 1986 American Academy of Religion convention. Donaldson is writing a book on faith and identity in recent women's fiction.

GEORGE GARRELTS is associate professor of philosophy and religious studies at Mercyhurst College in Erie, PA. He has a Ph.D. in religion from the University of Syracuse, where he specialized in religion and culture. He has been the director of the Films for Discussion Series at Mercyhurst for a dozen years and works extensively with international films, particularly films of social and religious significance. His most recent article, on "The Dismantling of the Ibo Myth in the Novels of Chenua Achebe," was published in the *Interdenominational Journal of Religion*. Dr. Garrelts teaches courses on myth and film, and on religion and film. His favorite film is *Woja Albert!*

HAROLD HATT, professor of theology and philosophy, is vice-president and dean of Phillips Graduate Seminary, Enid, OK, where he has taught since 1962. He teaches courses on film communication and on theological issues in films and includes film study in dialogue with theology. Hatt has a B.A. from the University of British Columbia, a B.D. from Southwestern Theological Seminary, an M.A. from Baylor University, and a Ph.D. from Vanderbilt University. He is the author of two books, *Encountering Truth* and *Cybernetics and the Image of Man;* the latter was translated into Spanish and German-language editions. He is currently president of the AAR/SW and of the Southwest Popular Culture Association.

NEIL P. HURLEY, S.J., is president-founder of INSCAPE, a non-profit institute dedicated to programs of "edu-tainment." Fr. Hurley holds three degrees from Fordham University, including a Ph.D. in political science, and has taught at Fordham, Notre Dame, Loyola of New Orleans, Loyola-Marymount, Florida State University, the Pontifical Catholic University of Santiago, and the National University of Chile.

He is the author of over a hundred and thirty articles covering religion, the social sciences, communications (particularly film), and future studies. His books include *Toward a Film Humanism, The Reel Revolution,* and two volumes in Spanish on media. His work on Catholic/Jesuit influences in Hitchcock's films, *Soul in Suspense,* is due from Scarecrow Press in 1991.

CHARLES B. KETCHAM is Thoburn Professor Emeritus of Religious Studies at Allegheny College. He received his B.A. from Mt. Union College, his B.D. from Drew University, and his Ph.D. from St. Andrews University, Scotland. He was a Fulbright Scholar at the University of Edinburgh and has spent post-doctoral years at Union Theological Seminary and Harvard. He has written five books, two of which are on film: *Federico Fellini* and *The Influence of Existentialism on Ingmar Bergman.*

ROBERT E. LAUDER, associate professor of philosophy at St. John's University, Jamaica, NY, has had several articles on film and theater published in *The New York Times* Arts and Leisure Section. A weekly columnist for *The Long Island Catholic* newspaper and the author of seven books, Fr. Lauder has also published articles on film and theater in *America, Commonweal* and *The New Oxford Review.* He has taught philosophy for twenty years at Cathedral College Seminary in Douglaston, NY, and has also taught at Princeton Theological Seminary, Queens College, and Brooklyn College. A specialist on Ingmar Bergman's films, he is the author of *God, Death, Art and Love: The Philosophical Vision of Ingmar Bergman* (Paulist Press, 1989).

JOHN R. MAY, chair and professor of English at Louisiana State University, is the co-author of two books on film—*Film Odyssey: The Art of Film as Search for Meaning* (1976) and *The Parables of Lina Wertmuller* (1977)—and the co-editor of *Religion in Film* (1982), published by the University of Tennessee Press.

ANN-JANINE MOREY received her Ph.D. in religion and social ethics from the University of Southern California. Her book *Apples and Ashes* (Scholars Press, 1982) is concerned with themes of individualism, community and gender in the American dream. She has published articles in the *Journal of the American Academy of Religion, Soundings,* and *Christian*

Century. Her second book (in progress) deals with religion and sexuality in nineteenth and twentieth century American fiction.

MICHAEL THOMAS MORRIS, O.P., while attending the University of Southern California on an art scholarship, studied film under Arthur Knight and continued his interest in the cinema as he pursued a course of theological studies in the Dominican Order. In 1986 he graduated from the University of California at Berkeley with a Ph.D. in the history of art. A professor at the Dominican School of Philosophy and Theology at Berkeley's Graduate Theological Union, he offers a popular course in religion and the cinema. Fr. Morris' biography of the art director and designer Natacha Rambova, *Madam Valentino,* is due out this year from Abbeville Press.

PHILIP C. RULE, S.J., holds a Licentiate in Sacred Theology from the Jesuit School of Theology, West Baden Springs, IN, and a Ph.D. from Harvard University. Fr. Rule taught at the University of Detroit from 1968 to 1980, and since 1980 he has taught at Holy Cross College. A former literary editor of *America* and former member of the National Catholic Film Office Review Board, he is currently on the Board of Directors of the Conference on Christianity and Literature. He teaches and publishes in areas of Romantic and Victorian literature, and film studies. Fr. Rule has taught "Film as Art: Appreciation and Criticism" and "Film: Form and Function," and his film articles include "Teaching the Film as Literature" (*Soundings*) and "Reflections on the Religious Dimensions of the Film" (*Christian Scholar's Review*).

PETER VALENTI, professor of communications and foreign languages at Fayetteville State University, holds a Ph.D. in English literature from the University of North Carolina at Chapel Hill, where he began teaching film. He completed further work at the Carpenter Center, Harvard University, under Nick Browne. His essays on film have appeared in such publications as *Film Criticism* and *The Journal of Popular Film;* his book *Errol Flynn: A Bio-Bibliography* was published by Greenwood Press in 1984. Currently he is completing a study of religion and the American classic cinema.

JAMES M. WALL is editor of the *Christian Century* magazine, located in Chicago, IL. He is the author of *Church and Cinema* and the editor of *Three European Directors* (both for Eerdman's). An ordained United Methodist minister, he has graduate degrees in theology from Emory and in religion and personality from the University of Chicago. A frequent contributor on film to his magazine and other publications, he has served as a member of ecumenical juries at film festivals in Berlin and Montreal and is president of Inter-Film North America, an organization which relates religion to film. Wall has taught courses on film and religion at various United Methodist seminaries, including Claremont, Garrett Evangelical Theological, and Emory.

Notes

Introduction

[1] Gabriel Marcel, *Homo Viator* (New York: Harper & Row, 1962), 32.

[2] T.S. Eliot, "Religion and Literature," in *Essays Ancient and Modern* (New York: Harcourt Brace & World, 1936); rpt. in *The New Orpheus: Essays toward a Christian Poetic,* ed. Nathan A. Scott, Jr. (New York: Sheed and Ward, 1964), 227. Additional references to this essay will be noted in parentheses in the text.

[3] Roger Angell, "Mean Streets," *The New Yorker,* February 18, 1980, 128.

[4] Robert B. Ray, *A Certain Tendency of the Hollywood Cinema, 1930–1980* (Princeton: Princeton University Press, 1985). Additional references to this work will be noted in parentheses in the text.

[5] Robert Detweiler, ed., *Art/Literature/Religion: Life on the Borders* (Chico: Scholars Press, 1983), 151.

[6] "The Great American Films," a program jointly sponsored by Filmex and the American Film Institute, 1973; "The 10 Greatest American Films of All Times," 1977 American Film Institute Survey: 1) *Gone With the Wind,* 2) *Citizen Kane,* 3) *Casablanca,* 4) *The African Queen,* 5) *The Grapes of Wrath,* 6) *One Flew Over the Cuckoo's Nest,* 7) *Singin' in the Rain,* 8) *Star Wars,* 9) *2001: A Space Odyssey,* 10) *The Wizard of Oz.*

Comic Rhythm, Ambiguity, and Hope in *City Lights*

[1] James Agee, *Agee on Film,* v. 1 (New York: McDowell, Obolensky, 1958), 10.

[2] H. Gene Blocker, "Another Look at Aesthetic Imagination," *The Journal of Aesthetics and Art Criticism* 30 (Summer 1972), 535.

[3] Neil P. Hurley, "Charles Chaplin," in *Religion in Film,* ed. John R. May and Michael Bird (Knoxville: University of Tennessee Press, 1982), 157–162.

⁴ S.K. Langer, *Feeling and Form* (New York: Charles Scribner's Sons, 1953), 332.

⁵ *Ibid.*, 351.

⁶ *Ibid.*, 328.

⁷ *Ibid.*, 331.

⁸ *Ibid.*

⁹ Robert Payne, *The Great God Pan* (New York: Hermitage House, 1952), 192.

¹⁰ *Ibid.*, 190.

¹¹ John Dart, "Film Comedy: A Way to Religion?" *The Los Angeles Times*, December 3, 1972, Section C, p. 1.

¹² *Ibid.*

¹³ Walter Kerr, *The Silent Clowns* (New York: Alfred A. Knopf, 1979), 346.

¹⁴ From a conversation in the fall of 1976 with Ron Robertson, a student of mine.

¹⁵ David Shepard, "Authenticating Films," *The Quarterly Journal of the Library of Congress* 37 (Summer/Fall 1980), 350.

¹⁶ Kerr, *The Silent Clowns*, 352.

¹⁷ Kerr backtracks somewhat on the matter in his discussion of the Mutual comedies (*ibid.*, 88), but note that he also reads the ending of *Modern Times* as an image of "no one going nowhere" (*ibid.*, 362).

¹⁸ Agee, *Agee on Film*, 262.

The Grapes of Wrath: The Poor You Always Have with You

¹ Quoted in *American Film Criticism: From the Beginnings to Citizen Kane*, ed. Stanley Kauffmann (New York: Liverite, 1972), 383.

² *Ibid.*, 385.

³ John Steinbeck, *The Grapes of Wrath* (New York: Penguin Edition, 1985), 536.

⁴ Robert Bellah, *et al.*, *Habits of the Heart: Individualism and Commitment in American Life* (New York: Harper & Row, 1985), 285.

⁵ Arthur McGovern, *Marxism: An American Christian Perspective* (Maryknoll: Orbis Books, 1980), 328.

⁶ Quoted in *Ancient Near Eastern Texts Relative to the Old Testament*, ed. James B. Pritchard (Princeton: Princeton University Press, 1955), 163–180.

⁷ John R. May, "Con Men and a Conned Society: Religion in Contemporary American Cinema," *Horizons* 4 (1977), 21.

⁸ Andrew Sarris, *The American Cinema* (New York: Dutton, 1968), 45.

⁹ Parker Tyler, "Mirage in a Sunken Bathtub," in *Great Film Direc-*

tors: A Critical Anthology, ed. Leo Brady and Morris Dickstein (New York: Oxford, 1978), 334.

[10] The truck and its journey through "alien land" also beg comparison with another Ford vehicle—the stagecoach with its band of passengers traveling through hostile Indian territory. As Gerald Mast observes, "the coach itself becomes Ford's metaphor for civilized society. Like the train in *The Iron Horsemen* and *Liberty Valance* and the truck in *The Grapes of Wrath,* the stagecoach is a machine built by human hands for the taming of the vast, uncivilized western waste." More to the point, Mast says that "despite the brilliantly exciting staging and cutting of the stagecoach's climactic battle with the Apaches, *Stagecoach* is a film about warm people and important human values." Whether it be the mythic west or a contemporary situation like the migration of workers, Ford's characteristic style is to deal with "warm people and important human values"—the "abiding verities" mentioned at the beginning of this essay. Gerald Mast, *A Short History of the Movies* (Indianapolis: Bobbs-Merrill, 1971), 299–300.

[11] Steinbeck, *The Grapes of Wrath,* 535–36.

[12] May, "Con Men and a Conned Society," 21.

[13] Louis Giannetti, *Understanding Movies* (Englewood Cliffs: Prentice-Hall, 1987), 59.

High Noon: On the Uncertainty of Certainty

[1] For this and other interesting changes from the script to the final screenplay, see George P. Garrett, O.B. Hardison, Jr., and Jane R. Gelfman, eds., *Film Scripts Two* (New York: Appleton Century-Crofts, 1971), 37–155. Amy's announcement that she is a feminist occurs on 142.

[2] J.R. Silke, "Zinnemann Talks Back," *Cinema* 2 (October–November 1964), 22.

[3] *Ibid.,* 20.

2001: A Space Odyssey and the Search for a Center

[1] R.P. Blackmur, *Henry Adams,* ed. with introduction by Veronica A. Makowsky (New York: Harcourt Brace Jovanovich, 1980), xxiv.

[2] *Ibid.*

[3] *Ibid.*

[4] James Monaco, *American Film Now* (New York: New American Library, 1979), 278.

[5] Pauline Kael, *Going Steady* (Boston: An Atlantic Monthly Press Book, 1970), 122.

[6] *Ibid.,* 123.

[7] Marsha Kinder and Beverle Houston, *Close Up: A Critical Perspective on Film* (New York: Harcourt Brace Jovanovich, 1972), 85.

[8] *Ibid.*

[9] Michel Ciment, *Kubrick* (New York: Holt, Rinehart and Winston, 1983), 131.

[10] *Ibid.*, 128.

[11] *Ibid.*

[12] *Ibid.*

[13] *Ibid.*

Citizen Kane: Descent into the Demonic

[1] Charles Higham, *The Films of Orson Welles* (Berkeley: University of California Press, 1970), 2.

[2] Pauline Kael, *The Citizen Kane Book: Raising Kane* (New York: Bantam Books, 1981), 110.

[3] *Ibid.*, 201.

[4] Joseph Conrad, *Heart of Darkness* (New York: W.W. Norton, 1971).

[5] Kael, *Raising Kane*, 63.

[6] James Naremore, *The Magic of Orson Welles* (New York: Oxford University Press, 1978), 61.

[7] *Ibid.*, 9.

[8] *Ibid.*

[9] Robert Carringer, *The Making of Citizen Kane* (Berkeley: University of California Press, 1985), 84–85.

[10] Charles Higham, *Orson Welles* (New York: St. Martin's Press, 1985), 153.

[11] Kael, *Raising Kane*, 59.

[12] Marc Alyn, "God in Contemporary Literature," in *New Questions on God*, ed. Johannes B. Metz (New York: Herder and Herder, 1972), 117.

Sunset Boulevard: Twilight of the Gods

[1] "In the Beginning," produced, written and directed by Kevin Brownlow and David Gill, *Hollywood*, Thames Television, January 1980.

[2] The actress Loretta Young, an ardent Catholic whose career began in the silent cinema and came to full flower in the golden age of talkies, points to a more specific reason for the demise of the Judeo-Christian ethic in American filmmaking after the war: the breakdown of censorship in an effort to be more realistic in film. "As I see it," she reminisces, "Hollywood started to go downhill when the power of the censorship

board was broken. Specifically, Otto Preminger introduced the word 'virgin' into the dialogue of a picture called *The Moon Is Blue* simply because he wanted to break the code. He told me that it was for artistic reasons, but I retorted that not everyone who breaks it thereafter would necessarily have his presumed good taste. Of course, none of us liked to be censored, but we saw the wisdom of it, respected it, or at least feared it. Now there are very few limits, and the very word 'censorship' is a dirty word." Just as Norma Desmond's career was shipwrecked by the development of cinematic sound, so too was Loretta Young's career cut short by that new cinematic morality which she considers the antithesis of Judeo-Christian religious values (telephone interview, August 29, 1988).

³ Steve Seidman, *The Film Career of Billy Wilder* (Boston: G.K. Hall & Co., 1977), 8.

⁴ Maurice Zolotow, "When Hollywood Took Its Gloves Off: The Making of *Sunset Boulevard*," *Los Angeles Magazine*, May 1977, 78–79.

⁵ Garson Kanin, "Recollection of and Conversations with Billy Wilder and Charles Brackett," *Hollywood* (New York: The Viking Press, 1974), 196–207.

⁶ Will Holtzman, *William Holden* (New York: Pyramid Publications, 1976), 30.

⁷ The mansion used in *Sunset Boulevard* was appropriately called "The Phantom House" and was located on Wilshire Boulevard, not Sunset. Owned by J. Paul Getty, it also served as a locale for the film *Rebel Without a Cause.*

The Godfather Films: Birth of a Don, Death of a Family

¹ William Murray, "Playboy Interview: Francis Ford Coppola," *Playboy* 22 (July 1975), 60.

² Quotations from the Genesis narrative are from *The Jerusalem Bible* (New York: Doubleday & Company, 1966), 18.

³ Robert K. Johnson, *Francis Ford Coppola* (Boston: Twayne Publishers, 1977), 116.

⁴ Pauline Kael, *Deeper into Movies* (Boston: Little, Brown and Company, 1973), 425.

⁵ In an interview in *American Film* (May 1979), p. 42, Mario Puzo tells how Coppola saw immediately that the ending of the original screenplay, following the novel, lacked dramatic power—the principal murders take place days after the christening. Puzo says that "in just two seconds" Coppola had the perfect cinematic solution: "We'll have them all killed while the baby is being christened."

⁶ When referring to the spiritual relationship begun through bap-

tism (the literal meaning of the film's title), I have used godfather with a lower case g. But for the relationship established by Vito and Michael as heads of the Corleone family—the basis of the film's deeper meaning—I have capitalized Godfather throughout the text.

[7] For greater clarity in reading about what needs to be seen, references to the intercut slayings are in parentheses. During the ritual interrogation itself, Michael dominates the frame.

[8] *The Godfather* is an heir of the great American romance tradition traced to Hawthorne's tales; in this instance, one thinks immediately of "Young Goodman Brown" and "My Kinsman, Major Molineux."

[9] The same threefold pattern can be found in the film's opening sequence, though the intercutting is by no means as obvious. Three members of the Godfather's extended family ask favors of him—Bonasera the undertaker, Nazorine the baker, and Johnny Fontane, Vito's godson. The brain-damaged Lucca Brasi, who visits the Godfather between Nazorine and Fontane, simply pays his respects and gives the don a gift for his daughter.

[10] Aeschylus, *Oresteia*, trans. Richmond Lattimore (Chicago: University of Chicago Press, 1955), "Agamemnon," 11. 757–60.

[11] Vito Corleone's story in time past has its own framing rituals—the funeral procession for his father in the beginning, as I've noted, and at the end the Palm Sunday celebration in Corleone, a mythic subversion of Vito's triumphant homecoming to revenge his family's extermination by Don Ciccio.

[12] At the first communion celebration, the "sacredness" of the relationship between the don and his extended family is, once again, ironically underscored by a threefold repetition of favors sought—Johnny Ola, Connie, and Frankie Pentangeli. As in *The Godfather*'s wedding sequence, the real business of the family transpires in the dark inner office of the don, not in the sunlit patio.

[13] The corresponding middle ritual in Vito's story is the procession of the Blessed Sacrament culminating the festival of San Rocco, in which the priest's benediction with the monstrance comments ironically on Vito's bloody elimination of Fanucci and his ascendancy as don.

[14] *The Godfather, Part II* was the first sequel to be named best picture of the year and, as a matter of fact, to win more Oscars than its predecessor. *The Godfather* was nominated for ten awards and received three (best picture, best screenplay adapted from another medium, and best actor for Marlon Brando); *The Godfather, Part II*, nominated in eleven categories, won five Oscars (picture, direction, adapted screenplay, art direction, and musical score). *The Godfather, Part III* was nominated for seven awards but won none. On the other hand, no discriminat-

ing critic has ever considered the number of Academy Awards to be the surest index of excellence.

The Wizard of Oz and Other Mythic Rites of Passage

¹ Mythos is the Greek term for "story" or "tale" to be distinguished from the Greek term *logos*, which alludes to a style of rational discourse and from which our understanding of the term discursive comes.

² Joseph Campbell, *The Hero With a Thousand Faces* (Princeton: Princeton University Press, Bollingen Series XVII, 1949).

³ Sir James George Frazier, *The Golden Bough: A Study in Magic and Religion* (New York: Macmillan Company, single vol. ed., 1940).

⁴ Campbell, *The Hero With a Thousand Faces*, 30.

⁵ *Ibid.*, 245.

⁶ *Ibid.*, 51.

⁷ Campbell points out that "the belly of the whale" is often connected to the image of the world navel. One recalls Dorothy looking out of the window of the house and saying, "We must be up inside of the cyclone!" Miss Gulch then passes by the window and is transformed into a witch—a further indication of things to come.

⁸ Campbell, *The Hero With a Thousand Faces*, 97.

⁹ *Ibid.*

¹⁰ Frazier, *The Golden Bough*, 593.

¹¹ *Ibid.*, 595.

¹² John A. Hutchinson, *Paths of Faith* (New York: McGraw-Hill, 1975). From the "Letter to the Reader," 13.

¹³ From the Baum novel text and the accompanying Denslow Maps: see Michael Patrick Hearn, *The Annotated Wizard of Oz* (New York: Clarkson N. Potter, 1973), 61, and cover maps.

¹⁴ Campbell's "world navel" corresponds to the center of the universe. It is interesting that Denslow's drawings for Baum's novel also place the Emerald City at the center of the Kingdom of Oz.

¹⁵ Campbell, *The Hero With a Thousand Faces*, 196–206. The sequence with the flying monkeys reinforces this idea.

¹⁶ Rudolph Otto, *The Idea of the Holy* (London: Oxford University Press, 1923).

¹⁷ Baum gives us several different options: an enormous head, a lovely lady, a terrible beast, and a ball of fire. Why did the film version pick only two of these four fantastic images for Oz? My guess would be that these two were thought to be the most visual.

¹⁸ " 'No one knows it but you four and myself,' replied Oz." See Hearn, *The Annotated Wizard*, 265. Suddenly the story becomes more than a simple children's fantasy. It presents in narrative form insights

about the human situation and philosophical trends similar to those found in Feuerbach, Nietzsche, Camus, and Sartre, more popularly identified with the "death of God" movement. The grandson of a Methodist preacher, Baum was thoroughly familiar with the writings of Nietzsche through his lifelong interest and involvement in the Theosophical Society. Baum wrote an article on theosophy in 1890, describing his own era as an "age of unfaith." "The Theosophists are searchers of Truth," he said, "and admit the existence of God—but not necessarily a personal God." *Ibid.*, 91ff.

[19] This reference is drawn from the script and later from the introduction to the film. Interestingly, Elton John, one of our more theologically perceptive contemporary songwriters, released an album titled "Goodbye Yellow Brick Road," in which the first selection is entitled "Funeral for a Friend."

[20] Hearn, *The Annotated Wizard*, 339.

[21] "Where in the world did *you* come from?" asks Aunt Em of Dorothy, a question that she answers not from her bed with a washcloth on her head, but from the farmyard itself. " 'From the Land of Oz,' *said Dorothy gravely.*" Hearn, *The Annotated Wizard*, 209.

The Treasure of the Sierra Madre: Spiritual Quest and Studio Patriarchy

[1] Gabriel Marcel, *Homo Viator*, trans. Emma Craufurd (New York: Harper Torchbooks, 1962), 153.

[2] Joseph Campbell, *The Hero with a Thousand Faces*, Bollingen Series XVII (Princeton: Princeton University Press, 1968), 38.

[3] The nadir of such selfishness is evident in the savagery of Dobbs' attack on Curtin after the two are alone with the gold. Dobbs' demonic fury, emphasized by unusually low camera angles and chiaroscuro lighting, demonstrates total lack of concern beyond the self. Contrast this episode with the more matter-of-fact qualities of the bar fight sequence with McCormack, entirely presented through conventional camera set-ups. In that sequence, the focus is on the settling of a debt and not a final stage in the degradation of an individual.

[4] Interestingly, the historical context of the film within the studio system parallels in some ways the narrative message of the film. Just as Dobbs' simplistic sexism is shown to fail, so also was the studio patriarchy doomed: 1948 confirmed the drop in theater attendance evident the previous year, and negotiations were initiated to begin scaling down operations. The end of an era had arrived.

[5] Marcel, *Homo Viator*, 153–54.

On the Waterfront: Rebirth of a "Contenduh"

[1] Cited in Neil Hurley, S.J., "On the Waterfront: Blending Fact and Fiction Not Always Successful—But Worked in This instance," *Daily Variety* (53rd Anniversary Issue), November 1986, p. 116.

[2] *Ibid.* I asked Malden in 1984 whether he had been influenced by his contact with Father Corridan, who was a special advisor on the set. He told me he had and that Corridan's influence had lasted "down to this very day."

[3] The involvement of director Elia Kazan, once a communist sympathizer, in the HUAC investigations of Marxist influence in Hollywood is treated in a well-documented book by Victor Navasky, *Naming Names* (New York: Viking Press, 1980). See index for the references to Kazan.

[4] In my "On the Waterfront: Blending Fact and Fiction," I pointed out that the role which won for Karl Malden a well-deserved Oscar only put him in center stage once, namely in this stirring scene of religious witness at great risk. However, Malden's fine portrayal was limited, by and large, to being a moral cheerleader, spurring others on. The real-life priest, Father Corridan, ran other risks of reputation, loneliness, misunderstanding and a sense of ultimate failure in the historical project he and his followers had set for themselves—namely, the replacement of the corrupt ILA by a reform union not part of the combine with "Mr. Big" and the collusive shipping interests. Father Corridan had to walk a tightrope, without any safety net, facing constant pressures and vested interests not only from the secular world, but also from within the Catholic Church through powerful men who were benefactors and close friends of ecclesiastics in high places. To his credit, Francis Cardinal Spellman, archbishop of New York, gave Father Corridan a fair hearing and was convinced of his innocence from charges that he did not wear clerical garb and engaged in fisticuffs. Another film could be made on the "waterfront priest," of whom Budd Schulberg was reported to have said in Father Corridan's obituary in *The New York Times* 93 (July 1984): "He was the closest I ever came to feeling what true Christianity was all about."

[5] In a bedside chat I had with Father Corridan shortly before his death, he talked about the film, accenting the inspired nature of this "non-story" episode, adding that during the shooting of the entire film there was an indescribable feeling among those present that a curious force was helping to direct the picture.

[6] Parker Tyler, "John Doe; or, the False Ending," in *The Hollywood Hallucination,* with introduction by Richard Schickel (New York: Simon and Schuster, 1970), 168–190.

[7] Budd Schulberg, " 'Waterfront'—More Than a 90-Minute Movie," *The New York Times Book Review*, April 26, 1987, p. 39.

[8] Herbert Schneidau, *Sacred Discontent* (Baton Rouge: Louisiana State University Press, 1976), esp. Chapter One, "In Praise of Alienation: The Bible and Western Culture," pp. 1–49.

[9] Tyler sees this as an entertainment symbol when translated into the Hollywood "happy ending."

The Art of "Seeing": Classical Paintings and *Ben-Hur*

[1] In this essay, my use of the term "image" is specific and derives from the writings of John Berger. For Berger, "an image is a sight which has been recreated or reproduced. It is an appearance, or a set of appearances, which has been detached from the place and time in which it first made its appearance and preserved—for a few months or a few centuries. Every imagery embodies a way of seeing." John Berger, *Ways of Seeing* (New York: Penguin Books, 1977), 9–10.

[2] For a fuller description of the discipline of *seeing*, see my introductory essay, "Art as Religious Studies: Insights into the Judeo-Christian Traditions," in *Art as Religious Studies*, ed. Doug Adams and Diane Apostolos-Cappadona (New York: Crossroad Publishing, 1987), 3–11, esp. 3–8. My understanding of the discipline of *seeing* has been shaped by Jane Dillenberger, "Seeing Is Believing," *Journal of Current Social Issues* 15:3 (1978), 68–73; and Joshua C. Taylor, *Learning to Look* (University of Chicago Press, 1957).

[3] Walter Lowrie, *A Short Life of Kierkegaard* (Princeton: Princeton University Press, 1958), 50.

[4] For this understanding of the relationship between classical paintings and advertising, and the psychological implications thereof, I am dependent upon Berger, *Ways of Seeing*, esp. 129–154.

[5] See my essay, "Dreams and Visions: Religious Symbols and Contemporary Culture," *Religion and Intellectual Life* 1:3 (1984), 95–109. For further clarification, see William Cenkner, "Understanding the Religious Personality," *Horizons* 5 (1978), 1–16, esp. 2. In both essays, symbol systems are interpreted as a socialization process.

[6] For example, see John Dillenberger, *A Theology of Artistic Sensibilities: The Church and the Visual Arts* (New York: Crossroad, 1986).

[7] Popular since the sixteenth century, sea paintings like Cuyp's by both the seventeenth century Dutch painters and Claude Lorraine influenced the development of the Luminist tradition of nineteenth century American painting. This style of sea paintings was therefore well ingrained in the American consciousness from the early nineteenth century. As with Cole's *Consummation of Empire*, Cuyp's sea scene is

mirrored by Wyler as a way of presenting an "authentic" background to his film. The visually recognizable and familiar make the story more "real" and more acceptable to the viewer. Two characteristics of a painting masterpiece, superb design and a dramatic situation (e.g. the sea battle), serve a film scene as well. The aim of the painter and of the filmmaker is similar: to create an interpretation of reality that is simultaneously universal and individual. That is to say, this *individual* sea scene is unique while it also relates to the *universal* history of sea scenes.

[8] Ellwood C. Parry, III, "Looking at Art: Thomas Cole's *Course of Empire*," *Artnews*, 82 (October 1983), 110–112.

[9] For a careful study of Raphael's place in American cultural history, see David Alan Brown, *Raphael and America*, exhibition catalogue (Washington, D.C.: The National Gallery of Art, 1983).

[10] The headline of the February 7, 1914 edition of *The New York Times* read: "Mr. Widener Pays More Than $500,000 for Raphael's 'Madonna and Child'." A reproduction of the painting was placed below the headline. *The New York Times* heralded the purchase as "the most valuable picture ever brought to this country." The painting itself, *The Small Cowper Madonna* (1504), is part of the Widener Collection, the National Gallery of Art, Washington, D.C. For an extensive analysis of Raphael's place in the development of American aesthetics and of American art collections, and specifically the purchase of this painting, see Brown, *Raphael and America*, 15–107.

[11] Charles I. Sanford, *The Quest for Paradise: Europe and the American Moral Imagination* (New York: AMS Press, 1979), 2.

[12] Kenneth Clark, *What Is a Masterpiece?* (New York: Thames and Hudson, 1979), 10–11.

Love and Duty in *Casablanca*

[1] This essay was presented as a paper at the Southeast American Academy of Religion meeting on March 11, 1989. I am grateful to those who participated in the discussion. I especially acknowledge my conversations with Prof. Wayne Floyd, Jr. and Prof. Scott Bates.

[2] There are many biblical models of the virtue of altruism. From the Hebrew Bible, for example, we have the figures of Abraham, Ruth and Esther. In Judaism altruism is most closely related to the concept of *zedakah* (charity) and *zedek* (justice). Charity is a consequence of belief in God; belief in God "shatters egocentricity" and leads to self-transcendence. See David Hartman and Tzvi Marx, "Charity," in *Contemporary Jewish Religious Thought: Original Essays of Critical Concepts*, Arthur A. Cohen and Paul Mendes-Flohr, eds. (New York: Charles Scribner's Sons, 1987), 47–54. The emphasis in Christianity on altruism differs

from that of Judaism. In the gospels the portraits of Jesus' life as well as his teachings in parables such as the good Samaritan hold up self-sacrifice as the ideal virtue. This virtue of self-giving love of the neighbor is most closely related to the virtue of humility over against hubris or pride, the first sin of Adam and Eve. Thus there is the sense that altruism overcomes an essential tendency in us toward self-love or narcissism. The emphasis on humility has dominated mainstream Christianity since the time of St. Augustine. In Judaism, humility finds its finest expression in the writings of Moses Maimonides, but it is not related to human sinfulness or narcissism; it is related instead to God's love (*hesed*). As Bernard Steinberg notes, "the norm of humility is an instance of the task of *imitatio Dei*." See Bernard Steinberg, "Humility," *ibid.*, 429–433.

[3] Robert B. Ray, *A Certain Tendency of the American Cinema, 1930–1980* (Princeton: Princeton University Press, 1985), 89.

[4] *The New York Times*, November 22, 1942, p. 1.

[5] *Ibid.*, November 27, 1942, p. 27, col. 1.

[6] *Ibid.*, November 29, 1942, sect. 8, p. 3, col. 1 (emphases mine).

[7] *Newsweek* XXIII: 11, March 13, 1944, pp. 90–92. As Sidney Rosenzweig has noted ['*Casablanca*' *and Other Major Films of Michael Curtiz* (Ann Arbor: UMI Research Press, 1982), 78], "given *Casablanca*'s unusual production history, its success is surprising." Ronald Reagan and Ann Sheridan were originally considered to play the roles of Rick and Ilsa. When the film went into production, the script was not complete; Howard Koch was called in to take over from the Epstein brothers. Even decisive features of the finished film were not settled until late. No one knew, for example, if Ilsa would stay with Rick or leave with Victor. And Dooley Wilson's singing "As Time Goes By," one of the most memorable parts of the film, was added almost as an afterthought.

[8] Ray, *A Certain Tendency*, 89–112.

[9] Rosenzweig, *Casablanca*, 81 (emphases mine).

[10] Barbara Deming, *Running Away from Myself: A Dream Portrait of America Drawn From the Films of the Forties* (New York: Grossman Publishers, 1969), 22.

[11] *Ibid.*, 11.

[12] See Rosenzweig, *Casablanca*, 80, who confirms the importance of Louis: "*Casablanca* is as much about Renault's conversion to the cause as Rick's. He has the best lines and, by not stopping Laszlo's plane nor arresting Rick, determines the plot's resolution."

[13] Ray, *A Certain Tendency*, 90.

[14] *Ibid.*, 45.

[15] E.g., see Ray, *A Certain Tendency.*, 93.

[16] Rosemary R. Ruether, *Sexism and God-Talk: Toward a Feminist*

Theology (Boston: Beacon Press, 1983), 195–96. "For Christian women," Ruether writes, "one of the most difficult barriers to feminist consciousness is the identification of sin with anger and pride and virtue with humility and self-abnegation. . . . Women become 'Christ-like' by having no self of their own. They become the 'suffering servants' by accepting male abuse and exploitation. They fear the beginning steps of asking who they are and what they want to do, rather than 'putting others first.' "

Notorious: Penance as a Paradigm of Redemption

[1] Frank S. Nugent, "Mr. Hitchcock Discovers Love," *New York Times Magazine*, November 3, 1946, p. 12.

[2] See François Truffaut, *Hitchcock* (New York: Simon and Schuster, 1967), 121–122, and Alfred Hitchcock, "Rear Window," *Focus on Hitchcock*, ed. by Albert J. LaValley (Englewood Cliffs: Prentice-Hall, 1972), 43–44. Both make specific reference to *Notorious*.

[3] Pius XII, *Mystici Corporis*, par. 103.

[4] Paul Anciaux, *The Sacrament of Penance* (New York: Sheed and Ward, 1962), 46.

[5] *Ibid.*, 54.

[6] Bernard Häring, *Shalom: Peace: The Sacrament of Reconciliation* (New York: Farrar, Straus and Giroux, 1967), 9.

[7] *Ibid.*, 93–94. Protestant treatments also stress the need for specific confession, but not of minor details. This is found in the high church approach of Max Thurian, *Confession*, trans. by Edwin Hudson (London: SCM Press, 1958), 123–124, and in the low church approach of George William Bowman III, *The Dynamics of Confession* (Richmond: John Knox Press, 1969), 39–44, 90–91. For a range of denominational perspectives on confession, see David Belgum, *Guilt: Where Religion and Psychology Meet* (Englewood Cliffs: Prentice-Hall, 1963), chapter 5.

[8] See William Rothman, "Alfred Hitchcock's *Notorious*," *The Georgia Review* 29 (1975), 885. See his development, 884–927.

[9] As if to signal the centrality of the drinking motif, Hitchcock makes his cameo appearance taking a glass of champagne at the bar. Since he had lost a lot of weight at the time, many viewers miss him. This was not, however, the cameo appearance he had originally planned. In line with the film's theme of love, he had wanted to appear as a deaf person walking down the street talking in sign language to his female companion. Just as they approached the camera, she was to slap his face. However, word got out and, because there was sufficient reaction from the deaf protesting that this would hold them up to ridicule, the plan was scrapped. Nugent, "Mr. Hitchcock Discovers Love," 64.

[10] Quoted in Charles Thomas Samuels, *Encountering Directors* (New York: G.P. Putnam's Sons, 1972), 233.

[11] Gene D. Phillips, *Alfred Hitchcock* (Boston: Twayne Publishers, 1984), 115.

[12] When asked to comment on this failure of Devlin to respond fully to Alicia's amorous advances, Hitchcock denied being an expert on love, and then added: "But I do know that many of the screen's conventions about love are completely ridiculous. For example, a man kisses a woman. Everyone in the audience expects him to follow it up with 'I love you' or 'I think you're wonderful.' Or to say something which shows that he has his mind on his, shall we say, work. In real life it is far more likely that his mind is elsewhere. He might be noting the time, or wondering what's cooking for dinner. And if he speaks at all it might be to utter some vagrant thought not connected with the kissing. In other words, I believe that people can behave physically in a certain way while talking about seemingly unrelated things" (Nugent, "Mr. Hitchcock Discovers Love," 13). Analogous to Hitchcock's insight is the church's teaching that we have not genuinely confessed until we have consciously taken responsibility for our actions.

[13] Eric Rohmer and Claude Chabrol, *Hitchcock*, trans. by Stanley Hochman (New York: Frederick Ungar, 1979), 84.

[14] Donald Spoto, *The Art of Alfred Hitchcock* (New York: Hopkinson and Blake, 1976), 164.

[15] *Ibid.*, 162.

It's a Wonderful Life: Divine Benevolence and Love of Neighbor

[1] For example, Bosley Crowther in *The New York Times* wrote that "for all its characteristic humors, Mr. Capra's *Wonderful Life* ... is a figment of simple Pollyanna platitudes." Quoted in Frank Capra, *The Name Above the Title* (New York: The Macmillan Company, 1971), 382.

[2] *Ibid.*, 383.

[3] *Ibid.*, 375.

[4] Stern's short story is in *The "It's a Wonderful Life" Book*, Jeanine Basinger in Collaboration with the Trustees of the Frank Capra Archives (New York: Alfred A. Knopf, 1986), 95–102. The final shooting script is also in this book.

[5] Capra, *The Name Above the Title*, 376.

[6] Charles J. Maland, *Frank Capra* (Boston: Twayne Publishers, 1980), 134.

[7] *Ibid.*, 151–152; Raymond Carney, *American Vision: The Films of Frank Capra* (Cambridge: Cambridge University Press, 1986), 387; Le-

land Poague, *The Cinema of Frank Capra* (South Brunswick and New York: A.S. Barnes and Company, 1975), 207.

[8] Carney, *American Vision*, 384.

[9] For my division of the film, I am indebted to Charles Maland's more detailed ten-part division in *Frank Capra*, 137–138.

[10] *Ibid.*, 145.

[11] Capra, *The Name Above the Title*, 453.

[12] Maland, *Frank Capra*, 136.

[13] Robert B. Ray, *A Certain Tendency of the Hollywood Cinema, 1930–1980* (Princeton: Princeton University Press, 1985), 184–186.

[14] *Ibid.*, 198–199.

[15] Carney, *American Vision*, 381–386.

[16] The extended flashback ends after the meeting with Potter. No mention of George's prayer in Martini's restaurant is made by the celestial powers in the opening moments of the film, and so I suggest that George's prayer comes after the prayers of his loved ones and after Clarence has seen the extended flashback.

[17] In an interview Capra confessed, "My life is . . . well, I'm getting a heck of a lot of help from somewhere! You know, no one will believe it, but before every scene I shot, I said a silent prayer. Hard to believe, I suppose." *New Orleans Review* 8:1 (Winter 1981), 75.

[18] Maland, *Frank Capra*, 148.

[19] Capra, *The Name Above the Title*, 375.

[20] *Ibid.*, 383.

One Flew Over the Cuckoo's Nest: A Salvific Drama of Liberation

[1] David Denby, " 'Cuckoo's Nest' Is Just An Adolescent Fantasy," *The New York Times*, December 21, 1975, Sec. II, p. 17.

[2] Vincent Canby, " 'Cuckoo's Nest'—A Sane Comedy About Psychotics," *The New York Times*, November 23, 1975, Sec. II, p. 1.

[3] David M. Graybeal, "On Finding the Cuckoo's Nest," *The Christian Century*, August 4, 1976, p. 688.

[4] *Ibid.*, 689.

Index

196